SURGEON HENRY'S TRIFLES

SURGEON WALTER HENRY

Surgeon Henry's Trifles

EVENTS OF
A MILITARY LIFE

Edited with an Introduction and notes by
PAT HAYWARD

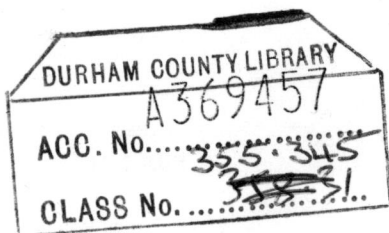
1970

CHATTO & WINDUS

LONDON

Published by
Chatto & Windus Ltd.
42 William IV Street
London W.C.2

*

Clarke, Irwin & Co Ltd
Toronto

SBN 7011 1569 6

Printed in Great Britain by
R. & R. Clark, Ltd
Edinburgh

CONTENTS

INTRODUCTION   *page*   1

1. Boyhood in Ireland   7

2. England · Commissioned · Sails for Portugal · Garrison duty
   Incitement to mutiny · A love affair   19

3. On the march · Joins 66th Foot · Storming of Badajos
   Attack by leeches · Another love affair   38

4. Adventures on the march · Battle of Vittoria   58

5. Surprise of Maya · The Nivelle · Orthes · Invasion of
   France · Thoulouse · Peace · Return to England   76

6. Leave · Sails for India · Madras · Calcutta · The Ganges
   A Tiger Hunt · Invasion of Nepaul   100

7. Life in India · Idleness and its consequences · Suttee
   Cholera · Ordered to St. Helena · Mauritius   123

8. St. Helena · Officers of the 66th received by Napoleon
   His conversation with them   143

9. Quarrels and scandals · Dr. O'Meara and Sir Hudson Lowe
   Attempt at bribery   161

10. A rapacious Brigadier humbugged · Death of Napoleon
    The post mortem · The route for England · Dolphin
    fishing   176

11. Garrison duty in England and Ireland · George IV · Lord
    Strafford's debt · Lord Enniskellin on riot control · Rude-
    ness of Lord Palmerston   192

12. Voyage to Canada · Quebec · The Ambassador looks for the
    lavatory in the dining room · Salmon fishing · Montreal   210

13. Cholera at Kingston · Toronto · Diet of snipe for a sick
    man · Political situation deteriorates · Sir John Colborne   228

14. Insurrection · The fighting at St. Charles and St. Denis
    'Le bon Dieu n'est pas patriote' · Reinforcements · In-
    surrection quashed · The author is promoted · The 66th
    leaves Canada   244

APPENDICES

I General Notes   262
II Chronology of Surgeon Henry's Life   271
III Notes on Regiments mentioned by the Author   273

Index   275

Frontispiece   Surgeon Walter Henry

MAPS

Spain and Portugal   27

The Campaign of 1811–13   45

The Campaign of 1813–14   66

The Ganges Valley   111

Upper and Lower Canada   225

INTRODUCTION

Walter Henry was born on the 1st of January 1791 in Donegal. He tells us that his family was respectable but not distinguished, and as his uncle was a doctor and he himself received a classical education it seems probable that he came from that professional middle class which is the most fluid, and at the same time most stable, element in the United Kingdom. He studied medicine in Dublin, Edinburgh and London but tells us nothing of his experience as a student. One can assume, however, that he must have worked fairly hard because he qualified soon after his twentieth birthday and he makes no mention of any diversion or indulgence after he left home. It is clear too that he read extensively, not only in the classics but in contemporary literature, a habit which he retained throughout his life. He took a keen interest in the countries in which he served and was a good linguist.

He seems to have been a competent horseman. He soon recovered from his early and unhappy experience with firearms, and enjoyed some excellent sport which served as a means of supplementing army rations or, on one occasion, of prolonging the life of a patient for whom he had prescribed a diet of snipes! His real passion in life was fishing. Trout and salmon, shark and bass, in fresh water or salt, it made no difference: if there were fish at hand the worthy doctor set about to catch them. Like most other healthy young men he fell in love whenever the occasion warranted it, but he seems to have anticipated Kipling's advice: 'pleasant the snaffle of courtship, improving the manners and carriage: but the colt who is wise will abstain from the terrible thornbit of marriage,' until he was in a position to support a wife. As a boy he was deeply and genuinely attached to his young cousin but she died when she was hardly more than a child. Her death affected him greatly, but one gets the impression that he recovered from his subsequent unsuccesful love affairs without any permanent wound; or perhaps he found it tactful to belittle their impact when he wrote his Trifles some years after his marriage. Of his successful courtship and family life in Canada he says nothing. We do, however, know that he married Leah Geddes about 1835, and thereby became part of a prominent early Canadian medical family, the Gambles.

1

Towards the end of his Trifles, he tells us of a fishing trip on which his wife and son accompany him. As she sat on the bank watching him, and was presumably treated to a minute by minute description of his prowess at dinner afterwards, one can safely assume that she was very much in love with him. She bore him five children, the eldest of whom was also christened Walter. He followed his father's profession and graduated in medicine at McGill College. He practised in Ottawa and died there in 1874, at the early age of 37, probably from tuberculosis. It seems that he was buried in the cemetery at Hull across the river, but all the records were destroyed when St. James's Church was burnt down at the beginning of this century. His other sons were John, who emigrated to Australia, Charles who became an inspector of the Quebec Bank and George who was employed by the Canadian Pacific Railway. There were two daughters, one of whom married Mr. Fred Hooper of Hamilton and the other, Mary, married Mr. J. H. Evans of Toronto.

His professional competence as a doctor must be set against the medical knowledge of the time and what little he tells us of his cases. His panacea for most maladies seems to have been to bleed his patient, which was the usual practice in those days. On several occasions when he mentions its success one is tempted to believe that the victim was so weakened by the loss of blood that he was forced to rest and so gave his constitution a chance to exert itself and achieve recovery thereby. As a surgeon he had plenty of practice in the Peninsula, where amputations were carried out almost in the front line. The glimpses, and unfortunately they are only glimpses, that one gets of the medical organization under Wellington are interesting. Except at the very beginning of his service, when he tells of the unfortunate episode over servant allowance, there is no criticism of the administrative arrangements. This was certainly not due to a docile nature on the part of the author who was no passive admirer of authority. He was perfectly willing, as he showed at St. Helena in the matter of the senior officer who ran a lucrative business in selling meat to the garrison, to take active steps in his own and his unit's defence. It is rather a well-deserved tribute to Sir James McGrigor the chief medical officer with the army in the field and the staff that supported him. It was only later when the whole logistic structure of the Army was destroyed by the parsimony, ignorance and stupidity of the Government that it fell into disarray and cost the country untold loss in lives and money during the Crimean War.

Henry must have kept a diary from the time he was commissioned until he was posted to Canada. During this period of his service, in Portugal, Spain, India and St. Helena, he paints a very vivid picture of regimental life, every minute of which he seems to have enjoyed. He was fortunate in his posting which was to the 2nd Battalion of the 66th Foot, a regiment with a high reputation in peace and war. In those days each regiment had its own medical staff whose personnel normally stayed with it until they died or retired, as is the rule in the Household Cavalry to this day. As a consequence the Medical Officer was very much part of the regiment. In Henry's case, after service in the Peninsula, he was posted to the 1st Battalion in India, where he took part in the campaign of 1816 against the Gurkhas. Meanwhile the 2nd Battalion had been sent to St. Helena as a guard on Napoleon, where the 1st Battalion joined them the next year. So Henry had the advantage of having served in both battalions. As the danger of war decreased the first and second 66th were amalgamated and reduced to normal regimental strength.

This involved a reduction from sixty-six officers who sat down to dinner in July 1817 to the normal establishment of about thirty-six shown in the Army List of 1820. The Commanding Officer at the time, and for many years later, was Charles Nicol, a man for whom Henry had a sincere liking and respect. We know from other sources that this was fully deserved; so it is reasonable to assume that he removed those who failed to reach his own high standards and maintained a happy and efficient mess as a result. This was particularly necessary at St. Helena where the strains and stresses of guard duty, the need to be constantly on the alert without the stimulus of active service and the friction existing between Sir Hudson Lowe and his prisoner had all the makings of a wretchedly unhappy station.

Certainly Napoleon did his best to make it so. The story of his quarrel with Sir Hudson Lowe is still a subject of controversy, but the 66th was hardly involved. Some of the credit for this must go to Surgeon Henry because a central figure in the affair was Dr. O'Meara, of whom Byron wrote: 'This stiff surgeon, who maintained his cause, hath lost his place and gained the world's applause.' As fellow countrymen and doctors they had much in common but neither national nor professional prejudice influenced the sensible opinion of the author.

After the dull but exacting duties of St. Helena the Regiment moved to the United Kingdom and thence to Canada. There the situation was different. Politically things were going awry. As was to happen in every other part of the Empire in succeeding years the people of the Colony were feeling their way towards independence. Whilst the mass of the population was mostly concerned with its own affairs, there were enough militants, both for and against the Government, to create what would now be known as an internal security problem. Henry's animadversions on politics hold little interest today except possibly for the dedicated political historian of the period, and they have been largely omitted from the present edition. His account of the military operations is much more interesting. The difficulties confronting Sir John Colborne and the measures he took to solve them sound a very modern note. Nothing is more trying to a soldier than what Admiral de Rigny before Navarino described as 'ces hostilités sans hostilités,' but the few British Regiments, assisted by the local militia, managed to restore order with a minimum of bloodshed and a maximum of good temper and restraint.

Not that life in Canada was without its compensations. The 66th was popular as well as efficient, so there were adequate social relaxations between operations; and for Henry there was always fishing. Here again substantial cuts have been made in the present edition. Though one feels that the author would have liked to erect a memorial to every fish he slew, the interest of his readers could hardly be maintained if they had to accompany him on each one of his fishing expeditions. But he enjoyed them, every minute of them, even when he was smothered in mosquitoes.

In January 1839 Walter Henry was promoted to Staff Surgeon and six years later was Deputy Inspector General of the Army Medical Services of Canada. He held the local rank of Inspector General from 1852 until his retirement in June 1855. Thereafter he lived at Belleville, then a small town on Lake Ontario between Kingston and Toronto until he died on 27th June 1860 in his seventieth year.

The original edition of his memoirs entitled *Trifles from my Portfolio* 'by a staff Surgeon' was published by William Neilson of Mountain Street, Quebec, in 1839. It was not noticed in England until the *Quarterly Review* of March 1841 which gave it seventy-seven pages, largely consisting of extracts. The author is described as 'a sturdy, jovial, humorous little Irishman and a skilful surgeon,' but the reviewer did not read his script very carefully. He mentions Henry's bet about Napoleon's escape from Elba but says that the Doctor lost it. In fact he won it. 'Moreover he ate it too, and a very good dinner it was,' as he tells us in a footnote to the English edition.

However, the end of the review is kindly if somewhat patronising: 'The author is evidently a worthy as well as a clever man, and we rather think, that, with some omissions, his work might be advantageously reprinted in England.' Surgeon Henry took the hint. The English edition entitled *Events of a Military Life* and published under his own name appeared in 1843. He had clearly taken some trouble to polish the work for a more sophisticated audience—to its detriment. In his account of his Peninsular experiences he quotes extensively from Napier but Napier is like old brandy, best taken neat. His involuntary assistance has also been removed.

The doctor's own text is too good to need copious notes which would only break the thread of his narrative. Three appendices have, however, been added. The first gives some general notes on personalities and events described in the text, the second a brief chronology of the author's life, and the third the better-known titles of some of the regiments mentioned. No attempt has been made to give the present titles because the spate of reorganizations and disbandments of recent years has complicated the subject far beyond the grasp of the ordinary reader—military or civilian!

Surgeon Henry's own spelling of the names of people and places has been retained where they are not too far removed from the current fashion to be unrecognizable. He refers to Stewart and Stuart as well as MGrigor and McGrigor impartially, but there is no doubt as to his meaning. Here and there he makes curious spelling mistakes which were reproduced in the English edition—chesnut for chestnut, Illiad for Iliad are examples. I have not drawn attention to what may have been a printer's error. He would not have liked it. Nor have I amended his punctuation.

I am indebted to Dr. Charles Mitchell of the University of Ottowa, Dr. Charles Roland of Chicago, Captain Martin Bates of

The Irish Defence Journal, Mr. MacIntyre, the librarian of Donegal County Library, Mr. Potts of the Ministry of Defence Library, Mr. Dineen of the Royal United Service Institution and Colonel Watson of the Canadian Defence Liaison Staff in London for helping me to trace what little is known of the author's life; to Mrs. David Emmett for typing the script and her father Mr. Bill Macgregor for proof-reading; and most of all to my wife for her sympathy and understanding.

1

Boyhood in Ireland

O THER arguments may be more cogent and logical, but the *'argumentum ad absurdum'* is often the most natural and convenient method of demolishing a faulty theory, or opinion. Thus to disprove the notion, that the elements sympathize with our little individual concerns, on this planet, and even honour the birth, or lament the death, of a great man, by a flourish or peal of the band of nature, as was long fondly believed, it is only necessary to state the fact, that when so utterly insignificant an atom of humanity as myself came into the world –

> The front of Heaven was full of fiery shapes
> Of burning cressets –

the atmosphere growled its '–fierce and far delight,' as loudly as it did when Oliver Cromwell and Napoleon Buonaparte yielded up the ghost. For, I have been credibly informed, that on the early morning of the 1st of January 1791, when the new year and myself were born together, there was a very terrible and uncommon accompaniment of rain, and tempest, and thunder, and lightning.

The moral world was, also, at that time, undergoing a storm far more dreadful, and of longer continuance, than the natural. Society was universally agitated, and more or less involved in the turmoil of the recent French Revolution, and all Europe was shaking still in this political earthquake. Paris was big with ominous and bloody events. The Abbé Sieyes was filling his desk with constitutions for nations of all ages and dimensions. Mirabeau was building up his tremendous reputation at the Jacobin Club. The emigrants were beginning their groans–the Marseillois their hymns, and the Poissardes furies their yells. Maximilian Robespierre was employed from morning to night in sharpening his dagger. In England, Pitt was employed in keeping down, with a strong hand, the surging sympathy of the mob with the lawless proceedings on the other side of the Channel; or fighting nightly duels with his great rival in the House of Commons, or in manufacturing colonial constitutions, and making and fencing the warmest and most comfortable nests for political rattlesnakes in Lower Canada. Austria, and Russia, and Prussia were engaged in those fearful Polish atrocities, which have since so palpably brought down on their heads, the vengeance of retributive justice. In short, all Europe was torn by the conflict of opposite opinions, interest, passions and prejudices; and in a state of universal hubbub, agitation, oscillation, perturbation, conglomeration, botheration and confusion.

Far removed from the chief scenes of all this strife, a little unplumed biped, myself, first saw the light in the secluded and pretty little town of Donegal, in the north-west of Ireland. It is not necessary, my dear reader, to tell you more concerning my lineage, than that it was respectable; and as to my ancestors, they were, at any rate, as numerous as those of the first duke in the land.[1]

My native town is pleasantly situated on a small, but clear and pretty river, the Esk, where it meets the tide. It is no trifling advantage in after life to have been in possession of opportunities of acquiring habits of confidence in the water and powers of skilful swimming in early youth.

Yet my first acquaintance with the water was not a little unpropitious. When about 4 years old, I was taken out by a maid servant, one fine evening in summer, for a walk. She, of course, was enjoined to take particular care of Master Walter and not let him run into the wet places, for various reasons known to the learned; amongst the rest, for fear of spoiling his nice frock and trowsers. Above all things, she was ordered not to let him go out of her sight. Now, there chanced to be a pleasant green lane near the town, and to this favourite spot Dolly forthwith directed her steps, in the hope of enjoying a small palaver with a young baker of her acquaintance, who made his appearance, punctually, according to appointment. Close to the place of meeting there happened to be a gate leading into a clean, flowery field, clear of cattle. Into this I was permitted to go for a hunt after the butterflies, whilst nurse and her lover remained in the lane. One side of my play ground was bounded by the river. Soon getting tired I sat down on this bank and begun to pull the bunches of primroses with which it was covered; but unfortunately, in reaching for one tempting and luxurious bunch, near the water's edge, I lost my balance and tumbled in.

After floating down the current a few yards, I providentially grounded on a shelving sand, and there I lay struggling and squalling. Although it could not be said that, like Don Juan on the beach, I was 'As fair a thing as e'er was formed of clay,' for I was never superfluously handsome, yet I soon found, in my utmost need a pitying Haidée in the more homely shape of Dolly, my nurse.

As soon as she had finished her conversation with her lover, Dolly began to think it was time to look after her charge; but he was no where to be seen. She explored the field unsuccessfully, till, on approaching the river, she, at length, caught a glimpse of poor Master Walter floating down the stream. Dolly, then, screamed with all her might, but the baker was out of hearing and there was no creature near, except an old goat, brousing on a bank. She ran down along the edge of the water, frightened out of her wits, and when the stream admitted of wading, rushed in desperately up to her middle, floundered to the shallow where I lay sticking in the mud, and dragged me to the shore.

The precise fib she invented, to account for my melancholy condition, when we came home, is not on record.

The River Esk, after a short course of four miles from its parent lake amongst the mountains, enters the great Bay of Donegal, a little below the town. On a steep bank above the bridge, the base of which is washed by the stream, stands a fine old castle of the early Tudor æra, formerly belonging to the great Earl O'Neill, but now, with the greater part of the town, the property of the Earl of Arran.

The northern side of the castle rises high and abrupt from the rocky bank of the river, and is very richly mantled with ivy which harboured a legion of jackdaws and sparrows. It happened that on a fine clear morning in February, having been presented, by my father, with a new gun and accompaniments, I determined to make war on these birds, and to distinguish my first feat in arms, by the slaughter of a whole hecatomb.

Having made a reconnaissance before breakfast, I ascertained that the enemy was in great force, though in a state of relaxed discipline, which boded an auspicious result from a sudden and bold attack. I determined, therefore, as soon as I should swallow down my porridge, to surprise their position.

Breakfast over, and powder-horn and shot-belt indued, I seized my gun and marched boldly to the attack. After creeping on my hands and knees, till within thirty yards of the foot of the castle wall, the rocky nature of the soil preventing more regular approaches, I halted and began to load. I know not whether it arose from inexperience, or nervousness, at the vicinity of the point of attack, or flurry from the unusual mode of progression, or haste, or a bad lock; but, alas, the melancholy fact is but too certain, whatever the cause, that instead of bringing down materials for half a dozen sparrow pies, I blew myself up!

I never could find data to calculate how high I had been projected. The powder-horn contained exactly a pound of treble strong Dartford. Its brass head was found, some days after, about a quarter of a mile off, but it could throw no more light on the subject.

My first recollection of this horrible business is dated from a tub of suds in our wash-house, into which I had been soused, to put me out. After swallowing more soap than was agreeable, both in decoction and infusion, the larger grains of powder were well sponged out of my eyes, nostrils, mouth, and throat, and I was put to bed. In five minutes my kind uncle Dr. R.[2] and my sweet cousin, his daughter, were at my bed-side.

When quite recovered I abjured the gun and learned to fish. In process of time I became a very successful angler, a fact which many a 'finny darter with the glittering scales' has had reason to know to his cost.[3]

From my early years I was a studious and reading boy, and had, fortunately, access to two respectable libraries, besides the more limited one at home. Reading, indeed, was my greatest enjoyment and I can still recollect the vivid delight with which I first perused the Arabian Nights and Don Quixote. My young heart used to beat audibly for Shecherazade; and the catastrophe of the poor Don, abjuring his chivalry, burning his books and dying penitent, made me melancholy for a week.

My parents were religious and taught me the Bible early; and, laughter-loving mortal that I am, I hope I have not forgotten their good lessons and that sacred instruction, assuredly the source and the spring of any humble merit I have ever possessed. Like uncle Toby, I was much struck with the military details, particularly the duel between David and Goliath and the siege of Jericho. Even in my more mature judgement I admire the picturesque and most interesting account of this splendid beleaguerment exceedingly;

the immense host of the Israelites moving seven days in solemn procession round the doomed city, preceded by the ark of the covenant and the sacerdotal trumpets; the solemn pause, on the seventh morning, only interrupted by the yet lingering echoes of the last blast charged with instant fate; the thunder-shout of an hundred thousand warriors, and the awful crash of the tumbling walls.[4]

The custom of reading in bed is bad and dangerous, yet such was the literary voracity with which I devoured any new book, that I often smuggled it to my couch and read as long as the candle lasted. Good Homer might take a nap over his Illiad if he chose; but I can safely aver that I never did, either in the original, or Pope's or Cowper's translation. On the contrary, as good often springs from evil, my wakefulness over a book in bed, on one occasion, saved our family from destruction.

When the people of France chose to mix up a cup of blood for themselves and force it down each other's throats, they averred, lustily, that it was sweet and delicious to the taste, and very invigorating to the constitution. Under this specious character they palmed it on the neighbouring nations; and, amongst the rest, Ireland, deceived by the imposition, desired, greedily, to have a portion of the Circaean beverage, which she drank with mad heedlessness. She got drunk, and rose in rebellion, as a natural consequence. At the commencement of the rising the insurgents were much in need of arms and, to procure them, used to pay nightly visits at houses where they supposed guns and pistols were to be found. Now, my father's house was one of these; and on the identical night selected by the party, to pay their respects to our quiet family, I was busily engaged fighting with Cortés against the Mexicans, and fancying I heard the hideous sound from the gong of the idol temple rejoicing over a sacrificed Spaniard. Suddenly a real sound of men's feet in the garden, under my window, arrested my attention. It was between twelve and one, and all the house at rest; but I started up instantly and awoke the family. As those were ticklish times, fire-arms were always kept loaded; my father seized a blunderbuss, and two men servants a gun each. A window was then cautiously opened, and a parley ensued; but, as the rebel party, apparently ten or twelve in number, insisted on all the arms in possession being given up incontinently, threatening death in case of refusal, and my father peremptorily declined the terms, the

11

negociations were soon concluded. The villains then prepared to force the back door, and one strong ruffian had already battered in two or three panels with a sledge-hammer, when a window above his head was suddenly opened, and my father shot him dead on the spot. Some desultory firing then took place; the gang uttered the most horrid threats of fire and extermination to all in the house; but, another of them being hit, they became alarmed, and, finally, decamped, carrying with them the dead body.

My uncle, the physician, was a man of letters and had a good library. Having lost his only son, who was surgeon of a man-of-war and died in the West Indies, and finding me docile and studious, he took a fancy to me, and I found myself, established in the vacuum in his heart, which the sad bereavement of his excellent son had left. One beloved daughter remained to console and bless her widowed parent. Her mother was dead. Catharine R. was three months younger than myself, and my playmate, friend, and confidante, from infancy. She was a pretty, graceful and clever girl, playful as a kitten, but of a very sweet and generous disposition. She was very frequently permitted to be my companion on my short angling excursions, with her little silk-haired dog, Cato.

My cousin, who died in the West Indies, had caught and tamed a large gray seagull, which he called Simon. After the death of his amiable master this bird became a great favourite with my uncle and all the family, and used to run about the yard quite domesticated and on good terms with the poultry. One of his wings was kept clipped; but, notwithstanding, he generally managed to take up a position on one of the high pillars of the gate. From this circumstance, my humorous uncle called him 'Simon Stylites,' who, as the learned reader knows, was an ancient Egyptian hermit that lived thirty years on the top of an obelisk.

There was a large fish-pond in the garden which was fed by a small rivulet. After my cousin's death it was much neglected and became covered with weeds. One day when we were all three walking in the garden, I proposed to have the pond cleared out, and promised to stock it with trout, which might be tamed and taught to come for crumbs from the hand of Catherine. The old gentleman embraced the suggestion and gave orders accordingly, whilst his fair daughter's eyes sparkled at the idea of feeding the finny pets.

When the pond was ready I took measures for catching a number of small trout and transmitting the little captives to their new abode; and in the course of a week I stocked it with some dozens. Three or four days after, my uncle went to inspect the condition of his new subjects, but was much surprised to find they had all disappeared. As his maxim was the indulgent English sentiment that supposes innocence without proof of guilt, no suspicion fell on Simon, who still marched about the yard among the turkeys with all imaginable gravity and propriety. I had my own private opinion on the subject, however, which was, by no means, favourable to Mr. Simon. In a few days a second batch of trout was procured, and, this time, a watch was set to discover the culprit. Alas, for honest appearances – my poor uncle had been *gull'd*, like cleverer people who trust implicitly to a grave face; for, the very next morning after the reservoir had been re-stocked, Simon Stylites was discovered in *flagrante delicto*.

There were various opinions as to the proper punishment to be awarded in the case. As to the offence being treated as a capital felony, it was altogether out of the question; for my uncle would rather fill up his fish-pond than suffer any thing to be done affecting the life of his son's favourite bird. At last, it struck me, that I might devise a plan to punish the offender for his gluttony, and cure him of the vice at the same time; which, according to the most enlightened jurisconsults, would be accomplishing the grand desiderata of criminal justice.

Next morning, I fastened two small trout on unbarbed hooks and threw them into the fishpond with lines attached to them; then, hiding myself behind a lilac on the bank, with the lines in my hand, I awaited the result. I had no occasion to wait long; for, at the same time as the day before, the sage-looking bird strutted down the gravel walk to the edge of the pond, and proceeded to reconnoitre with all due precision. Having soon discovered the decoy-fish, which were near the surface, down he darted on them, instanter. When I saw that he was fairly caught, I started up and pulled the lines, and soon had my friend Simon floundering about in a state of astonishment. After playing him as long as I considered proper, for the purposes of justice, I extricated the hooks from his mouth and liberated him with an admonition. Now, although advice in such cases is generally thrown away, and many an asthmatic Judge might save the valuable breath he thus idly wastes on emancipated criminals, this was, by no means, the case with my reprimand. On the contrary, it produced the most salutary effect on the morals of the seagull: the result would have delighted old Jeremy Bentham, could he have witnessed it; the fish flourished, and the reformed Simon Stylites never visited the forbidden precincts again during the rest of his life.

All the world knows that Molière always read his comedies to his old woman before producing them on the stage, and judged by the effect on her what he might expect from the audience. So, to compare great things with small, I never mounted a new fly without making it pass an ordeal, though not exactly of the same nature. As I had no old woman, and even if I had, her optics would scarcely answer, I was obliged to employ a venerable cat.

This tabby was somewhat particular in her tastes. She loved milk and fish as well as ordinary cats, and often regaled herself with a tender mouse when she could; but she differed from her race in being fond of flies. When I found the light favourable, and grimalkin opening her eyes after a doze on the rug, I used to suspend the fly to be examined opposite a small crack in the window pane in the full light of the sun. The slight current of air, through the crack, agitated it sufficiently to give it the appearance of life. If it was destined to be a killing fly, the old lady looked greedy, twirled her long moustaches and struck the rug three or four times with her tail. If otherwise, she took no notice, but resumed her nod. Under the sanction of her approval I proceeded to my sport with all the confidence of a Roman, to whom the Augur had promised victory.

The valley of the Esk was inhabited by a moral, industrious, hardy and good-looking population, who were, chiefly, Protestants. I have heard with concern that many of this estimable peasantry have, since then, emigrated to America and Australia.

In those days my memory was retentive, and I had Virgil, and Horace, and Milton, and Shakspeare, and most of the English Poets, at my finger-ends. Cowper was an especial favourite, and I love him still; *cum grano salis.* I have often wondered why some sensible physician of his acquaintance did not attack his hypochondriac delusions through the liver and stomach–undoubtedly the *'fontes malorum.'* And with every sincere respect for true religion, in the value of which I am a cordial believer, I have the presumption to be of opinion, that had I lived at Olney, my blue pilling the poet would have done him far more good than all the heavy lectures his friend Newton so mercilessly showered upon him.

When Scott appeared I devoured each successive poem with the most hungry avidity, and considered them all great efforts of genius. Nine-tenths I now esteem namby-pamby. But the battle-piece in Marmion, and a few other portions, still maintain their ground.

One beautiful morning in June, I strolled up the valley as high as the lake, purposing to return by the opposite bank of the stream. At this time, I was yet only a trout-fisher and innocent of salmocide. But I felt that morning such an exuberance of 'lusty life' and high spirits as could only be presages of my approaching good fortune. When I reached a favourite place where I had frequently caught some fine trout, I heard a sudden splash in the water, and, there, without doubt, were the large expanding circles on the surface, caused by the rise of a salmon. I had only a small rod and slender silk line, but they were good of their kind, and I determined to dare the contest. Approaching the place, then, with some such feeling as the harpooner experiences when poising his weapon for a plunge into a whale, or the matador when preparing to give the *coup de grâce* to a bull, I threw my flies lightly over the spot where the fish had risen, whilst my heart palpitated violently and my whole frame trembled with excitement. Up he darted at the fly, but I struck too soon and missed him, and a second time I was equally unsuccessful. After giving him a little leisure to compose himself, I again placed the tempting object within his reach, and once more he dashed at it, but carelessly and contemptuously, as if he purposed, by a stroke of his tail, to wet the nimble wings that had eluded him before. This last and lucky time, I hooked the fish, but by the edge of the tail—a most untoward place; for, thus hooked, every fish has tenfold advantages and chances of escape.

When I found the salmon fast on the line, I felt something akin to the sensation of being in the clutch of a tiger. Whiz, whiz, whiz, sounded the reel—away, away, away, darted the fish, like John Gilpin, or Mazeppa. Fortunately, the bank of the river was the edge of an extensive meadow, clear of trees, so that when my line was run out I could run too. After an arduous struggle of two hours, I fairly tired him out, and landed him on a shelving bank. He was a fine fish of twelve pounds, fresh from the sea; and as I stood over him in triumph, where he lay gasping on the sward, the feeling was only comparable to the exultation of Achilles bestriding the corpse of Hector

There was a mill on the Esk, about a mile from my native town, the neighbourhood of which used to be capital fishing ground. But, as there is nothing mundane without alloy, there was one small draw-back. The miller's ducks and geese were always in my way—swimming and splashing about in the mill-course and frightening away the trout. Provoked with their spoiling sport, I used sometimes to throw my flies amongst them and hook one of them by the foot. The frightened bird would attempt to fly away, but, after allowing it a little play, I would catch it, take out the hook and let it off.

This was all very well when no champion for the feathered people was in sight; but I had a certain latent and unpleasant apprehension of evil from the miller's wife—a cross and masculine lady, the terror of all the little boys in the neighbourhood—who would be likely to punish on my ears the indignities sustained by her ducks. One day, whilst in the very act of amusing myself with one of the poultry, I descried this formidable dame with a child in her arms, on the other side of the mill-stream. The quacking of the bird soon attracted her attention, and, 'sending her voice before her'—in a volley of curses, like one of the Homeric heroes, she ran to a plank that crossed the stream, with the too evident intention of passing to my side and taking certain liberties with my person. As it would have been very unmilitary to permit this hostile movement without interruption, I straightway threw down my rod, and ran to defend the *tête du pont* on my own bank; and when I found she was storming the pass and already half-way across, I pushed aside a prop on which the plank rested; when the enemy lost her footing and was tilted into the water.

In an instant I felt the most bitter compunction and that intolerable consciousness of deserving to be hanged. The mother managed to scramble to the bank, but, in her fright she lost hold of the poor infant, which was hurried down by the current straight towards the sluice that opened on the mill-wheel. Being resolute to repair the mischief I had done, I jumped in, and in a few strokes reached the unconscious little creature just as it was entering the immediate suction of the sluice. I seized it, swam to the shore and then delivered it to the mother, with a full confession of guilt, entreaty for pardon and promise of amendment.

By this time the miller, attracted by his wife's screams, made his appearance, and I prepared for a very comfortable drubbing. But after the first burst of passion they both behaved with great magnanimity. I pleaded my own cause as well as I could; and as the place where the plank crossed the stream was not deep, an absolutely felonious *malus animus* could not be established. Evidence as to good character and respectable family, too, was not wanting; and the promptitude with which I had rescued the poor child was in my favour. Finally, I was forgiven, and a treaty of peace was established, in which the interests of the ducks and geese were guaranteed for the future. When all this was happily completed, I was invited to dry my clothes at the kitchen fire, before which half a dozen oaten-cakes were standing. One of these was presented to me as a peace-offering—the infant was undressed dried, and soon soothed to sleep; and a little silver rattle from the town, the next day, won the mother's entire forgiveness.

One Saturday, Catharine and Cato got leave to accompany me. to a famed haunt of trout, called the 'Common Hole,' where a small river joins the main stream. When we reached the confluence of the rivers—Catharine being busily occupied in manufacturing wild-flower nosegays, or hunting the brilliant June butterflies over the field, assisted by little Cato, who appeared to relish the sport as much as his mistress—I soon hooked a large trout and was playing it with great care, altogether absorbed by my sport; when I heard a loud scream of terror, and on looking up I was horrified to behold poor Kate running towards me without her bonnet, exclaiming, 'O, Walter—the bull—the bull!' whilst a furious black brute was pursuing her, at the distance of a couple of hundred yards, tearing up the earth with his horns and bellowing frightfully. With desperate energy I seized the fishing-rod, and after directing my cousin to run for her life to the gate of the field, I advanced as boldly as a palpitating heart would permit, to meet the bull. It was, indeed, a forlorn hope—still, I cherished the idea, that the human voice has a magic power of subduing the fiercest animal, which I had recently picked up in the course of my reading; accordingly, I strained my voice to the loudest shout possible, and ran menacingly at the fierce beast, brandishing my fishing-rod. Whether his ear was annoyed at the shrillness of my treble, or his eye magnified the long rod into a formidable weapon, I know not; but he stopped, when within ten yards of me glaring on me and tossing off the sward in fragments from his horns. As soon as he had ascertained the real insignificance of his foe, he began to bellow afresh, lowering his head for a last rush, and I gave myself up for lost. As I was

17

turning towards the hole where I had been so peacefully enjoying myself five minutes before, with the intention of making a run and a plunge into the water, all at once, my dear little ally, Cato, came into play. The courageous little animal now ran up within a few feet of the bull's horns, barking as fiercely as he could and making an important diversion in my favour. As soon as I saw the beast's attention momentarily occupied by his puny antagonist, I took to my heels and arrived at the gate in time to assist my poor panting Kate, who had scarcely strength of breath left to climb over. Presently, up came the bull roaring, in pursuit of Cato; but, like many other run-aways, I shewed a firm face in my intrenchments; and having plenty of ammunition at hand, in the form of a heap of broken stone for mending the road, I opened a sharp fire on the enemy's forehead through the bars of the gate, and, after one effective shot in the eye, succeeded in beating him off.

2

England · Commissioned · Sails for Portugal · Garrison duty · Incitement to mutiny · A love affair.

I HAD now received a respectable country education, was decently instructed in my mother tongue, and had made a tolerable progress in the classics. I was thus as well prepared as boys generally are, for the more severe studies of the university; and it was determined in a family conclave that I should repair to Edinburgh, study medicine at that prolific *'officina medicorum'* – graduate and in due time establish myself as my uncle's successor.

But man can only propose – a higher power disposes. An untimely death carried off my cousin in the bloom of her youth, and my poor heart-broken uncle soon followed her to the grave – the victim of a grief that would admit of no alleviation or comfort. As a climax, my revered mother shortly after was cut off by that relentless destroyer of all that is beautiful in form or angelic in disposition – consumption.

I gave up all idea of home practice – entered Trinity College, Dublin, but with the intention of still prosecuting medical study – passed a winter in Edinburgh; and finally embarked at Newry for Liverpool, with the object of completing my surgical education in London.

I spent a year in London, where I was a pupil of Sir E[verard] H[ome],[5] a great gun of his day, though by no means the best man or best surgeon in the world. I owe him little, but I owe a cleverer man, at that period young in fame, much. Even then, some thirty years ago, green and inexperienced as I was, I had a presentiment that Sir Benjamin Brodie[6] would attain to the distinguished eminence which he has since reached.

Having obtained from the chirurgical wisdom of Lincoln's Inn Fields an authority to cut up all the King's liege subjects, who chose to permit me, I determined on entering the army and visiting the Peninsula; where Lord Wellington was at the time 'grimly reposing' behind the lines of Torres Vedras, and waiting for a false move on the part of Massena, whom he there held in check. It is true, the whig *quidnuncs* of the day gave me or any body else small hope of joining the English army; except in the way of meeting it in the Bay of Biscay after being driven out of Portugal. But, notwithstanding their gloomy forebodings and craven-croaking, I resolved to try.

Accordingly, with my credentials in my hand, I went to the Horse Guards, and from thence was referred to a tribunal sitting at No. 4 Berkeley-street, Berkeley Square. The wise men on the medical bench there, having examined me, and reported that I could physic as well as bleed, I was in due course gazetted 'Hospital Mate' for general service to His Majesty's Forces. The title grated on my ear at first, as cacophonous to the last degree; but one gets accustomed to disagreeable sounds. It has sunk, since, beneath the growing intelligence of the age, like any other barbarism of the middle ages.

Next day, I went to an army tailor to order my uniform. The awful black feather in my cocked-hat was calculated to raise unpleasant ideas, and I considered it scarcely fair for the Horse Guards' people to put me in mourning, prematurely, and by anticipation for any accidents amongst my patients.

I recollect that I was interrogated afterwards in Silver-street, in Lisbon, by General P[ea]c[oc]ke,[7] about this identical black feather. It was very long and pliant, and on a wet or windy day used to whisk about my eyes; so that under these circumstances, I always doubled it up into the fold of the crown of the hat to keep it out of the way. In this state the General met and accosted me— 'You are a medical officer, Sir?' 'I am, Sir.' 'Then, where is your black feather, Sir?' 'There it is,' I replied, flapping it across his nose. The General rode on.

About a week after my appointment, I was ordered to Portsmouth, to embark for Lisbon. I travelled in the same coach with a facetious brother *medico* bound to Cadiz, of the name of M[artin]-d[a]le.[8] At the inn where we stopped to dine my companion electrified the contents of two coaches by emptying his snuff-box, more than half full, into his soup, and swallowing it with much gusto. He let me into the secret afterwards, but I could never see much to admire or imitate in burning one's mouth for the sake of exciting a little momentary wonder. It was a common trick, it seemed, to astonish strangers, and was managed by having two similar boxes, one containing snuff and the other pepper.

After waiting several days at Portsmouth for a fair wind, I sailed in the transport Mary, John Hogg, Master, with four officers, bound to Lisbon. I record Mr. Hogg's name for two reasons — first, he quarrelled with me one day after dinner for telling him in the course of a conversation on Heraldry, that his crest was a boar's head — and, secondly, because the said Hogg's name was the most happy example of the identity of designation and person — sound and sense — appellation and character, that I have ever had the good fortune to meet.

One clear Sunday morning in the beginning of May, 1811, we proceeded through the Needles with a fleet of three hundred sail, escorted by a frigate, the name of which I forget. All the morning and afternoon we bore down channel gallantly, and in the evening we had the pleasure of witnessing a pretty chase. An American brig that had got permission to profit by the convoy, finding that some of the fleet were heavy sailers, and that the easterly breeze was freshening and promised to continue, took it into her head to cut our acquaintance. No doubt she thought she might leave us when she pleased, and that our frigate would hesitate at quitting the fleet to pursue her, so near night, and exposed to the chance of meeting one or two Dunkirk luggers, then supposed to be close at hand. However, for once, Jonathan reckoned without his host. As soon as the frigate saw the American making off she fired a gun, and a little after a second, without effect. Upon this the convoy which had been under single-reefed top-sails before, hoisted more sail, shook out her reefs, and dashed away in pursuit of the brig. After half an hour's trial of speed, the fugitive, finding the frigate was fast gaining on her, lay to; and, no doubt, paid dearly for the two shots — as for the scolding she got from the captain of the convoy, it was given gratis.

One morning at breakfast, when I got up to manufacture some egg-cream, and had a large tea-kettle full of boiling water in one hand, and a tumbler with the egg in another, the ship gave a fearful roll, sending me and my kettle to the other side of the cabin. I then endeavoured to anchor on one of the standing berths; but, both hands being engaged, I could only use my elbow, and it would not hold, consequently, back in a second I was sent by the recoil of the vessel; and, alas! a third time launched, *nolens volens*, on this perilous navigation. All this time my four fellow-passengers were at the table, throwing up their feet to keep out of the apprehended

21

danger, and screaming with a sort of hysteric laughter, in which, however, fear was a principal ingredient. After two or three more turns across the cabin, I fortunately made good a landing on my chair in safety, and without spilling a drop either of the water or the cream.

Our dinners, of course, were generally enlivened by similar little interludes between the acts. Often our soup-tureen, impelled by some extraordinary ground swell, would start from its moorings, smash half a dozen decanters and tumblers in its passage, and then unrelentingly pour its scalding contents into the Vice-President's lap. Then Captain Maunsell of the 39th, would exclaim—'any *more* soup Hooper?'—'Ogh, no, bad luck to you, don't you percaive I have got my *ne* plus ultra.'

On the 16th May we made the Rock of Lisbon; soon after were boarded by a Portuguese pilot, and after passing the imposing array of forts at its mouth, we advanced up the Tagus with a delightful breeze and anchored off Belem Steps.

This scenic capital does certainly display many beauties to a stranger as his vessel drops anchor in the broad stream at its feet. There, however, he ought to stay, satisfied with distant admiration; for though all is majestic and magnificent without all is stench and filth within.

My first business, naturally, was to look out for a lodging; accordingly, after reporting myself at the proper places, I repaired to the Town Major's office for a billet; and, having procured one, sallied forth from thence to establish myself in my quarters—a matter occasionally analogous to the dangerous invasion of an enemy's country.

Previous to leaving England, I had purchased a Portuguese grammar and dictionary, with the intention of studying hard on the voyage. But a transport in the Bay of Biscay is somewhat different from the grove of *Academus*—consequently, my progress was not great. On reaching my '*Patrone's*' door—as they quaintly but kindly call one's host in Lisbon—I found on mustering my acquirements in Portuguese, that the sum total amounted to half a dozen words and one sentence—'bread,' and 'wine,' and 'water,' and 'fish' and 'tea,' and 'how do you do?'

Thus accomplished, I arrived in front of a good-looking house in the Rua dos Plaçeres, in Buenos Ayres—the best part of Lisbon. I was admitted with politeness by a well-dressed servant, and shewn into an anti-chamber, where sat a gentlemanly-looking Fidalgo, with the Maltese cross on his breast. These were favourable circumstances, and those first appearances of respectability and courtesy were not belied by the subsequent deportment of my worthy host. After the introductory bow to each other, we were both not a little puzzled to find that our literary acquirements had not furnished a mutual channel of communication. He knew about as much English as I did Portuguese, and was unacquainted with French. 'Twas true, the excellent Fidalgo had picked up a few oaths, which he had heard amongst the English soldiers; but these expletives were not much calculated to make our ideas intelligible to each other, or to keep up a good understanding between us. In this dilemma we had recourse again to the eloquence of courtesy and the countenance—bows '—and smiles, and sparkles of the speaking eye'—till, his knight's cross having haply suggested to me that he might understand Latin, I accosted him as well as I could in that language. Fortunately, I had been taught to pronounce in the broad, Continental, and not the English manner—so, he understood me at once, and a *medius terminus* being thus established between us, we chatted away as classically as we might on the events of the day—the *'bellum internecinum adversus Gallos'*—the great *'Dux* Wellington' the *'exercitus Britannicus'*—the *'Rex Georgius'*—the *'spes Lusitaniæ'* and so forth, for half an hour, until we became cordial cronies, and the good old gentleman finished by inviting me to dinner.

By the assistance of my good host, I acquired in the course of a week as much Portuguese as relieved the Latin occasionally, or sometimes superseded it altogether. He was besides very useful to me in many other respects; acting as my guide in pointing out the lions of the Lusitanian metropolis, and introducing me to several of his friends, after our acquaintance had ripened into intimacy. He was, I believe, a true patriot—loved his country, was cordial to the English—deprecated the convention of Cintra, of which he could not speak with patience, and abominated Junôt and the French; who had insulted him and stolen his plate and pictures. In fact, I felt then and afterwards—and still feel—under the greatest obligations to this warm-hearted gentleman; and as I never could repay him in his own country, nor any other, I shall now do all in my power in the way of gratitude, by consigning the name of Don Manoel Joze Mascarenhas to the limited immortality of my book.

When I first landed I had called on Dr. B——,[9] the principal medical officer, and an old school fellow of my father—who received me as graciously as his nature permitted. After a short conversation, in the course of which he directed me to call the next morning for farther instructions; and when I had risen from the chair, preparatory to taking my leave, we were both startled by a shrill, violent, and prolonged female shriek from the upper part of the house. The principal medical officer suddenly turned as pale as a sheet; and, exclaiming, 'By G— she has killed herself!' rushed out of his office and ran up stairs. Another loud scream met his ear almost immediately, and perceptibly accelerated his steps; whilst I was left, hat in hand, deliberating whether it behoved me to disappear, or to wait for the denouement of what promised to turn out something sufficiently tragic.

I was not left long in suspense, for in two minutes a frightened female servant came running down stairs, half a dozen steps in one and requesting me to hurry up without delay. On entering the bed-chamber, I found the doctor and another servant supporting and soothing a very handsome young lady, who was pale and faint, and bleeding profusely from a wound in the left breast. As the chief *medico* was so dreadfully agitated that he could be no use, he requested me to examine the wound and take the proper measures for dressing it and staunching the bleeding. I found that the patient had stabbed herself with a stiletto; fortunately, the point had struck against a rib and glanced off, producing a deep flesh-wound, but not penetrating the chest. She had, moreover, and it was a pity, pierced a very white and well formed bosom, and the blood was running down her side on the bed in a considerable stream. I soon succeeded in stopping the bleeding; the fair suicide was then undressed, after the usual restoratives, and put to bed. She was obstinately silent in answer to the reiterated questions of the doctor; but it appeared to me she did not receive my announcement that the wound was not fatal, in the mood to be expected from a person still determined on self-destruction, but quite the contrary.

The history of the case was this. Dr. B— had had this lady, an extremely pretty Portuguese, living under his protection for a considerable period; but, on making preparations to embark for England, he wished to cut the connection. The overture he made to this effect was very unpalatable to his mistress, who desired to accompany him, and even hoped to be made his wife in process of time. It appeared that on the morning of my call, there had been a recent and violent altercation between the parties. He swore she should not go with him, and she said and swore she would. The ungallant *medico* then flew into a passion, called her a fury, and a fiend, and abused her as far as his limited Portuguese would permit. In reply, she vowed she would destroy herself, and that he should have her life to answer for, and then asked pardon of the 'Virgem purissima'—the above catastrophe was the result.

I attended the fair lady for a week. She soon recovered, and I have my own suspicions that previous to stabbing herself she had carefully studied the anatomy of the rib which her poniard encountered, and which saved her life. At any rate she failed in her great object—the doctor pensioned and discarded her—and she returned to the opera.

About this period there was great lack of medical assistance, both with the main army in the north of Portugal, and in Beresford's corps, quartered in Spanish Estramadura. The battles of Fuentes d'Onore and Albuera had filled the hospitals with wounded and there were many sick. There chanced at the time to be a large detachment of the 11th regiment at Lisbon, preparing to join their head quarters in the north of Portugal, without a regimental medical officer. It was therefore arranged that I should embark with them for Figueras, a town at the mouth of the Mondego, and accompany them up the river to Coimbra, where I was directed to report myself and await farther orders.

The weather was fine when we embarked at Belem in the beginning of June, 1811; and we had a pleasant voyage of two days to Figueras. There, the detachment was put in flat bottomed boats, and we proceeded up the vine-banked and beautiful Mondego to Coimbra.

Having reported my arrival to Dr. T—t, then at the head of the medical staff at Coimbra, I was directed to cross to the other side of the Mondego and take charge of a ward of about a hundred poor wounded fellows, lately brought in from the front, and now quartered in the Francisco Convent.

The second morning after I had established myself, in passing under some fine chesnut trees near the convent gate, I saw a goodlooking Portuguese lad lying on his back in the shade, taking a comfortable *siesta*. It immediately occurred to me that I wanted a servant, and that here was the very '*criado*' I required, dosing away his time for want of a master; accordingly, by way of introduction, I touched him gently in the side with the toe of my boot. Antonio started up—collected a frown on his handsome brow at the freedom I had taken; but strangled it instantly and put a smile in its place, when he saw my red coat and cocked-hat. We then entered into amicable conversation, and I asked after his acquirements. Although he could neither make spatterdashes nor play on the fiddle, like Sterne's La Fleur—he said he could cook, and brush my clothes, and polish my boots, and groom a horse. He had no certificates, for he had never been in service—but he had an honest as well as comely face; and trusting to an ingenuous manner and this natural recommendation, I hired him at once—appointed him my Major Domo and factotum, and directed him to look after my rations.

When my morning hospital duties were over, I strolled up the river-side to the 'Quinta das Lagrimas,' and thence to the 'Fonte dos Amores'—the former the traditionary abode, and the latter the scene of the murder, of the celebrated Ignes de Castro.

It is not very usual to jump the one step from the sublime to the ridiculous, but it is common enough to descend from this elevation to the occupations and amusements of ordinary life. Thus, after the contemplation of the sad story of Ignes, in returning along the river my eye was attracted by some lively fish playing about and glancing in the water. Instantly my sentimentalities took wing—the old angling predilections resumed their ascendency—I hastened home—put in order the cane-rod that I always carried with me—repaired to the river-side—began to fish—and in an hour succeeded in persuading a dozen good sized dace to accompany me home to dinner.

I found that my valet had not overrated his culinary qualifications. He made some tolerable soup out of the tough ration beef, and fried the fish nicely with *azeite*, fresh drawn from the olive trees on the neighbouring hill. A bullock's heart roasted, was also very properly cooked; and when the cloth was removed I sipped my ration wine philosophically over a dessert of delicious grapes and oranges. Thinks I to myself this is mighty pleasant campaigning.

Part of the Santa Clara Convent had been given up for the use of the sick and wounded, but the remainder was occupied by the nuns. I frequently attended the chapel to hear these sisters' singing, which certainly was admirable; but, so many heretics being in their immediate neighbourhood, they appeared to be preserved with more than ordinary care from all possibility of the most harmless intercourse. Even the usual *grille* and turning box were blocked up. However, to console us for this privation, report said they were mostly old ladies, with one young beauty, one acknowledged beauty amongst them, who, crossed in love, had thrown

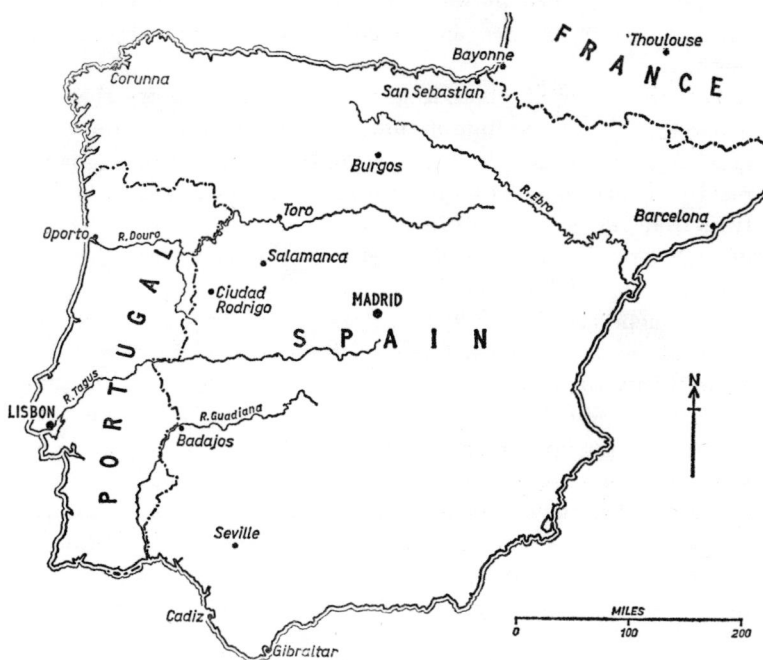

FRANCE
Thoulouse
Bayonne
Corunna
San Sebastian
Burgos
R. Ebro
Toro
Barcelona
Oporto
R. Douro
Salamanca
Ciudad Rodrigo
MADRID
SPAIN
PORTUGAL
R. Tagus
LISBON
R. Guadiana
Badajos
N
Seville
Cadiz
Gibraltar
MILES
0   100   200

herself into the convent. Such is the witchery of a fair face, even an ideal one, over all the senses that in listening to the choir in the chapel, I always associated Donna Theodora's idea with one voice pre-eminently sweet; although, for aught I know to the contrary, the said beautiful lady might have a note like a pea-hen.

When I was in Coimbra there was a fountain in the garden of the Santa Cruz Convent of Augustine Friars, within the city, which all the English officers greatly admired; for it was a pleasing and cool retreat to the convalescents from the great heat of the town. The fountain was a circular sheet of water, some thirty yards in diameter, surrounded by a verdant wall of clipped cypress, forty or fifty feet high; and having a little circular island in the middle in which grew one orange tree, worthy of the garden of the Hesperides. There was a comfortable seat at the bottom of the verdant enclosure for the refreshment of the Padres; and, to do the whole Santa Cruz establishment but justice, they threw their gates open in a very handsome manner to the English. They permitted us to bathe in the fountain; and our common habit was to swim round the tiny island until we were tired, then land and return loaded with as many oranges as we could manage to carry in our teeth.

Few rivers can produce frogs in greater abundance than the Mondego; the winter inundation affording this noisy fraternity great facilities in the breeding season. In the quiet hamlet where I resided, I was screened by its situation and the shade of the fine trees from the great heat of the town; but I was in the very focus of the frogs. When I awoke, stunned by the terrific croak, croak, croak, of some billions of these reptiles, it seemed to me that all this tremendous uproar could not be an occurrence of ordinary seasons; and as I could not sleep, I thought I might as well form some theory to account for it. After two or three hours puzzling my brain, I found out what satisfied me then, as the veritable cause of all the uproar. In the year 1811, the whole nation of frogs were keeping an universal jubilee, in consequence of the recent expulsion from the kingdom of their cannibal enemies, the French.

Coimbra at this time contained nearly a thousand British sick and wounded, so that there was a fine field for practice. We had many bad surgical cases, and not a few extraordinary recoveries after terrible round-shot wounds. Amongst these, there was a patient of mine, a grenadier of the 77th Regiment, who had been wounded at the affair of El Bordon, when this regiment and the 5th Foot behaved so beautifully, retreating in square before overwhelming numbers of French cavalry, never losing their formation, carrying off their wounded over three or four leagues of open country. A cannon-ball had struck him on the back, but, as it was nearly spent, his knap-sack and the tin vessel over it had turned the shot out of its direct course; but it had ploughed its way downwards, carrying the tin with it, and cutting every thing soft of the poor fellow's hinder parts sheer off as clean as with a carving knife. There was great bleeding at the time, but he fainted, was carried off by his comrades, and the nearest surgeon tied up the large arteries, when he recovered. He was soon after sent down to Coimbra.

The cure was necessarily tedious, but it was at length happily completed; and nature had furnished him with new skin over the enormous wound about as extensive as the hide of a calf. When I left Coimbra he was beginning to move about slowly on crutches; still very lame from the great loss of muscle. At parting he expressed much gratitude for my attentions, and in return I wished he might get a good pension and a soft-bottomed chair for the remainder of his life.

In the month of July, apprehensions being entertained at headquarters that another retreat on the lines might be necessary, from the junction of the French army of the south and that of Portugal, orders arrived to clear the hospitals and send the sick to Lisbon. Accordingly they were broke up, and a large detachment of two hundred was placed under my charge. We embarked on the river, were put on board a transport at Figueras, and arrived without accident at Lisbon.

My first care after returning to Lisbon, was to visit my fine old 'Patrone,' the Knight of Malta, and I soon found myself comfortably re-established in my former habitation.

In the course of a couple of days I was directed to do duty at an hospital under the charge of a German staff surgeon, whose name it is not necessary to mention. I soon found that my worthy Teutonic chief was much fonder of *schnapps* than of surgery; and from keeping late hours, not particularly punctual in his morning visits at the hospital; in fact, sometimes staying away altogether three or four days. This was exactly what I wished, for it gave me the real management and most of the practice of the establishment. I recollect that on one of the few occasions when we met in the morning, I pointed out to him a man with a bad wound in the leg, which would not heal, and required amputation to save his life. The vinous staff surgeon, unfortunately, was not in the best operating condition, for his hand shook sadly; so he deferred the matter till the next day. At the appointed time, the jovial German was again absent: after waiting for some time in vain, I took off the limb myself with the assistance of a smart orderly. The day after, the staff surgeon and myself went round the wards together, and when he came to the patient, who had worn for some time what was technically called a cradle, to protect his leg from the weight of the

bed-clothes, and which now concealed the stump; he accosted him
–'Well, my goot friend, how duz your leck?' 'Faith, your honour, I
was aised of it yesthurday, and I now only feels a thrifle of a pain
in aich of my toes.' The doctor stared a little, but was satisfied
with my explanation, and we then went to his quarters to lunch.
Afterwards he amused me with his violoncello on which he played
skilfully; we dined together and went to Saltire's theatre in the
evening.

Few mortals approach half a century without having to lament
numerous youthful indiscretions. One of my early follies I may be
permitted to narrate.

About the month of August, 1811, some general order of Lord
Wellington respecting a certificate from the principal medical
officer before the monthly allowance for a servant could be drawn
from the Commissariat by the junior medical officers, excited great
wrath among the young doctors. The obnoxious order directed
that this allowance should only be issued if the P.M.O. considered
that a servant was absolutely necessary–an awkwardness of
expressing the order, probably attributable to the bungling of
some clerk at head quarters. However, the *medicos* took fire at
what they considered an insult, and a meeting of 'Hospital Mates'
took place at Lecor's Hotel, to deliberate upon the subject. The
medical staff at Lisbon was strong at this time–the meeting was
attended by sixty or seventy persons, and I happened to be placed
in the Chair.

After a prolonged discussion and much impassioned dilating on
our grievances, branching out into very miscellaneous oratory, a
committee was appointed by ballot to draw up a petition and
remonstrance, to the Commander of the Forces against the recent
order. The committee, of which I was a member, *ex officio*, carried
into effect the directions of the meeting, and submitted the result
of their labours to their constituents at another general meeting
held at the same place a week after. The petition was there
approved, and it was unanimously resolved that it should be presented by the committee to Dr. B—, the P.M. Officer in Lisbon,
with a request to forward it to Lord Wellington's Military Secretary. After the business was thus despatched to our entire satisfaction, we had a hot supper, and finished the evening with singing
and jollification.

At the appointed hour the committee waited on Dr. B— with

the petition and remonstrance, which we considered quite a *chef
d'œuvre* of composition. The doctor was the gentleman whose
mistress had stabbed herself, and who was now waiting the arrival
of his successor to embark for England. He received us civilly, put
on his spectacles and proceeded to read our laboured document,
which we were nearly certain he would approve, and even admire.
When he had done he coolly replaced his glasses in their case, and
then accosted us—'Why, d— your young bloods, you fools—what
have we here—a petition and remonstrance to the Commander of
the Forces from a parcel of d—"Hospital Mates"—be off, and be
d— to you—you may think yourselves lucky that I do no more than
quash your folly—thus!' And with that he tore our eloquent appeal
into a thousand pieces and flung them in our faces.

When we had left the house and proceeded a few yards down the
street a messenger called me back. The doctor then addressed me—
'and *you*, Sir, have been such a d— ignoramus and blockhead as to
become president of this wise deliberative meeting, and to sign
your name first to your remonstrance—why, Sir, if I forwarded the
petition *your* commission would not be worth that snap—the
others might be overlooked, but you would be made an example of,
by G—!' He then, in a more friendly tone, pointed out to me the
impropriety and danger of bodies of officers meeting to deliberate
without lawful authority. The doctor soon changed the subject—
asked about my hospital—laughed a little concerning the convivial
propensities of my immediate superior, the German—told me my
patient, the fair suicide, had been dismissed—asked me to dinner
the next day, and we parted very good friends.

That evening a meeting was summoned at the hotel to report
proceedings respecting the petition, and we had a very full attendance. I took the Chair, and began with as much power of face as I
could muster, to relate the transactions at the P.M.O's. office—
repeating his precise words and mimicking his manner as well as I
could. When I finished, there was, first, a murmur of disapproba-
tion, which, however, did not last long, but was soon drowned in a
loud and general laugh. It was then proposed and carried; 1st.
That the consideration of our grievances should be postponed
sine die; 2nd. That an inquisition should be forthwith made into
the quantity of *Collares* in the cellar; and 3rd. That a large instal-
ment should be mulled and produced immediately. The weather
abounded in radical heat calling for corresponding moisture—the

wine was delicious and not strong–temperance societies had not been born–the night was short and the morning sun lighted us to our homes.

Exactly opposite to Don Manoel's house there resided two good-looking Portuguese girls, who passed the greater part of their time, when the shade of the house in the cool of the evening permitted, in their handsome gilded balcony. I watched their manœuvres with a good deal of attention, and found that their principal amusement consisted in playing tricks on the Gallegos, or Gallician water-carriers, passing beneath, with their little painted barrels on their shoulders. No sooner did a Gallego approach than these damsels would accost him–'tio! tio!' Uncle–uncle–the familiar term used to the lower classes. The man would stop and look up; then–I shudder whilst I relate a deed so unlady-like and atrocious–the playful girls would giggle and spit in his eye. The water-carrier would retort by a squirt from the pipe of his barrel about the ladies' ankles, and this was considered great fun on both sides. Yet, my '*Patrone*' told me these ladies were of respectable family and irreproachable character.

As our respective balconies were only separated by a narrow street, I soon introduced myself, and we generally had a little conversation every fine evening, which was wont to become more animated as the increasing darkness screened us from observation. Mutual compliments were then interchanged; I praised the brilliancy of the ladies' eyes, and their fine persons; unusual in Lisbon, where dumpiness is a common characteristic of the women. I perceived that my lively neighbours were much at a loss to discover a laudable quality about me, and were obliged to content themselves by saying, '*vos merced tem muito bonitas dentes*'–you have good teeth.

Except occasionally playing a modinha set to music, on the guitar, I firmly believe these girls never read, nor worked, nor drew, nor visited, nor went out, except to church; nor did anything but lounge through the house, look out of the windows, loll on the couches–make love when they could, and amuse themselves with the Gallegos. And such I found out was the general routine of unmarried female life amongst the higher classes in Lisbon.

According to my '*Patrone's*' statement, the French, when in occupation of Lisbon, must have behaved infamously ill, and pillaged openly and universally. They seized all the church plate they could find, and were not particular in respecting what belonged to private individuals. The forced contributions exacted by Junôt were enormous–Don Manoel had paid at one time four thousand crusadoes, and smaller sums on two or three occasions–he had also lost part of his plate; but when he discovered the rapacity of the new masters of the kingdom, he secreted and saved the remainder. His pictures suffered–but he cared nothing for any that had been taken away, except one Murillo–a scripture-piece which he prized highly.

Butchers' meat at this time was of very indifferent quality in Lisbon, but there was an excellent fish-market; and Antonio, who had conducted himself remarkably well hitherto, was a good fish-cook, so that ichthyophagism was the order of the day. As to wine, we had the strong white wine from the south shore of the Tagus– the Porto-feitoria red wine–Calcavellos, and the delicious Portuguese Claret–Collares–all very reasonable–Champaigne, Claret, Port, Madeira and Sherry, were to be had, but at such prices as did not suit my finances–nor did the hot and heady nature of most of them harmonize any better with my humble and undisciplined taste. I luxuriated amongst the grapes and oranges, as most strangers do on a first visit to Lisbon.

After a residence of four months, spent most agreeably in the Portuguese capital, I was ordered to Aldea Galega, a village on the other side of the Tagus at the commencement of the high-road to Elvas. There was a strong detachment of Royal Marines quartered there, of which I got medical charge. In the course of a few weeks the three officers and the greater part of the detachment were withdrawn and only a sergeant's guard remained. By some mal-arrangement in the Inspector of Hospitals' department, I was not relieved, although I represented that there was nothing to do. Here then I continued in the double capacity of principal medical officer and commandant, having under my authority a commissariat clerk, a serjeant, twelve marines and Antonio.

I happened to occupy a very good quarter in Aldea Galega, in fact, the best house in the town; and what was better, there was an extremely pretty young girl in it, named Theodora, the daughter of my host, with whom I could not well help falling in love, being the only British Officer in the town. Accordingly, we commenced a vigorous flirtation, though under the disadvantage of an inmate in the house, a maiden aunt of the fair Theodora; who, as nearly the last of the almost extinct tribe of Duennas, concentrated in her breast and deportment all their watchfulness and malignity.

But love laughs at Duennas. My trusty Antonio conveyed one day a note to my mistress, written in choice Portuguese, filled with the usual amatory hyperboles and soft fibs at which Jove is said to laugh; and concluding by soliciting a short meeting on the stairs, where I might, if only for a moment, hear the dulcet sounds of her voice–(our amour hitherto having been confined to the eyes)–and assure her how much I was devoted to her charms, &c. &c. &c. I took the liberty of enclosing her a fishing-hook, fastened to a long thread, which I implored her to employ in dropping me an answer at night from her bed-chamber window, immediately above mine, and to preserve it carefully, as affording us a medium of future correspondence.

The old song says–

> I took it in my head
>   To write my Love a letter,
> But, alas! she cannot read,
>   And I like her all the better.

So my poor Theodora could not read; but she either found some female confidant to read my billet for her, or with her sex's sagacity conjectured the mystic meaning of the hook; for, as soon as it became dark, down came the line with a beautiful red rose fastened by the stem, which the most obtuse understanding could not avoid considering–'*le premier gage d'amour*'.

We met on the stairs. I exhausted my stock of Portuguese in whispers of love and devotion; and the amiable Theodora had just acknowledged in return that she esteemed and loved the '*valorosos Inglezez*'; and had blushed no insuperable objection to myself in particular; when the old Hecate, her aunt, suddenly made her appearance. Poor Theodora was thunder-struck–she wept, and embraced her aunt's knees, and kissed her shrivelled hand, and begged hard for concealment of the matter from papa. I implored the old lady by the most moving considerations I could shape into decent Portuguese, to be good-natured and propitious to our mutual flame, assuring her that my intentions were honourable, and even daring to compliment her on the kindness of her heart and benevolence of her countenance, although, in truth, she had the visage of a Gorgon. But flattery and entreaty were equally lost labour. With what was intended for a withering scowl, she called me a '*maldito eretico*', and seizing the trembling girl by the arm, she hurried her to her apartment by the application of five or six terrific slaps on the back. Notwithstanding this cruel treatment, the hook and line brought me that night another rose, and I returned a note as affectionate as possible.

But treachery was at work. Next day the Juiz de Fora, or chief magistrate of the town, sent for me, and after embracing me much more cordially than I wished—for he was redolent of tobacco and garlic—he made a thousand apologies for the painful necessity he was under of changing my quarter; but, as a compensation, he could give me a billet on the next best house in the town. The fact was, he assured me, a Portuguese General Officer was every hour expected at Aldea Galega, and the best quarter in the place, which I occupied, was for him. Hereupon I remonstrated, and argued that it was not a little hard to turn out the chief doctor and commandant, permanently quartered in the town, for the accommodation of any Brigadier for only one night. The Juiz was superfluously polite—he bowed and smirked, and used the blandest language, but concluded by saying how much-soever he regretted the necessity—I *must* turn out. After half an hour's debate he continued inexorable. I then waxed wrath, and I fear, swore lustily, that I defied him and his friend the General, *à l'outrance*, and would not budge an inch. The fat little magistrate then flushed up into a towering passion—looked very livid and apoplectic, and swore by one-and-twenty thousand *Diabos* he would oust me, *vi et armis*, and so we parted.

But the commandant of Aldea Galega, who suspected trickery, was not to be bullied out of his good lodging and the vicinity of his *carissima*. I immediately posted a marine sentry on the door of the house, with specific directions to defend the garrison and repel any attack from the enemy. For two days the post was thus held by regular reliefs—but no General made his appearance—in fact, no General came at all; for it was all a plot to turn me out of the house, probably to break off the little *liaison* with Theodora. So I triumphed over the conspirators and dismissed my sentry: but my poor mistress was sent out of the way and I saw her no more.

By this time I had purchased a good-looking Portuguese horse, and found, to my great satisfaction, that my trusty Antonio groomed him well and turned him out very smartly. The rides around the town were pleasant and the road dry, but rather sandy. The umbrageousness of the fine cork tree forests on the road to Elvas afforded thick shade and cool rides, even in the hottest part of the day.

In the beginning of December, 1811, I was once more ordered to Lisbon, where I found my old apartments, at Don Manoel's, occupied by a brother *medico*–consequently looked out for lodgings elsewhere; and as I had been lately tired of idleness at Aldea, I volunteered to be resident attendant in a convent full of sick near the Campo d'Ourike.

The Christmas day of 1811, at Lisbon, was one of the most brilliant and beautiful days that the sun ever saw, and he has seen not a few in his time. I enjoyed the delicious time the more for having sat up half the preceding night, witnessing the gorgeous ceremonies of Christmas Eve in the 'Igreja da Renya'. The church had been then crowded almost to suffocation; and the heat and confinement–the fumes of incense and the innumerable lights, mixing with the un-aromatic exhalations from four or five thousand garlic-eating people–were good preparations for enjoying the pure Atlantic breeze, the magnificent prospects and rich sunshine of Cintra.

On my return I dined with a medical friend residing in the San Jeronymo Convent in Belem. San Jeronymo is the Patron Saint of Lisbon, and watches continually over its safety–preserving it from fires, earthquakes, inundations and such calamities. His zeal and vigilance of late years admit here of no question; although it is confessed that in 1755 he slumbered on his post, and did not awake until his statue was pitched from its pedestal prone upon its face. He was also, it cannot be denied, a little remiss in permitting the entrance of Junôt and his band of marauders; although it is averred that he did all in his power to remedy the evil by procuring favourable winds to waft Sir Arthur there to drive them out. On the whole, San Jeronymo is a respectable Patron Saint–much revered in Lisbon; and who, since his canonization, has done as much good as any saint in the calendar.

In the month of December I was appointed assistant-surgeon to the 66th regiment and directed once more to proceed to Coimbra. In consequence of the severe loss this excellent corps sustained on the bloody field of Albuera, it was formed into a provisional battalion, with two or three other weak corps, and laboured under this disadvantage during the remainder of the Peninsular struggle–though only joined in battalion, for the greater part of the time, with the 31st regiment. The 66th, for its strength, was one of the most efficient corps in the army–it always fought well–was well-behaved and on good terms with the inhabitants in quarters, and had few sick. A high compliment was paid to this regiment, by the Duke of Wellington, during a sharp little affair on the advance from Coimbra to Oporto, in 1809. In riding past Capt. Goldie,[10] (now Colonel Goldie, of the 11th Foot) then commanding two companies, the Duke stopped and halted them, saying, 'You may take your men back, and tell your commanding officer, they have fought like lions today.'

3

On the march · Joins 66th Foot · Storming of Badajoz · Attack by leeches ·
Another love affair

Mounted on my bay horse, Liberdade, with my baggage
on a mule in charge of Antonio, I set out from Lisbon,
on the 23rd January, 1812. Our first day's march was a short one
of two leagues to Saccavem; next day we passed through Alhandra
and saw the eastern extremity of the far-famed lines of Torres
Vedras. We admired (as who does not) the foresight and sagacity
that had appreciated the strength and value of these mountain
bulwarks, and the skill and secrecy with which they had been
rendered impregnable.

We witnessed a great deal of misery amongst the poor inhabitants on this march, who were unanimous in their exclamations of
bitter hatred to the '*malditos Frenceses*'. The cutting down of the
olive trees for fuel was one charge constantly reiterated against
Massena's troops. The poor people said they did not mind so
much the burning and breaking up of their furniture, or even
making bonfires of their houses, as the wanton destruction of the
trees from which their revenue was mainly derived, and which
took so long a time to arrive at maturity.

When we reached Coimbra, Ciudad Rodrigo had fallen, and
troops and artillery were moving to the south, where preparations
were making for investing Badajoz. The regiment to which I now
belonged, I found, was quartered in Spanish Estremadura, somewhere near Merida. I was directed to proceed without delay to
join it.

I retraced my steps to Thomar—crossed the picturesque Zezere
at Punhete, and proceeded from thence to Abrantes along the
right bank of the Tagus, which here is literally golden-sanded—to
appearance. It is, I believe, only the mica which has been washed
out of the granite during the long course of the stream, nearly all
the way from Toledo.

Halting for a couple of days at Abrantes, which was a large
depôt of sick, I had the pleasure of meeting many old acquaintances, and of visiting all the hospitals. This is a very convenient

station for sick on many accounts—chiefly the healthy character
of the place and the direct water communication with Lisbon.

Proceeding on our march, the faithful Antonio and I crossed
into the Alentejo—had a shot at a wolf without hitting him, near
Gaviao, and reached Elvas on the 20th March. At this time the
last siege of Badajoz was just commencing—Lord Wellington's
head quarters were at Elvas—the town was full of staff, and all
was bustle and note of preparation. The weather was very wet,
and I pitied the poor fellows up to their middles in the trenches.

At Elvas I learned that the 66th was quartered at Merida—the
direct road would be through Badajoz, but as that route was not
then practicable, I was ordered to march by the circuitous line of
Campo Mayor and Albuquerque.

When we arrived in Albuquerque the cannonading at Badajoz
had begun, and the next morning, the weather being fine, all the
world was out on the walls of the castle (situated on a high hill)
to witness the exciting spectacle. Although twenty miles distant,
every shot could be heard distinctly; and at first, before a broad
pall of smoke covered besiegers and besieged, every thing going
on could be seen with a glass. When I mounted to the castle, after
breakfast, I found a great crowd of well dressed spectators with
many ladies. Deep interest was painted on every countenance;
and no wonder, for many of those now assembled were inhabitants
of Badajoz, and had obtained permission from Phillippon, the
French Governor, to quit the city when it was first invested;
leaving their homes, and some their husbands and families,
behind.

Yet, though concern and apprehension were manifest in the
countenance, there was nothing unmanly in the demeanour of
the male part of the assembled crowd, nor any silly expression of
violent emotion on the part of the ladies. Their whole conduct, as
well as that of the men, produced an impression on my mind
favourable to the Spanish character.

There was one singularly fine and handsome woman, Donna
Thereza Solvielta, and two sweet girls her daughters, whom I
particularly observed. When they took their position at the top
and directed their eyes towards the beleaguered city, I observed
that every shot, as the sound boomed sullenly on the ear, paled
the lovely cheeks of the two young ladies, but the mother stood
the fire better. At the first report there was a faint exclamation—

'*O Virgem purissima!*' from one of the daughters; but they all soon became composed, and as I was beginning to feel an interest in the group, and my uniform as a British officer was a sufficient introduction, I accosted Donna Thereza, and thus commenced a most agreeable acquaintance with a very amiable family. When I informed them that in all probability no bombs would be thrown into the town, and that the English fire would be entirely directed against the ramparts and defences of the place, and thus that there was scarcely any danger of their house being hit, which was in the square near the cathedral–they were much consoled, for they had feared a general bombardment. It appeared that the husband and two boys remained in Badajoz. After listening and reconnoitering through a glass until we were tired, I walked about with the ladies until the sun became hot, and then escorted them home to their lodgings in the house of an old female relative.

The rain that fell lately had swollen the rivers crossing the road to Merida so much that they were unfordable, and the bridges had fallen in the wars–I was thus detained three days at Albuquerque. The morning was spent on the hill, listening to the firing, and speculating about the siege with my new friends the Solvielta family. At length I bade those interesting ladies adieu, and Antonio and myself set out for Merida.

The cannonading sounded in our ears the whole way. We found more difficulty than we had expected in fording the rivers, and I very nearly lost my fine mule and all my baggage in crossing one of them. After three or four unpleasant passages of this description we reached Merida, where I joined my regiment, commanded by a gallant soldier, Major Dodgin,[11] and was formally introduced to the officers.

Merida is a very ancient city–was the seat of a Provincial Military Government under the Romans, and is still full of fine Roman remains. There is a long and beautiful bridge over the Guadiana, of the time of Charles the Fifth, but on a Roman foundation–a Roman and a Moorish aqueduct–a large piece of an amphitheatre–the remains of a Naumachia, a Presidium in a very perfect state of preservation, with several busts of Roman Emperors in the niches, amongst which I discovered the heads of Trajan and Galba–a Triumphal arch–the portico of a Temple of Mars with '*Marti D.O.M,*' on the base of the pediment. This portico is quite perfect: it stands in front of a Church of Dominican Friars, and immediately under the old inscription is the following: *'Jam non Marti sed Jesu Christo, D.O.M., consecratum est'*. The amphitheatre has been used not long ago as an arena for bull-fights—a small improvement on the bloody spectacles formerly exhibited, but still most barbarous, and evincing the little improvement that fifteen or sixteen centuries of a corrupted christianity have produced on the national morals.

In the course of a day's rambles through the town I descried a handsome white marble Façade of a Temple of Diana, built into the front of a modern house, which, from certain indications, afforded by the conduct of two or three young damsels at the windows, was unquestionably more devoted to the worship of Venus Urania than that of the chaste goddess. Here, at any rate, Paganism might triumph on the superior purity of its morals.

But on this occasion I had little time for antiquarian explorations—Soult, at this time, was collecting what force he could to relieve Badajoz, now hard pressed—which the covering army, under Sir Rowland Hill, was determined to prevent—consequently a fight was expected, and it became necessary to clear the hospitals and send all incumbrances to the rear. The sick of the second division, therefore, were ordered to Altar de Chao, an hospital station in the Alen-Tejo; and although I had only just arrived, after a march of five hundred miles, I was directed to take charge of the convoy.

The siege of Badajoz was still going on, and this march, as well as that by Albuquerque, were of high interest, from the vicinity of the route to the invested city. Our road now described a segment of a circle round it, within the former course and much nearer, and its lofty citadel was visible from every elevation of the way, standing above a heavy canopy of smoke which overhung the ramparts and lower parts of the town, as well as the besieging batteries. Generally, about three o'clock in the afternoon, there was a suspension of firing on both sides for a short time, to allow the guns to cool. Then the smoke would be wafted away by the wind, and the whole fortress become distinctly visible. Soon a salvo would thunder from the breaching batteries, and be immediately answered by the garrison, and then the incessant roar of the heavy artillery on both sides would proceed without intermission as before.

I reached Campo Mayor on the 6th of April, with my convoy

of sick, and was much pleased to find that the poor fellows had all improved wonderfully in health during the march. Indeed, the good effects of locomotion in recovering very debilitated subjects, were strikingly displayed during the whole Peninsular struggle, but never more than on this occasion. The convoy consisted of one hundred and twenty sick, thirty or forty of whom were so ill of bad continued and remittent fevers, that it was necessary to tie them on the mules' backs, lest they should fall off through weakness. Others were supported by men of the escort sitting behind them; but at the end of the second day's march these enfeebled subjects would ride by themselves bravely and vigorously, and call out lustily for their rations. I am convinced that the lives of several amongst them were saved by this march, and the recovery of the rest was materially accelerated. To be sure ours was a march cheered by the most exciting military music all the way; and the sound of the twenty-four pounder salvos, with the occasional glimpse of the smoke-wreathed city, and the French flag still flying on the citadel, formed a cordial more tonic and stimulating and restorative than all the elixirs in the world.

On the 6th of April, the last day of our march, the cannonade was much louder and closer than usual, and as I rode along I became more and more convinced that a crisis was approaching. On our arrival in the evening, at Campo Mayor, we found the whole population in a state of intense excitement and anxiety. It was generally known that Badajoz was to be stormed during the night; and as we were only seven mile distant, even the pattering of the musketry could be distinctly heard in the calm of the evening, between the heavy reports of the battering artillery. As the night advanced every accidental swelling of the sound was deemed the signal for the terrific conflict at the breach. I know not how the intelligence was received, but most certainly there were reports in circulation that night, at Campo Mayor, that the castle was to be escaladed by Sir Thomas Picton and the third division.

During this eventful night few eyes were closed in Campo Mayor; the priests were performing divine service and imploring success in the churches, and the entire adult population were either engaged in prayer, or traversing the streets, in extreme agitation and alarm. All this time the thunder of the bloody conflict sounded awfully, and as the work of death advanced, and the air became cooler and stiller, the report of the heavy artillery appeared actually to shake the roofs of the churches over the trembling masses crowded within. The scene altogether was one that cannot easily pass from the memory, for it was marked by astonishing sublimity. I hurried from one church to another; but all were alike–all were filled with people praying with extreme fervency–weeping, sobbing, exclaiming–enquiring wildly and anxiously for intelligence, or listening intently to the loud and confused sound of mortal strife.

At length day dawned, and with it came an ominous calm and lull. Did this bode good or evil? Was the city taken, or had the storming parties been shattered and repulsed, and had the garrison ceased its fire because the besiegers had retired from the reach of the guns? For a long time nothing could be descried on the wide plain between the two places–at length a horseman was seen galloping full speed along the road. The agony of suspense then became almost intolerable: but when he approached nearer and was seen to stop suddenly, stand up in his stirrups and wave his hat repeatedly round his head–a shout of ten thousand '*Vivas!*' rent the air, prolonged and reiterated along the fortifications until lost in the overwhelming pealing of all the bells in the city.

My military dress procured me two or three score of warm embraces–the pale countenances of the women brightened up and their dark eyes beamed out brilliantly. Never were fair ladies so condescending and so affectionate, and I believe, if I had chosen, I might have kissed half Campo Mayor. '*Viva os Inglezez!*' was in every mouth. At length getting satiated with the numerous accolades, and remembering that my day's march was a short one, I delayed the starting of my sick convoy for a couple of hours, and determined to gallop over to Badajoz.

I reached the bridge over the Guadiana in three quarters of an hour, but my surprise was great; instead of finding every thing quiet, and every body occupied in attentions to the wounded and preparations for burying the dead, as I had expected, I beheld a scene of the most dreadful drunkenness, violence and confusion. Parties of intoxicated men, loosed from all discipline and restraint, and impelled by their own evil passions, were roaming and reeling about; firing into the windows–bursting open the doors by the discharge of several muskets simultaneously against the lock– plundering–shooting any person who opposed them–violating, and committing every horrid excess, and sometimes destroying each other. There were many Portuguese, but the majority were English soldiers; and amongst these, two regiments of the third division, the eighty—and—[12] were disgracefully conspicuous.

I proceeded amongst the desultory but dangerous firing, by the *detour* of the Talavera gate to the main breach. There lay a frightful heap of fifteen hundred British soldiers, dead, but yet warm, and mingled with some still living, but so desperately wounded as to be irremovable without more assistance than could yet be afforded—there they lay stiffening in their gore—body piled upon body—involved, intertwined, crushed, burned, and blackened—one hideous and enormous mass of carnage.

At the foot of the castle wall, where the third division had escaladed, the dead lay thick, and a great number of corpses were strewn near the Vincente Bastion. Several were scattered on the glacis of the Trinidad Bastion, and a number who appeared to have been drowned, were lying in the cunette of the ditch, at that place. But the chief slaughter had taken place at the great breach. There stood still the terrific beam across the top, armed with its thickly bristling sword-blades, which no human strength nor dexterity could pass without impalement. The smell of burned flesh was yet shockingly strong and disgusting.

Joining some of the medical officers who were assisting the most urgent cases, and amputating limbs shattered by roundshot, I remained during the morning and forenoon; then hastily eating a biscuit, partially blackened with gunpowder, and taking a mouthful of wine from a soldier's wooden canteen, I returned to my charge at Campo Mayor. The bells were still ringing merrily at intervals, and every body was rejoicing—rejoicing! after what I had just witnessed!

I hastened to get my party in motion, and with many bitter reflections on the calamities of war, proceeded on the march. When I arrived at Chao I had an attack of low fever, which was fortunately of short duration, and in a few days my trusty Antonio and his master retraced their steps towards Estremadura.

When we had advanced about a league on our first day's march towards Elvas, we saw at a distance a large body of men approaching. It was the French garrison of Badajoz, about three thousand five hundred in number, on their route to embark for England. There was a striking difference in the appearance and bearing of the veterans from that of the young soldiers. The former had a bold and self-confident look, that said '*N'importe—c'est la fortune de guerre—notre temps viendra.*' The poor young conscripts, of whom there appeared a fourth-part, on the contrary, looked completely *abuttus*; and their furtive, timid glances, betrayed the fear of discovering a loaded gun or a Portuguese knife in every object around them.

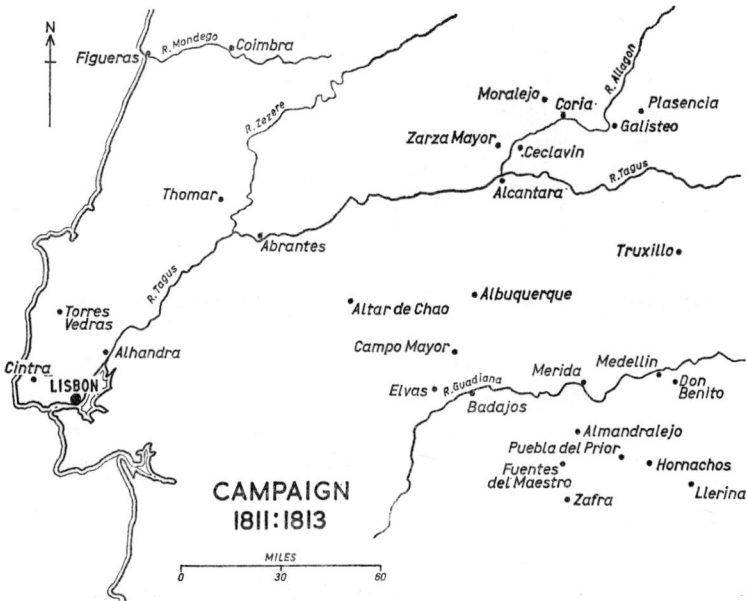

CAMPAIGN
1811:1813

On our return through Elvas, the town was full of wounded; yet, in passing through the hospitals one would form a very incorrect opinion of the miseries and agonies that followed the storm, from the appearance of the patients. To have been wounded and to have escaped with life from such a tremendous conflict—involving a display of the most sustained, unflinching and perfect valour, in the course of many ages—was, in itself alone, a cause of pride and gratulation. *They* were untainted with the pillage of the devoted city, and the thousand atrocious crimes comprised in that fatal word.

At this time there was a strong muster of medical officers in Elvas, and the hospitals afforded a fine field of practice and great professional facilities in acquiring surgical confidence and experience. I obtained permission to stay there a fortnight.

On our return through Badajoz, I entered that ill-fated place with very painful feelings. All was still gloom and dismay. Almost every individual of any respectability in the city had been outraged, either in his property or the sanctity of his family, relations or friends. Happy were the ladies that had left the town before its investment. Those beautiful Solvieltas—had they remained! and from my heart I rejoiced at their escape.

Although the British and Portuguese troops—but chiefly the former—bore then, and still bear the principal share of the odium, the lower classes of the inhabitants were also chief performers in the horrid tragedy. The rascally mob—the disgrace of all large cities—as soon as the magazine of brandy in the cathedral was opened, joined, when they became half-drunk, in all the brutalities of the time. Having superior local knowledge, they conducted the English and Portuguese strangers to the houses of the principal and richest inhabitants, and when the doors were burst open, shared in the spoil and the crime.

Yet, originally, the blame lay with the Spaniards themselves, and even during the storm they provoked the wrath of the assailants. Had not Mendizabal behaved like a coward or a fool, Badajoz would never have fallen into the power of the French. When covering the place in an almost unassailable position, under San Christoval, defended by two rivers, a fortress and a fort, he suffered himself to be surprised by Soult, with half his force, and himself and his army to be driven from their strong post and scattered all over the country. And this rout was the more shameful, as he had been previously warned by Lord Wellington and advised to be on his guard against Soult, but with true Spanish pride and mulishness scorned the good advice, and affected to believe that the French General would not dare to attack him. Aaing, even after the dispersal of Mendizabal's army, had the Governor held out three days longer—assured as he was of speedy succour—the town could not have been taken by the French. But the truth is, the magniloquent Spaniards, to use a vulgar expression, scarcely ever shewed any pluck.

I believe it is true that the troops of the fourth division, who got into the town by escalading the San Vincento Bastion, when straggling through the deserted but illuminated streets, were fired upon out of the houses by the Spaniards. It is natural that this would be mentioned to their comrades, and, when the whole allied force burst into the city, be a pretext, if not an extenuation, for many of the excesses that were committed.

On the 22nd of April, I rejoined my regiment at Almandralejo. Sir Rowland Hill's head quarters were there established.

In the beginning of May, the cavalry picquets of our division posted near Hornachos, being considered a little too much exposed, the light companies of General Byng's brigade were sent to a small village called Puebla del Prior, to support them. I was directed to accompany the detachment.

One day a brother officer and myself rode to Hornachos, a town two leagues farther in front, which was occasionally patrolled by both armies. It was a silly excursion, for we might both have been shot or taken prisoners; and as it was we were chased by two of the enemy's dragoons, but being better mounted and in lighter riding order, we soon found we could distance our pursuers if we chose; we consequently checked our horses and tried to inveigle them into an ambuscade. But they were old hands, and when they found how matters stood, they deliberately turned and went back to their patrol without even wasting a cartridge on us.

After passing a fortnight quietly at Puebla, we were disturbed one day whilst at dinner, by the approach of a strong body of the enemy's cavalry, before whom our advanced picquets were slowly retiring. They came close, but did not attack as they had no infantry; and it afterwards appeared that this little demonstration was a mere reconnaissance to feel our force—Sir Rowland having at this time marched to destroy the French *Tête du Pont* and forts at Almaraz on the Tagus.

When Sir Rowland Hill returned, after the successful accomplishment of his object, with little loss, we advanced in the direction of Zafra and the Sierra Morena. At Usagre, we had the mortification of witnessing the defeat of two brigades of British heavy cavalry, by about an equal number of French, from the top of the church tower. This sight caused great disgust, as from the superior physical strength of our men and horses they ought to have been more than a match for their adversaries. The French were commanded by General L'Allemand, and the British by General S—,[13] who was much blamed at the time for absolute deficiency of personal intrepidity in leading on his men. In the evening the wounded began to arrive at the village, and I sat up all night dressing their hurts–mostly sabre-cuts.

In the end of June, my commanding officer, Major Dodgin, was attacked with a violent inflammatory fever, and I received orders to convey him to Badajoz, and attend him there. Notwithstanding extensive depletion from the temporal arteries, and other measures necessary to subdue ardent fever in a patient of very large and robust frame–strong as a horse and weighing twenty stone–he became violently delirious. Under the hallucination that he had been appointed aide-de-camp to Sir Rowland Hill, he insisted one morning on dressing himself, mounting his horse and proceeding back to camp. After fruitlessly attempting to reason him out of this project, I found I must employ stronger measures; accordingly, having first removed the Major's sword, pistols and trowsers out of the way, and left him in charge of two servants, I proceeded to the general hospital in quest of more assistance and a straight-waistcoat.

Here I found a certain pragmatic staff-surgeon, named B—, whom I begged to afford me the necessary aid, and also to give me his personal help in subduing the Hercules with whom I had to do. Now it so chanced that the staff-surgeon in question had attended General Walker, who was so badly wounded at the storm. The patient had had several ribs broken, but recovered; and his doctor being a good draughtsman, had made a sketch of this remarkable wound, and was, unfortunately, when I called, engaged in giving it the finishing touch. I waited a few minutes, but seeing him still intent on his work, I then requested that he would leave off his sketch and accompany me to my refractory patient's lodging, or he might get away, and in the powerful sun that was then broiling us, soon ride himself to death. 'My dear Sir,' he replied, 'just wait one instant; it will not take more than one moment. Look there, what do you think of that? Is the colouring too high? I had much difficulty in managing that flesh–hah, hah! *both* ways–hah, hah, hah! Doesn't that rib *relievo a leetle* too much–Eh? Certainly it does–don't you think so? I'll just soften it down a little.' At last, after a quarter of an hour's shading down General Walker's too prominent rib, out we sallied with two orderlies and a straight-waistcoat.

Now, I had anticipated mischief from the delay, and was not mistaken. When we came to the top of the short street where the

Major lodged, we were both horror-struck at seeing him dressed in his blue frock and cocked-hat, leading his large black charger out of the door and preparing to mount. We all ran down the street as fast as we could but he was on horse-back before we reached his quarter. The staff-surgeon then accosted him, representing very eloquently that the Major was not in a condition for a journey in the hot sun—that he would fall from his horse on the road, &c. &c. The Major told him to begone—that he was a meddling fool or a madman thus to interrupt him when ordered on duty—and then finding his opponent still resolute, he set spurs to his horse and charged the poor doctor. The latter jumped to one side in great alarm and disappeared through a low window, that was fortunately open. The patient then proceeded in a canter down the street towards the ramparts, and afterwards turned to the right in the direction of the Elvas gate, but I ran by a near cut and arrived there before him. I found some difficulty in explaining to the Spanish Lieutenant, who commanded the guard, the nature of the case; but at length he did as I wished, and when the Major arrived, looking very pale, the gate was closed and there was no egress. He fumed, and fretted, and threatened the officer—but it was all in vain; then turning his horse he galloped towards the Talavera gate, taking the same circuitous course by the ramparts. There, also, he was anticipated, for whilst I ran to the one, I had sent a servant to the other. A good deal fatigued by all this exertion in the burning sun, and weakened by loss of blood, the patient rode home, lay down on a couch and called for his writing desk. He then began a letter of charges against me for forcibly detaining him in Badajoz, but not being able to finish it, and soon writing diagonally instead of across the paper, he gave over, lay down and fell fast asleep. He slept nearly thirty-six hours, when he awoke convalescent—free from all complaint but weakness, and recollecting nothing that had happened.

It appeared that when I went to the hospital he started out of bed, soon mastered all opposition, and proceeded to dress himself. He was very angry at the removal of his sword and trowsers, and I had imagined that the absence of the latter would be an impediment to escape not easily got over—but I was wrong. The Major made one of the servants surrender the trowsers he had on, banging him with a stick until he took them off, and such was his strength and determination that he fairly cowed them both into submission. The man's trowsers were too small, but he forced them on, though at the expense of some fearful rents in the thighs, and, indeed, the Major might as well have been altogether *sans culottes*, as invested with the tattered concerns. He then went to the stable, saddled his horse himself, and actually brought him into his bedroom, which was on the ground-floor, until he found his cocked-hat. Had we been one minute later, or failed in blockading him at the gates, the poor patient would, in all probability, have ridden till he dropped dead from his horse.

After this adventure the Major soon recovered and proceeded to join the regiment, but without his surgeon. It was the month of August, when the banks of the Guadiana are annually afflicted with bad remittent and intermittent fevers—I caught the disease, struggled against it for a little, but at last was obliged to surrender at discretion.

I had no particular desire to employ the facetious rib-painter, so I confided myself to the charge of a young *medico*, a friend and countryman who watched me with the most kind and sedulous attention. From a desire to save the vital fluid and economize strength, he would not bleed me from the arm or temporal artery, as I wished; but when the symptoms of determination to the head became urgent, he sheered and shaved my curly locks one hot afternoon, and attached three dozen of leeches to my poor caput. A few hours after, they carried me into the yard, placed me erect, and poured four or five-and-twenty buckets of cold well-water over me from a third story window. After this terrible shower-bath, I was rubbed dry and put to bed. For the first two hours I was not quite sure whether my head had not been carried away in the flood, for I felt as if there was no living part, and all was numb and cold above my shoulders—but there was violent reaction during the night, and I became delirious the next morning.

However, I was not destined to leave my bones in Badajoz—there were but too many British bones there already. By the blessing of Providence, which, laughter-loving mortal that I am, I am not ashamed to acknowledge—I at length recovered, but, in the dreadfully hot weather we then had in Estremadura, the convalescence was tedious.

On this occasion, I lodged in the house of a kind-hearted young Priest, Don Juan Joze Martinez, who had two sisters living with him, and a third, the Abbess of a convent in the same street. The young senhoras were exceedingly kind and attentive; perhaps the more so, when they discovered from my servant that I was an Irishman, which, in Spain, is synonymous with Roman Catholic. However, to do these good ladies justice, although they were undeceived in this respect, they did not relax the least in those thousand little affectionate acts which my helpless situation called for, and those soothing offices of female kindness, so delightful to the object, when on a bed of sickness in a strange land. But they were very urgent in their endeavours to convert me from my heresy and bring me within the pale of their own church, seasoning each cup of the nice broth they prepared and administered with good advice on this subject, and often calling in their brother to their assistance. He was stronger-minded and more liberal, however, than these dark-eyed maidens, and used to reply to their entreaties, '*Deixa lo, deixa lo, Pobrecito*'–'Let him alone, poor fellow–we must cure him first and convert him afterwards.'

When I became convalescent, a strange Spanish gentleman called to see me. He said he had been requested by his wife and daughters to enquire concerning my health, and to express on their parts grateful thanks for the attentions they had received at Albuquerque. It was Don Ignacio Solvielta, and as soon as I recovered sufficiently I called on my fair friends. It was pleasing to learn that their house had remained untouched during the siege; and in the sack and pillage of the storm, although the door had been blown open, a bag of a couple of hundred dollars was the amount of their loss.

My *Patrone* gave me a graphic description of the state of his family during the dreadful two days, when Badajoz was the prey of a drunken and infuriated soldiery. He had sagaciously anticipated the plunder, and provided two purses–a larger and a smaller–placed his sisters on the top of the house and then destroyed the ladder–after these precautions the doors were secured and the courageous Priest quietly awaited the result. About eight o'clock, the first morning, a party of half-drunken British soldiers, in yellow facings,[14] blew off the lock of the street door, rushed in and seized him, and demanded his money. He pleaded poverty, but they presented their muskets to his breast, and at last, by horrid threats, extorted the smaller purse. Then they searched the house, destroying or pillaging whatever struck their fancy; at length they went away and the door was barricaded as well as circumstances permitted. In the course of the first day another party—also British and with the same facings, broke through the poor Priest's defences—roamed through the house, and afterwards by threats of instant death, forced him to surrender the larger purse of dollars. The door was then left open, but the house was no more molested. The poor trembling girls remained all that day and night on the roof, and did not venture down till some degree of order was restored in the town.

During the siege two twenty-four pound shot had penetrated the back wall of the house and lodged in the front, without doing farther injury than piercing a wooden partition and demolishing an arm-chair, from which one of the sisters had just risen. The Priest intended to keep them both, though, as he remarked, they were not in the habit in his church of preserving relics so substantial.

A veil was thrown purposely over the sufferings of his sister the Abbess, and inmates of the convent, which was never withdrawn, for when I ventured to enquire if they had escaped insult and outrage, my *Patrone's* brow grew black. It was then only I could fully appreciate the fine character of the man. Smarting under recent violence and spoliation, and, moreover touched, as there was too much reason to believe, in a point on which Spanish honour is so peculiarly susceptible, he yet had the good sense not to confound the innocent with the guilty, and the magnanimity still to treat me with the greatest tenderness when lying helpless under his roof.

At this time the heat of the weather was extraordinary in Estremadura—the Fahrenheit thermometer rising to 97 degrees in the shade at Badajoz. Under these circumstances it was not easy to recover strength fast; but, having heard that the army was about to move to the front, I became anxious to join, and marched ten days before I ought to have set out. The consequence was an attack of ague on the road; and though the temperature in the sun could not have been less than 130 degrees, my teeth danced and chattered for an hour or so, like a pair of castenets, and I was forced to halt in a village on the road, named Santa Martha.

At this time the army was six months in arrears of pay, and, consequently, a good deal of inconvenience was occasionally experienced from narrow finances, particularly when absent from one's regiment. Two or three days after my arrival in Santa

Martha, when taking a farewell look at my last dollar, and devising some plan of ways and means suited to the emergency, a mounted soldier of the 66th arrived in the village, with a letter from Fuentes del Maestro, where the regiment was quartered. It was Colonel Nicol's[15] servant with a very kind letter, giving me unlimited leave of absence, and accompanied by three doubloons, which he thought I might require; and which, it appeared afterwards—such was the scarcity of money—he had been obliged to borrow from a Turkish Sutler who accompanied the Division.

I record this trait of my most esteemed friend, now General Nicol, because, in the first place, it is gratifying to my own feelings; and secondly, because it was one of a series of similar acts of thoughtful and unostentatious liberality and kindness towards his officers, during a quarter of a century that he commanded the regiment.

At length I rejoined the 66th at Fuentes del Maestro, just in time to accompany it on the advance of the Division in the direction of Llerena; but, on some intelligence being received of the concentration of a strong force of the enemy on our right, the Division was countermarched, and our Brigade, consisting of the Buffs or 3rd Foot, the 31st, 57th and 66th, returned to their old quarters at Fuentes del Maestro.

The day of our return was hot, and the road had been very dusty, with a good deal of wind. When the Brigade reached the immediate neighbourhood of the town, they halted and piled their arms until the men were furnished with billets. Near this spot was one of the old fountains from which the place had taken its name, which was a square enclosure, now in a ruinous state, and half filled with grass and weeds, but still containing clear water. The thirsty soldiers, fatigued with the heat and long march, flew at once to this reservoir, and kneeling and placing their hands on the low wall that surrounded it, they dipped their dusty muzzles up to the ears in the cool element and quaffed away like fishes. 'The consequence was awful in the extreme.' Next morning about one hundred and fifty of them came to the different regimental hospitals, and at first their cases looked rather alarming, for they were all spitting blood. On examination it was ascertained that they had fished up three or four hundred leeches from the old fountain, which was full of these little wretches. These blood-suckers had attached themselves in the mouth, nostrils, throat, gullet, and even the stomach; higher or lower, according to the vigor of their own adhesive powers, or the strength of suction of the drinkers. We had a bloody day at the hospitals, although no lives were lost, except the leeches, and very hard it was to eject them. Some were noosed with a silk ligature by the tail and torn off, though many were thus cut in two, leaving the head still sticking. Several were dislodged by a strong solution of salt, and tobacco was used to others. Powerful emetics were necessary to oust the knowing ones that had reached the citadel of the stomach. At last the enemy were finally beaten from all their positions with great slaughter.

The whole corps of Sir Rowland Hill, consisting of sixteen or seventeen thousand men, was now set in motion towards the Sierra Morena, to dislodge the French from a rich tract of country to the west of those mountains, and push up the valley of the Tagus and even advance upon Madrid. We marched on the 27th of August, reached Llerena on the 29th and Don Benito on the 6th of September.

The English had never been in Don Benito before, and thus we enjoyed the good effects of the first burst of patriotism, friendship and hospitality of the inhabitants, after the long and oppressive occupation of their town by the enemy. Nothing was seen or heard but patriotic songs—swearing to the Constitution before the ugly picture of Ferdinand the Seventh, '*Viva los Inglesez!*' and *fêting* and dancing. The people seemed to be all mad with joy. On the night of the 12th of September, when we were all busily engaged at a ball, the Marquis of Worcester arrived with despatches from Head Quarters to Sir Rowland Hill; in half an hour the party was broken up, and early in the morning the corps was put in motion for Truxillo. I recollect well the terrible wetting we all got in a thunder-shower as we were leaving the town, and when the sun had nearly dried our clothes during the march, our lower integuments were again dipped mid-thigh deep in fording the Guadiana.

A large depôt of provisions, and stores, and an hospital, were established at Truxillo. To my great mortification, the medical officer who was to take charge of the hospital, fell sick; I was directed by the staff-surgeon of the Division to take his place and remain in charge at Truxillo, whilst the 66th regiment, with the whole Corps, moved on Madrid.

I lodged in the mansion of the Conde de Q—, a descendant of Pizarro; a little old man, who, in right of his ancestor, always wore a small gold key outside the flap of his right coat pocket, of which he was very proud. He was very grandiloquent, as most Spanish gentlemen are–formal, courteous and pedantic.

The Conde de Q— had two daughters unmarried–Donna Francesca and Donna Bernarda, with the latter of whom, who was the younger and prettier, I soon found myself falling desperately in love. My time was fully occupied during the whole of the day, for I had two hundred sick, and a number of officers to attend, with only one incompetent Spanish Hospital-Mate to assist me; but the evenings were devoted to dancing–forfeits, blind man's buff, alternating with lessons in Don Quixotte, singing and the guitar.

It is customary in Spain to take one's chocolate in bed very early in the morning, and as I have generally found it good policy to conform to peculiar national customs wherever I have been, when innocent and not prejudicial to health, Antonio would sometimes bring it to me, fuming and fragrant, by day-light. But more frequently the fairy-footed Bernarda, accompanied by Francesca, would appear at my bed-side, bearing a little silver salver, on which was a small gilded cup of chocolate, so thick and rich that the little delicate parallelopiped of toast, its unvarying attendant, would stand upright in the middle. There would the lovely sisters remain '–twin cherries on one stalk' in all honest confidence, laughing and joking, and lisping their beautiful language, till I had finished my chocolate–a matter which I was never in a hurry to accomplish.

Let no man of vain imagination, nor woman either, entertain for a moment, a thought prejudicial to the amiable couple, for no sweet brace of sisters on record, chaste as '–the icicle that hangs from Dian's Temple'–could have uniformly comported themselves with greater propriety.

I remained three months at Truxillo, and were I not afraid of swelling out my book to inexpedient dimensions, I could detail numerous incidents, some comic and some tragic, but all amusing enough at the time, in which I was engaged. Many love passages also must be omitted–how I had a Spanish rival in my admiration of the fair Bernarda–how she confessed I need fear no supplanting in her heart–how I was threatened with *cuchillo* if I persisted in my presumption–how I received an anonymous letter, warning me of a plot to assassinate me, when paying a night-visit to a sick officer—how, with the assistance of the trusty Antonio and two of my hospital orderlies, the plotters were discomfited and soundly drubbed—how I discovered my little rival amongst them, and how I treated him on that occasion, professionally and *secundem artem*, by administering myself a good stiff dose of bark, *with the stick inside*—how I triumphed, and, alas! how, in the midst of my rejoicing, I was suddenly ordered to break up the hospital establishment at Truxillo and proceed to Elvas.

Young men under the influence of strong passions have done, do, and will do silly things, I presume, to the end of the chapter. On leaving Truxillo, I was prevented by an accident from making a fatal mistake early in life, and thus shading irreparably its whole complexion afterwards.

It was arranged that my mistress should elope with me on a fixed day, and a priest was to be ready at a village six leagues off, to unite us the same evening. As there are no post-chaises nor other procurable vehicles in that part of Spain, and the ladies must travel on ass-back or mule-back, I had purchased a quiet female donkey to carry her fair load. As this whole matter was *sub silentio*, for we feared the opposition of the Conde, Antonio negociated that the owner of the animal should bring it to the stable late on the evening preceding the intended escapade. At the time appointed, the donkey was grazing in a field with several others; and, just before the proprietor had caught her, a fight and general row took place amongst the *bourros*—the quiet animal selected for me received a kick in the *mêlée* from one of her he-relations, that lamed her effectually—no ass was forthcoming when required, and time pressed, for Soult was advancing and our army in full retreat from Burgos. No other suitable conveyance could be procured at a short notice, and thus our scheme failed, and the ignoble kick of an ass knocked the best concerted plan in the world to pieces. 'What great events from trivial causes spring.'

After bidding farewell to as lachrymose a pair of sisters (poor girls!) as ever wept in each other's arms, I conducted my sick to Elvas, accompanied by a good-natured little doctor of the Buffs, and a gigantic officer of the 71st, Ralph Dudgeon, somewhere near seven feet high, but every inch a good fellow. On the march the little boys and girls followed him as a prodigy, and every body stared up at him as if looking at a steeple. The roads at this time were infested by numerous bands of robbers, formed chiefly of deserters; but we marched in battle array, and although we had one alarm in a thick cork-tree wood, the rascals were frightened at our imposing appearance, and made off on the approach of our little but compact column.

At Badajoz I failed not to call on the good Priest, my former kind host, and was concerned to find that one of the amiable sisters was suffering from a Tertian fever. Having prescribed for her and left her a supply of good medicine, (invaluable in Spain,) we marched to Elvas.

4

WHEN we reached Elvas we found that the most alarming reports were in circulation as to the defeat and dispersion of the British army, and the approaching advance of the enemy in overwhelming force into Portugal. It was even feared that another retreat to the lines of Terres Vedras might be necessary. I was ordered to remain and do duty in one of the general hospitals until farther orders.

In the course of a few days these rumours ceased, for certain intelligence arrived that the army was once more established in its old frontier positions, covering Portugal. Sir Rowland Hill's Head Quarters were at Coria, and General Byng's Brigade, in which was the 66th, was stationed at Marolejo, a small town in the neighbourhood. I was then directed to march to that place.

We crossed the Tagus at Alcantara, where the river runs deep and rapid between two high rocky banks. The bridge is a fine relic of Roman power and skill; and, until the main arch was blown up two years before, was in good preservation, with the marble slab, even, yet perfect as from the sculptor's hand, telling who were Consuls and in what year of Trajan's reign it was built.

The Engineers had constructed a rope-bridge over the broken arch, which, from its great elevation, elasticity and broad span, shook under the passenger rather unpleasantly. When Antonio and I crossed, the day was very windy, and the bridge more than usually tremulous and unsteady; and although we dismounted, I was not without apprehensions, as a sudden gust would sweep violently through the deep gulley in which the river ran boiling below, that the slender flooring under our feet might be blown from its moorings, and all upon it tumbled into the Tagus.

Lord Wellington having now placed his army in winter quarters, was on his way to Cadiz, to concert measures with his brother the Marquis Wellesley and the Cortes, for a more perfect control over the Spanish armies, and the improvement of their very defective organization. We met him and General Alava the morning we

crossed the Tagus, on the road between Zarza Mayor and Alcantara. After they passed us an aide-de-camp rode back and made
enquiries about the bridge. I advised the party to dismount, and
Lord Wellington and General Alava to get out of the coach in
which they travelled, assuring him that if the gale increased much
their only safety would be in holding by the mules' tails. Where-
upon this gentleman, no less a person, I believe, than that most
distinguished officer, Lord Fitzroy Somerset,[16] laughed at my
good advice; and it certainly must have been a laughable thing to
see the great Wellington and General Alava clinging to the *os
coccygis* of a mule.

The next day an event occurred on the march, by no means of a
laughing nature. As we were moving quietly along a plain, thickly
covered with a cystus shrub—Antonio, my English *Bat-man*,[17] and
the baggage a little in the rear, a musket ball whistled suddenly
by, somewhere between my face and the horse's head, which made
us both prick up our ears. I looked round, and there, plain enough,
was the puff of smoke, about fifty yards from the road, amidst the
tall shrubs. Incontinently I galloped on towards a little elevation
in the road, and by the most extraordinary good fortune, not two
minutes after, descried the head of a small column of cavalry
coming along, half a mile off. They belonged to Don Julian
Sanchez, and had been specially ordered to destroy a band of
brigands, supposed to be in the neighbourhood. I told the officer
in command what had occurred, and we all hastened to the place
where the shot had been fired. The dragoons dashed into the
cystus very gallantly, and soon came upon a body of a dozen robbers, who shewed fight bravely enough, but to no purpose. The
country was open, for the slender shrub was no greater hindrance
to the movements of cavalry than a field of wheat—and the disparity of force was so great that none of them could escape. After
a short but animated affair, of which we were near spectators, the
whole band were killed or made prisoners. I saw three of the gang
afterwards strangled at Coria.

In this piquant little business, one dragoon received an ugly
wound in the arm, which I dressed on the spot. Two of the prisoners had received some sabre-cuts, which I also offered to dress,
but their ferocious captors would not permit it.

It had rained heavily lately, and every stream was much swollen
presenting numerous obstacles in our way, which we generally had

to ford—the bridges being 'few and far between.' Here again
my portable goods and chattels were in imminent danger, but
Antonio forced the passages in gallant style, assisted by an honest
Bat-man, yclept Jonathan Wild,[18] but no relative, that I ever
heard, of the prince of burglars. At the end of a long dreary day's
march from Zarza, we reached the miserable town of Moralejo.

Here General Byng's Brigade were resting after the fatigues and
privations of the Burgos retreat, although the indifferent rations,
muddy streets and wretched hovels of this village, afforded but
slender facilities for recovering health and efficiency. However,
our Brigade had suffered little, comparatively—the men having
been well taken care of and well fed on the retreat, whilst others
were starving, under the watchful eye of the best Brigadier, assisted
by Mr. Edwards, one of the best Commissaries in the service.[19]

A branch of the Allagon, a large tributary of the Tagus, ran
through Moralejo, which I soon explored, and found it contained
good dace and barbel that served to eke out the rations, and
nothing else was here procurable. Antonio managed, however, to
turn the tough, lean, ropy beef into something like soup, and thus
the programme of dinners was fish—soup—*bouilli*—Sunday—fish,
bouilli, soup—Monday, and so on through the week.

We remained but a short time in Moralejo, and then moved to
Coria, and afterwards to a large straggling village called Ceclavin.
Coria is a walled city containing nine or ten thousand inhabitants—the walls are of Moorish origin with several round towers,
but all in a ruinous state. The hill on which the city is built rises
precipitately from the former bed of the River Allagon, which is
now dry—the course of the stream having been in some way turned
from its ancient channel into another, half a mile distant, though
the bridge still stands oddly enough over the old course, and the
river has now to be crossed by a ferry. The local tradition is, that
Saint Somebody, whose name I forget, to whom the cathedral is
dedicated, foreseeing that in the course of time the church's
foundation would be undermined by the river, miraculously
changed its course one night, and in the morning the astonished
inhabitants beheld the stream running in a new channel at a
respectful distance. Certainly the puissant Saint left his miracle
incomplete, for, beyond all question, he ought to have endowed
the river with the power of carrying off the bridge on its back.

A Canon of the Cathedral in relating this story, told me confidentially,–'The people believe the legend, and we don't wish to undeceive them–they are the more devout for their faith. Between you and me the river's course was changed by the earthquake of 1755.'

During this winter amateur plays and various festivities were got up at Coria, which continued to be Sir R. Hill's Head Quarters. A pack of fox-hounds came out from England for the worthy Commander, and hunted once or twice a week, until they were broken up by a singularly unfortunate accident.

One very fine day there was a strong field–we found and had a splendid run of nearly two hours, with only a short check–every body well up. At last Mr. Reynard, being hard pressed, made for his earth in a steep bank of the Allagon, but feeling somewhat flurried with the long chase, the animal, wise as he was, forgot his topographical marks, and, instead of descending to his hole obliquely, he went sheer down a perpendicular bank, one hundred and fifty feet high, and was followed by five couple and a half of the best of the dogs. They were all killed instantly, and Sir R. Hill, the huntsman and two or three of the leading horsemen had a narrow escape; for the bank was most treacherous, giving no indication of danger until almost too late.

Here, as every where else in Spain, black eyes were so universal that any other colour in a lady's seemed as strange as if nature had given her three, instead of the usual number. I recollect one evening at a *Tertulla* in Coria there chanced to be a very fair English woman present. She was pretty and graceful enough to be remarkable even amidst much Spanish grace and beauty, but nothing was said of her fair skin and classic features. The buzz through the room about the lovely foreigner was–'*Mira, mira! aquella senhora tiene ojos azules!*' with a soft lisp on the last mellow word. 'Look, look! that lady has blue eyes!'

During this winter measures were being quietly taken to promote the comfort, improve and preserve the health, and increase the efficiency of the British and Portuguese regiments. We were all in high spirits–cheered by the good news from Russia; and the reverses of Napoleon there had a momentous bearing upon the war in the Peninsula, inasmuch as in all probability large draughts from thence would be required to reinforce the dispirited and diminished forces of their brethren in the north. The time was thus becoming favourable for a grand combined movement to push

61

the enemy out of the kingdom. With secrecy and his usual consummate sagacity, did the great General who commanded us,
prepare for the grand and final hunt over the Pyrenees.

There is a little old walled town called Galisteo, situated nearly
equidistant between Coria and Placentia, where two of the regiments of our Brigade were quartered during the early spring
months. At this place I was attacked by my old enemy the Tertian
ague, which I dosed in the regular way with all the usual remedies
for a fortnight—but all in vain—at twelve o'clock every second day
my teeth began to chatter. Thinks I to myself—this open attack
on the enemy will never do—let us try a manœuvre. Accordingly,
at half-past eleven I prepared a tumbler of hot spiced wine—
ordered my horse to the door—got into the saddle and drank it
off, and then proceeded in a canter over the extensive plains in
the neighbourhood. When it approached twelve, although the sun
was powerful, I could feel the ague-fiend's cold fingers grasping
my loins—I then put spurs to *Liberdade*—pushed him into a full
gallop—and at length, by dint of perseverance and good management, I fairly distanced my villainous pursuer. I tried this plan
with equal success the next time, and on the return of the third
Tertian period, was delighted to find that at twelve o'clock my
feelings continued comfortable—my spine did not turn into an
icicle, nor my grinders commence their former hornpipes.

On my recovery, *comme d'ordinaire*, I reconnoitred the river at
the bottom of the hill and picked up a considerable number of the
usual dace and barbel. But the Spanish and Portuguese streams
afford little variety and but poor sport, for, except the Bidassoa,
I never met with a trout in any of them.

In April we moved to Placentia, a clean and respectable city
with a singular cathedral, the front of which presents the archi-
tectural anomaly of the florid Gothic, Composite and Corinthian
Orders.

During Passion Week the large windows of the cathedral and
all the interior had been hung with black, and the light carefully
excluded. On Easter Sunday morning the principal inhabitants
and a large number of British officers having filled the spacious
interior to crowding and overflowing, the dark veil was suddenly
withdrawn, amidst the loud and triumphant notes of a magnificent *Te Deum*—the sun shone in brilliantly through the painted
windows, and all was at once, as if by magic, changed from the

most melancholy gloom to the most gorgeous splendour.

On the following day we had a military spectacle, in strong contrast to the rejoicings of the Sunday. The whole Division was assembled in a large plain to witness the execution of a soldier who had shot his Captain, and with the same ball, badly wounded a Serjeant. The same night, such was the vivid impression of this scene on the mind of one of the 66th–though the murderer belonged to another corps–that he awoke his comrade, and told him that he had seen the devil carrying off the soul of the criminal, and at the same time calling him by name, and warning him to avoid a similar fate–which was certainly very unfiendish. The poor man went to sleep again but awoke soon after in the same terror, from some similar dream; and then appearing to have quite lost his senses, he jumped out of bed, ran into the street, and drowned himself in the river. There was an officer of the 66th of very dark complexion and prominent eyes, who chanced to be Subaltern of the day, and had visited the quarter of this man when he first awaked. To his appearance in the room the officers unanimously ascribed the catastrophe, and the innocent D—y ever afterwards retained the nick-name of the devil. Oddly enough, the poor fellow was afterwards drowned himself. (At St. Helena, see p. 158 Editor)

On the clear, sun-shiny morning of the 19th of May 1813, the Corps of Sir Rowland Hill was put in motion from Coria and Placentia through the Pass of Banos towards Salamanca. The weather was beautiful; and this long march, which only ended in the Pyrenees, was commenced under the most favourable auspices.

On our approach to Salamanca, during the last day's march we perceived at a great distance, on the other side of the Tormes, a Column of the enemy deliberately retiring. Lord Wellington was in front and immediately detached some Cavalry and Horse Artillery across the river to cut them off. The day was clear, and when the advance of our Division halted on a rising ground near the left bank, we had a distant view of the chase. A Column of French Infantry moved along resolutely, with some Cavalry on their flanks and in the rear; and even when the guns opened and our Dragoons came up, they could make no impression on the square of determined men who preserved their formation; but they dispersed the enemy's Cavalry, and took about two hundred stragglers prisoners, with six guns, that we had the pleasure of seeing in the great square in Salamanca the same evening. This was a good beginning.

We encamped on the right bank of the Tormes, a mile from Salamanca; and in the evening a party of our officers rode into the town. We were unwilling to leave this fine old city so soon, but were ordered off the next morning, and marched six leagues to camp near the village of La Urbada; where we halted five or six days to give time to Sir Thomas Graham and the left of the army to advance. It was very plain that there would be no child's play this campaign, for large masses of men were moving concentrically on the main French communications with their own country, and prepared to overwhelm any isolated resistance. Concentration, then, must be the game of the enemy, and when the rival masses came within each other's attraction—to drop my figure and take another—then we should have the tug of war.

The whole of Sir Rowland Hill's Corps and the Light Division were here encamped. It was a fine game country—open, generally, but with picturesque copses and young woods here and there, affording ample cover and food.

The evening of the day we marched from Salamanca threatened to be a hungry one, for, except a little wine and two or three biscuits, our rations were out, and we could expect none till the next morning. My faithful Antonio, who hated hunger as much as Sancho Panza, looked longer-visaged than usual by an inch or two; and as the punctual Jonathan Wild heaped before the animals their ample allowance of glossy and succulent green forage, there was a great temptation for wishing to be a horse for half an hour. Just as Antonio paraded the last biscuit and a cup of wine for my dinner, we heard a loud and prolonged shout close to the tent; and when I ran out to see what the matter was, I had scarcely cleared the tent-cords, when a hare that had been started in the purlieus of the camp—after a spring of some seven or eight yards, came bounding against my breast. It certainly was an ungenerous and indefensible act, and must be considered most cruel and barbarous treatment of a helpless prisoner so early in the campaign, but truth is truth, and must be told—poor puss was in the soup-kettle in five minutes.

There were certainly some doubts started as to property, but there were fortunately no game laws in Spain, and when the soup was boiling, possession was plainly in my favour. It would have

been useless to enquire after the proprietorship, where, being a
'*fera naturae*,' none could have had existence. Through my whole
life I have found the advantage of decision and promptitude of
action, from matters of life or death,–to the most trivial–even
the splitting of a hair.

When the army was well advanced on the left, and every thing
ready, we broke up the camp and moved on Toro, where we crossed
the Douro. The bridge had been destroyed, but was temporarily
repaired, so as to admit of Infantry passing over; whilst the Artillery and Cavalry crossed at a ford a little below. The water was
inconveniently deep for the smaller baggage animals, and several
poor donkies got out of their depth and were lost. One of our
soldier's wives, mounted on a good stout ass, swam her animal
gallantly a quarter of a mile down the river, directing its course to
a shelving bank on the proper side, which she reached in safety
amidst a volley of cheers from the Division.

Meanwhile in every town we passed through the inhabitants
received us joyfully, standing at the doors of the houses with
pitchers of cool and delicious water in their hands, which they
distributed to the thirsty men, and accompanying this kind attention with looks and expressions of cordial friendship, '*Viva los
Inglezez!*' rang in our ears all the way. In this agreeable style we
chased the enemy before us for the next ten days until we came
close to Burgos, where they seemed inclined to make a stand, and
some fighting of no great consequence took place in the heights
near the town. Next morning, the 13th of June, we heard a loud
report, which was caused by the blowing up of the castle: a very
delightful sound, for Burgos had become a word of ill omen, and
we anticipated much trouble here. Little did we then know the
dreadful loss the French themselves suffered by that calamitous
explosion–the crushing of a column and the death of three
hundred men. The precipitate destruction and abandonment of a
place they had formerly successfully defended shewed fear and
weakness; and we now could start, inspirited afresh, on the
glorious hunt across the Ebro.

When we approached Pancorvo, a place of some strength, on
this celebrated river, situated on the high road from Burgos to
Vittoria, we struck off by a path to the left; and after passing
through a most difficult and formidable defile of two leagues,
crossed the Ebro at the Puente d'Arenas without any opposition.

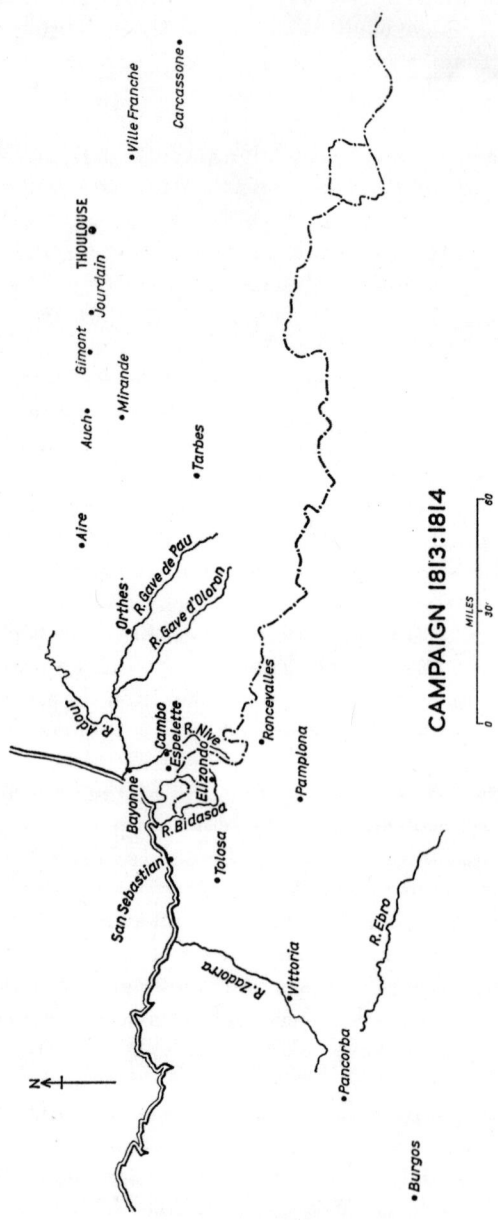

CAMPAIGN 1813:1814

Carcassone
•Ville Franche
THOULOUSE
Gimont
Jourdain
Auch•
•Mirande
•Tarbes
•Aire
Orthes•
R. Gave de Pau
R. Gave d'Oloron
R. Adour
Cambo
Espelette
Nive
Elizondo•
•Roncevalles
Bayonne
R. Bidasoa
•Pamplona
San Sebastian•
•Tolosa
R. Zadorra
•Vittoria
R. Ebro
•Pancorba
•Burgos

MILES
0   30   60

N

There was another proof that the French were much frightened, and quite bothered out of their judgement; for two or three hundred men might here have stopped our whole army, and gained a couple of days to enable the retiring masses of the enemy to retreat in better order.

We advanced slowly from the Ebro on Vittoria, where rumour said the French army was collecting and appeared determined to fight. Our Columns were now converging—the lateral routes were difficult for Artillery—the enemy concentrating—it was therefore necessary to move cautiously. Some little affairs had taken place, and a couple of French Divisions getting entangled in the intricate country to our left, had come in collision with our Light Division; but had effected their escape with trifling loss. All classes cheered us as we passed; and though, from the long march the mens' shoes were worn out, and blistered feet among the soldiers, and sore backs among the horses and mules had become more numerous than was agreeable—the whole army was in the highest spirits. Scientific combinations had been carried into effect in distant, but harmonious movements of different Corps and Divisions of the Allied Army, without any disturbing impediment—all had been inspired with the confidence, and almost the certainty of success under their great leader: whilst two or three little brilliant Cavalry affairs—the panic of the enemy—the acclamations of the inhabitants—and the beauty of the weather, were the scenic accompaniments of this first act of the grand drama.

Such was the deep impression produced by the important events of the 21st of June 1813, that every thing of which I was that day a witness, remains as fresh in my memory as if it only occurred yesterday.

On that celebrated Sunday morning there was a little light rain about day-break, followed by some mist and fog; which, however, did not last long, and were followed by a remarkably fine clear day. Having, from the commencement of the campaign, been attached as assistant to staff-surgeon Wasdell,[20] in medical charge of the Second Division, I moved with the Head Quarters, and thus always occupied a house when they were stationed in any village. On this occasion, as we all anticipated something to do this day, I awoke before day-light and looked out of the window at the camp of the Division, half a mile below—but nothing was to be seen but the dense vapour—after another hour the mist was clearing away–the men were striking the tents and getting under arms –in half an hour more the whole was in motion towards the village of Puebla, where there was a bridge over the Zadorra, a branch of the Ebro, about two leagues from Vittoria.

As we were crossing the clear stream of the Zadorra at Puebla, (it was of a far different colour before the day was over,) I glanced into the water and saw a number of lively dace playing about, apparently altogether careless of the great events taking place in their neighbourhood. Morillo's Spaniards had seized the bridge and crossed before the British, and we now heard a little firing beginning on the heights on our right; said to be the scene of a victory gained by our Black Prince, and hence called '*los montagnos Inglezez.*' By and bye the firing thickened–we passed one or two dead bodies of French soldiers on the road, and the whole Column moved towards the table land above the river in compact order.

When we reached the top a grand and spirit-stirring spectacle met our view. We saw the extensive line of the whole French army posted on a range of heights about two miles off, in order of battle, with Vittoria in the centre. The position appeared to be nearly four miles in length–the greater part of the troops were in column –some in line; and the Artillery was disposed in batteries on the most commanding points. Numbers of mounted officers were moving about slowly from one part of the field to another.

This was the first time I had seen a powerful army prepared for battle; and the sensation was exciting, exhilarating and intoxicating. I was young and ardent, and felt strong emotions in anticipating the approaching combat and the probable discomfiture of those imposing masses. I longed to join in the struggle and 'throw physic to the dogs.'

When our Division had advanced along the high road to Vittoria, within long cannon-range of the enemy's position, we were ordered into a field to the right, and then halted. The word was then given, 'With ball-cartridge prime and load!' In the meantime Sir Rowland Hill and a large staff, including the staff-surgeon and myself, rode forward to a small height whence there was a better view; but the crowd of mounted officers having attracted a shot from one of the enemy's nearest batteries, the greater part of us were ordered away, and only Sir Rowland and two or three of the senior officers remained.

The contrast between the aspect of the two armies at this part of the field was striking enough. On one side the dark and formidable masses were prepared at all points to repel the meditated attack—the infantry in column with loaded arms, or ambushed thickly in the low woods at the base of their position—the cavalry in lines with drawn swords—and the artillery frowning from the eminences with lighted matches. While on our side all was quietness and repose. The chiefs were making their observations, and the men walking about in groups, amidst the piled arms—chatting and laughing, and gazing; and apparently not caring a pin for the fierce hostile array in their front.

Soon after this the Brigade of Colonel O'Callaghan, consisting of the 28th, 34th and 39th regiments, attacked the village of Subijana d'Aliva, and having there suffered a heavy loss, I was ordered to the assistance of their surgeons.

We collected the wounded in a little hollow, out of the direct line of fire, but within half masket-shot—unpacked our panniers and proceeded to our work. This Brigade had, I believe, between four and five hundred men put *hors de combat* in the course of an hour; so, we were fully employed. A stray cannon-shot from a distant battery would drop among us occasionally, by way of a hint to inculcate expeditious surgery. Spring wagons were in attendance, in which we placed our patients and sent them to Puebla, the nearest town, where Dr. McGrigor,[21] then at the head of the medical department of the army, had made the most judicious arrangements for their reception and comfort.

When we had attended to all the wounded of this Brigade that we could find; including the large proportion of officers—several of the latter hit mortally—a message came to the staff-surgeon from the heights on our left; for a long time the scene of a bloody struggle: that there were a large number of wounded, and that they required more medical aid. There the 50th, 71st and 92nd regiments had been sent early in the day to assist Morillo and his Spaniards; but, strong reinforcements having joined the enemy on the hill, those gallant Corps were hardly pressed and suffered great loss. I was again detached and ordered up the hill on this urgent requisition.

I had been so entirely occupied, professionally, for three hours, that I was quite in the dark as to the state of the engagement; except that, latterly, the sound of the firing appeared louder and closer than at the beginning.

As I galloped up the hill, a round shot passed so near my head as to make me bob instinctively; though, as Napoleon is made to tell his guide at Waterloo, the bob might as probably be *in* the line of the ball as *out* of it.

The death of Colonel Cadogan of the 71st, was as glorious as that of Wolfe. After he received his mortal wound, he reclined with his back against a tree, his glazing eyes directed towards the enemy, and his last moments, like Wolfe's, cheered by the account of their defeat. After witnessing this fine scene with deep emotion, and working hard for two hours with the medical officers of the Brigade, I returned according to my orders to the depot of the wounded near Subijana, whence I had set out. Every thing now appeared changed—the firing was far advanced towards Vittoria—the enemy had abandoned several points of his position and seemed to be in full retreat.

In front of the village of Subijana d'Aliva, which had been taken early in the action, by Colonel O'Callaghan, there was a wood, about four hundred yards off, which was full of French Tirailleurs. Between this wood and the village was a large cornfield, without any hedges or enclosures, or cover of any kind more than the green wheat: and here I could not help thinking then, (and I am of the same opinion still;) that there had been very needless exposure and wanton waste of life, without the possibility of any good being derived from it. I saw myself, early in the action, parties detached from the village, where they had good cover, into the open field, and there fruitlessly and fatally contending with the fire of the Voltigeurs from the wood and the Artillery from the main French position. So ignorant, even, did these brave men appear of the true danger of their situation, that they enhanced it a hundred fold, by absolutely *grouping themselves* in little masses through the field for mutual protection; each of which objects formed a target not to be missed by covered Infantry, and scarcely by Artillery. Such was the loss sustained in this point, that in one part of the field, not more than about two acres square, I counted one hundred and fifty men either killed or very badly wounded.

Here the staff-surgeon, two other surgeons and myself, set to work afresh, after swallowing some wine and biscuit; and here we remained collecting, dressing, amputating and sending to the rear, till seven o'clock.

70

When our work was done and we had picked up every wounded man in the neighbourhood of Subijana, we mounted our horses, that had been regaling themselves all the time in the wheat, and pushed on for our own Division, now, with the whole army far in front. At this time the French were flying all across the country, having been cut off from the main road to France by Tolosa. We passed Vittoria a mile on our left, where the plunder of King Joseph's Treasure and Baggage was going on, and our Dragoons were getting drunk with his Tokay.

It was now sunset and the pursuit still continued. Most of the enemy's Artillery and Baggage had fallen into our possession, but there was still one large convoy, escorted by some Cavalry, that appeared to have a fair prospect of escaping in the approaching darkness. A troop of Horse Artillery, commanded, I think, by Captain Bull, galloped up and unlimbered within range on a rising ground near the road, whilst we stopped to see the result. The convoy was at this time entering a small defile in the road, when the Captain pointed the first gun, exclaiming–'Now for the first carriage.' He made a beautiful shot, for the ball killed the two front mules in the leading carriage, and thus stopped the whole; and before the impediment could be removed our Dragoons were up, and the whole convoy was captured.

After such a day's work there was a great deal of confusion at nightfall–soldiers and officers straggling about, unable to find their Corps. The Staff-Surgeon, a Mr. Frith, Chaplain to the Forces, and myself, strayed about the country three hours after dark, fruitlessly endeavouring to find the Second Division. Regiments, Brigades and even Divisions, became intermingled; and it was at least mid-day after the battle before this confusion was remedied. In the course of our wandering that eventful evening *we* also got our humble share of the plunder; for we picked up a sheep, a keg of cognac brandy, and I stumbled over a piece of superfine cloth that made me afterwards a pair of inexpressibles, of which I was sorely in need.

After wandering till midnight to no purpose, we fell in with some stragglers of the Buffs and 57th, who kindled a fire, skinned and dressed our sheep, and broiled us a chop upon the coals. They divided their biscuit with us, and we gave them a share of our cognac. After this we wrapped ourselves in our cloaks and slept profoundly after a good day's work.

The reunion of a Corps of Officers after a hard-fought and successful day, is an event of a highly interesting and affecting nature—all the worser passions and tendencies are subdued, under the influence of the exhilaration of the moment, the joy of escape from the late danger, and the delightful consciousness of recent good conduct and intrepidity. Other of the social charities, also, mix with these emotions—sorrow for the dead and sympathy with the wounded. After mutual congratulations and enquiries, I was pleased to learn that although the regiment had its fair share of the fighting, and had lost about fifty killed and wounded out of three hundred and fifty, only two officers had been hit, and neither mortally.

On the evening of the 22nd of June, we started again on a fresh chase; but as the enemy were then in light marching order—having been relieved from the encumbrance of Baggage and Artillery—there was not much chance of catching them.

At Salvatierra we found that three bed-ridden old people had been murdered that morning in cold blood by the retreating enemy, apparently without any provocation, and from shear wanton cruelty. We pushed them without any respite as fast as the horrible state of the roads would permit—broken up as they were by rain and the previous passage of the French disorderly masses—up to the strong defiles leading to the Passes of the Pyrenees, some of which they attempted to defend.

In approaching Pampeluna, during a very heavy thunderstorm, I chanced to be riding along in company with the 34th Regiment, in conversation with one of the officers named Masterman. Peal upon peal bellowed above us, whilst the reflection of the brilliant lightning from the then clear barrels of the soldiers' muskets, momentarily blinded us. Just as the thundercloud appeared to be directly in the zenith, a flash more terrible than any that had preceded it irradiated the column, and when I recovered my sight, I beheld the poor fellow with whom I had been conversing the instant before lying under his horse's feet. He was quite dead! He had escaped the murderous capture of Subijana, where so many of his comrades fell a day or two before, only to be selected from among thousands as the victim of this fatal bolt!

Nothing could be more ardent than the demonstrations of joy in every town we passed. This was the first time since the era of the Black Prince, that English soldiers had been seen in these romantic and secluded valleys, and we were absolutely treated as if we had dropped from the sky on some benevolent mission. As we marched through the streets the windows were crowded with women, cheering and waving white hankerchiefs and tossing out loaves amongst the soldiers; whilst the men stood at the doors, serving out wine to the officers, or handing goblets of deliciously cool water from their porous earthen vessels, to the men. For with nice discrimination, they would not give wine to the soldiers without the permission of the officers. All this time the bells of Churches and Convents would ring away with all their might.– Shouts of 'Viva los Inglezez!' filled the air, whilst every little urchin that could utter a sound, mingled his shrill treble in the general acclamation.

On the morning of the 6th July, the Corps of Sir Rowland Hill entered the fine vale of Bastan–quite a gem amongst the Pyrenæan valleys–which was still occupied by two French Divisions, whom we proceeded to drive from several successive positions. There was a good deal of desultory fighting all the day–for the enemy had still some stores in the pretty town of Elizondo, which they were withdrawing, and consequently defended the approaches to the place with great obstinacy. The staff surgeon and myself, moved with the advance; having our mule and surgical panniers close up, so that we very frequently attended to the wounded amongst the light troops engaged, before they could be seen by their own medical officers, who were with their regiments, a little way in the rear. In one case, where it was necessary to amputate the arm below the elbow, the patient, a fine-looking Light Bob of the 50th Regiment, said not a word whilst I was operating, but bore the pain with the greatest fortitude. At length when it was all over, he looked at the mutilated hand, and exclaimed with an oath–'I would bear it all ten times over, if I could ram that bloody hand into my piece, and blow out the cowardly villain's brains with it that shot me!' On inquiry we learned that the poor fellow had good reason for his indignation; for it appeared that the Light Company of the 50th had surrounded a farmhouse in which about a score of French had sheltered themselves. Finding they could not escape, they held out a white handkerchief from a window, as a signal of surrender–the firing then ceased on both sides; but when the first of the English, who happened to be my patient– entered the door, a rascal discharged his musket at him–shattering his hand which he threw up instinctively to save his head. The remainder then made a rush out, and in the surprise of the moment most of them escaped.

We entered Elizondo late in the evening, with the Light Companies and Staff of Sir Rowland Hill, whilst skirmishing was still going on at the other end of the town. Head Quarters were fixed here during the night; and the same tumultuous acclamations of joy and welcome met us as every where else.

In riding through Elizondo, and passing a good-looking house, a Priest saluted us, and begged we should do him the favour of spending the night at his house; and sharing the dinner he had prepared for some of his *'carissimos amigos, los valientes Ingle-zez'!*–his most dear friends, the valiant English. As we were both hungry and fatigued, it is scarcely necessary to observe that we required little pressing. So our horses were put in a comfortable stable, and were soon up to their ears in provender, whilst we sat down to dinner with his reverence and his niece–a very pretty *muchacha* of seventeen. Our good host had just dug up his plate, and some famous old wine that were buried in the garden four years before; and, certes, we passed a merry evening with this jovial and patriotic ecclesiastic. In the exhiliration of his joy for the emancipation of his native valley from the French yoke, under which it had so long groaned–assisted, perhaps a *little* by the *'Vinho vejo,'* the excellent Priest got slightly fuddled, and sang us several Spanish songs. In return he asked for 'God save the King' from us; of which he said he had heard much by report. My friend, Wasdell, having declined, and the Priest being very urgent, the task devolved on me–and very much did the old gentleman admire and encore my poor performance–and very sweetly did the sloe-eyed *muchacha* lisp out her pretty admiration of it–until the evening,–like all parties, and the chorus, ended happy and glorious.

Next day we advanced to Maya, one of the grand Passes, amidst the same exciting circumstances of partial fighting and cheering by the villages through which we passed. As the evening advanced, and the French retired to the top of the Pass, there was literally an engagement in the clouds; both parties being enveloped, and a bickering musketry fire kept up amidst their picturesque and voluminous folds. There were not many casualties; but staff surgeon Wasdell and myself, thought it necessary to sit up all night in the Church of Maya, to dress any wounded that might be brought in. At sunrise the next morning, Lord Wellington passed through the village to the front; and in riding past the church, he sent for one of the surgeons. I went out, and for the first time, had the honour of a short conversation with his Lordship. He was pleased to hear that so few men had been hit, and that their wounds were, for the most part, slight. He then rode on, saying courteously—'Good morning—go on with your duties.'

The enemy descended to his own side of the mountain during the night, and in the morning the British Troops stood proudly on their summits looking down upon the fertile plains of Gascony.

5

Surprise of Maya · The Nivelle · Orthes · Invasion of France · Thoulouse · Peace · Return to England

W HEN the French were fairly driven over the Pyrenees, and the British Army established in those strong gorges of the mountains forming the Western Passes, the Head Quarters of Sir Rowland Hill remained at Elizondo, whilst those of Sir Wm. Stewart, commanding the Second Division, were advanced to Maya, a small village about a mile from the Pass. Staff Surgeon Wasdell and myself were attached to the latter, and were quartered in Maya.

We passed the first fortnight very pleasantly; riding about and exploring the magnificent mountain boundary where we were stationed. Unfortunately, clear weather was not common in those elevated regions, and it was not very often that we could enjoy that bird's-eye view of France which we anticipated in approaching the Pyrenees.

At this time Napoleon, finding that matters were going on very badly in Spain, and that his brother had been ignominiously driven from the kingdom, sent Soult from Germany, to set them to rights. He invested him with the high Commission of Lieutenant of the Emperor, and directed him to organize the army afresh, and chase the Leopard, as he called the British Lion, from the presumptuous position he had taken on the borders of the 'Sacred Territory,' or holy land of France.

Soult travelled with great expedition–stimulated by a desire to distinguish himself, and wipe off a score of affronts he had received from the English. He soon re-established order and confidence in the beaten troops; proceeded to throw strong masses of troops in the immediate vicinity of the Passes of Roncesvalles and Maya; and lost no time in making a determined effort to pierce at once our extensive line in two or three places with superior force, then take the different posts *en revers*, beat them in detail, relieve Pampeluna and St. Sebastian; and, following up his advantages, force the English back to the Ebro.

According to the best military opinions, this was all well conceived and practicable; but one or two elements of success in the calculations were only contingencies, not very likely to happen. The French must fight far better than they had yet done, and the British worse—Lord Wellington, too, must be bothered in his nerves and fail in judgement.

On Sunday morning, the 25th July, we were alarmed at Maya, by a report that the enemy had appeared in force near Los Alduides; a post in the mountains, three leagues to our right, whilst every thing appeared quiet in our immediate front. On receiving this intelligence, Sir Rowland Hill, Sir William Stewart, and the whole of their staff rode off to the right; and the day being fine, almost every body in Maya followed in the same direction; so that at twelve o'clock I found myself the only commissioned officer in the village.

Being an unusually clear day, I mounted my horse and rode towards the top of the Pass, where the Brigade was encamped, to take a peep at Gascony. On my way I met the *Bat-men* of the 50th, 71st and 92nd regiments on their mules, going to the rear for forage—an unhappy journey for their masters. The day was still as well as clear, and as I proceeded I heard a shot or two from the top of the mountain, which in a few minutes thickened into a sharp fire of musketry. The picquets, I found, had been attacked and driven in; and when I reached the top I met the troops in motion to support them. It soon became plain that the enemy was in great force—pushing strong columns up the hill, preceded by a swarm of light troops.

It was the Count D'Erlon who commanded here, and the business had been managed skilfully by the feint at Los Alduides—this being the real point of attack. Notwithstanding a gallant resistance, the Count established himself with fourteen or fifteen thousand men at the summit of the mountain, to the right of the Pass; and in two hours from the time I had left Maya, the camp of the First Brigade, (whose mules had gone to forage,) tents and contents—the town of Maya,—the Head Quarter Baggage—the Commissariat and Hospital Stores, &c., &c., lay below him absolutely at his mercy.

It was very plain that without energetic measures I should lose my own goods and chattels with the rest: so 'Self-love and social being here the same,' I galloped down the mountain to Maya, at some risk of my neck. None of the staff had yet returned, and the servants were in great confusion and alarm. I immediately directed every thing to be packed up and sent to the rear with the greatest expedition; and took upon myself the whole responsibility. I also hurried away the Commissariat bullocks and biscuit, but had no mercy on the rum, as the mules employed in removing it would be wanted to carry the wounded, that were now beginning to drop in. Accordingly, the Commissariat Conductor set to work staving the casks, and we had soon a stream of old Jamaica running down the steep street into the rivulet at the bottom, fit to turn a mill. I wonder how the little fishes liked their grog.

The wounded now began to arrive fast. Many had been dressed by their own medical officers, but a large proportion required instant attention, which was paid them as far as the time and my ability permitted – the slighter cases being sent away on foot, and the more serious ones on mules. The enemy allowed us longer time than I expected in these operations; so that when a few of his sharpshooters began to make their appearance close to one end of the long straggling street – the Governor – my humble self – with the last of his convoy, was moving leisurely, and without any confusion, out at the other.*

Dire was the consternation of the poor inhabitants when they saw us retreating through the beautiful valley of Bastan, which had been the scene of such gratulation and triumph on our advance three weeks before. Many of them, male and female; and almost all the inmates of the convents – abandoned their homes and retired with the army. It was a painful sight to see the poor Nuns quitting their Convents and mixing with the troops in the dusty roads – their pale faces hectic with unwonted exertion, alarm and exposure. To the credit of our men, it ought to be told that great kindness, tenderness and inviolable respect were shown to them

---

* Colonel Napier, in his immortal History of the Peninsular War, repudiates the idea that the disaster at Maya was a surprise; adding that, although 'General Stewart was surprised, his troops were not; and never did soldiers fight better—seldom so well.' This I humbly conceive they might do, even though surprised. To my certain knowledge, everybody in Maya, and I believe in Elizondo too, was surprised. And that the officers of Colonel Cameron's Brigade, when expecting an attack, should send their baggage animals two or three leagues to the rear for forage, and thus deprive themselves of the means of carrying off their personal effects, appears to be, *salvo inclyto Auctore*, the most surprising thing of all. (Author's footnote.)

on this retreat–the soldiers carried their little bundles and helped them along; and it was pleasing to observe the unsuspecting confidence with which many of these old ladies trusted themselves and their portable property to the protection of our rough grenadiers. Assuredly, it was a high compliment to the character and discipline of the British Army.

As we passed through Elizondo, a large proportion of the population joined us in the retreat. I called at the house of our worthy host, the Priest, who had so kindly entertained us, but had only time for five minutes' conversation at the door. Poor fellow, he looked very desponding, and I have seldom seen a greater contrast than between his lugubrious face now, and his jolly and rubicund phiz, when roaring out the chorus of 'God save the King.' The pretty niece had been sent to a relation near Pampeluna. When I bade the fine old fellow good bye, I advised him to bury his plate and wine once more, adding that we should all be back in a fortnight again to tax his hospitality–'*Oxala a Dios! Oxala a Dios!*' 'God grant it–God grant it!' and then embracing me warmly and giving me his benediction, we parted.

We halted, confronting the enemy, the whole of the next day, that we might cover a movement of troops in the rear from the neighbourhood of St. Sebastian to Pampeluna, or its immediate front; and in the evening the whole of Sir Rowland Hill's Corps retired through the mountain pass of Lantz in the same direction; but such had been the difficulty of this lateral movement that we fell in with the Seventh Division on the narrow road, and some confusion was thus occasioned. As night fell it began to rain heavily, and became so pitch-dark that no object could be seen a yard off; and the horses were trusted to pioneer their riders along the side of the mountain, where a false step would be destruction. My pole-star was the white tail of the staff-surgeon's horse, just before me, of which I caught an indistinct observation now and then, when I stooped and looked attentively. At length both Divisions were obliged to halt in the middle of the night on the ground where they stood on the mountain side–from absolute inability to proceed.

From the 25th July to the 2nd August, was a week of hard fag and fighting. Sir R. Hill's Corps continued to retire before the Count D'Erlon on the 27th, 28th and 29th–still shewing him a formidable front–covering the movement of troops to the right, and keeping up a communication with Lord Wellington's main force in front of Pampeluna. During this time the staff-surgeon and myself, being both well mounted, were not idle. On the night of the 29th, Sir Rowland posted his Corps on a strong range of heights, five or six miles to the left of the position of Lord Wellington, and there anxiously awaited orders and the course of events.

At day-break on the morning of the 30th, every body was on the *qui vive*. We had been apprised of the repulse of the enemy on the 28th—the 29th had passed quietly; but we all expected something decisive on the 30th. As soon as it was clear, the staff-surgeon and I mounted and joined a large assemblage of staff, who, with Sir Rowland at their head, were on their way to a high hill, two or three miles to the rear; whence they hoped to be able to descry the important operations on the right. For, by this time, a very heavy musketry fire and cannonade was going on there merrily; and we could see a cloud of smoke, but nothing else. After remaining on the hill nearly an hour, and plying his glass perseveringly, Sir Rowland ordered a movement of the whole Corps to the rear—apparently with the object of connecting himself more closely with the Head Quarter Force, from which he was too distant.

However, this order was countermanded; for, soon after the reconnoissance from the hill, and Sir R. and his staff had returned to the strong ridge where the troops were posted, the heads of several of the enemy's Columns were seen moving simultaneously on the position—coming from our right, and apparently determined to attack us. Light troops were immediately thrown down the steep and wooded side of the hill, and other active measures taken to give them a warm reception; but it appeared to me at the time that Sir R. anticipated being forced, and did not like to hazard the loss of his Artillery; since, though a Brigade of English and another of Portuguese Artillery were close in the rear of the heights now threatened, they were not ordered up; although they might have done considerable execution amongst the approaching Columns, of which we had from the top the finest view possible. But, for this, no doubt, there were the best reasons at the time.

The French dashed at the hill gallantly—throwing out clouds of skirmishers, who forced ours back on the main body at the top. At one point near the centre of the position, they pushed so hard

that the Light Companies came running in, close to where the
General and his staff stood; and it required their utmost efforts to
turn them back. On this occasion I distinctly saw Sir Rowland
himself, turn right about face, three or four of the 50th Light
Company, who, panting with heat, and with faces blackened with
powder, had been forced up by superior numbers. Additional
skirmishers were sent down at this point, and the enemy was
repelled.

It was now three o'clock, and the sound of firing, far to the
right, was still heard occasionally; though the interest in affairs
there, had been for some hours absorbed in what was going on
before our eyes. Hitherto the enemy's efforts had been unsuccessful; but he was now seen prolonging his attack to our left,
where from the great extent of the position few troops could be
posted. At length, after a long struggle, the French established
themselves on the hill, and prepared to advance along its crest;
when Sir R. Hill retired his Corps in good order to another position two miles in the rear.

This was a sharp affair, although, from the thick cover, there
were few casualties, and the regimental medical officers attended
to their own wounded. The staff surgeon and myself were close up
to the line at the top of the position, all the time the action continued, with our mule and surgical panniers; but we had little to
do, except look at the fighting.

In the evening news arrived of a severe engagement having
taken place that morning, a little way in front of Pampeluna,
where the enemy had been defeated with great loss. At the same
time an order arrived for Staff-Surgeon Wasdell, to detach a
medical officer to the village of Barrioplano, to collect there the
wounded of both armies, and forward them in spring wagons to
Vittoria. I was sent on this duty, on which I was employed five
days and nights, with scarcely an hour's intermission–divorced
from my baggage and Antonio; whose face I had not seen for a
week already–and employing a heap of wheat in a barn, when I
was permitted to snatch half an hour's sleep–literally as bed and
board–for I got nothing else to eat.

A very large number of wounded were brought in here on this
occasion; all the disposable spring wagons with the army, and a
great many carts and mules, being employed in collecting them
at the villages near the extensive field of action, and conveying

them to the Church of Barrioplano; (situated on the high road, a mile from Pampeluna,) as to a central point. Here their wounds were examined—dressed—the limbs that required it, amputated—and the patients again put in the wagons and sent to Vittoria. Such was the urgency of circumstances, that for the first two days, I had no medical assistance here; but afterwards abundant aid was afforded by two cavalry assistant surgeons.

During this busy time, my brother assistant, Shekelton, (a worthy man, now flourishing in Dublin,) rode over to Barrioplano, to consult me respecting the case of our mutual friend and brother officer, Major Goldie, who lay at a village three or four miles distant, under his charge, desperately wounded by a musket ball through the lungs. It appeared that the ball had lodged somewhere in the chest, and the symptoms continued alarmingly dangerous. The patient had been most judiciously and tenderly treated, and his life saved, hitherto, by enormous bleeding, to the extent of three hundred ounces in two days.*

It chanced one morning that two spring wagons full of wounded French officers, prisoners, were brought in, and very soon after, two more with our own people, principally of the *Chasseurs Britanniques*; a corps composed chiefly of foreigners. I was then busy in the Church with a batch of wounded soldiers that had arrived earlier, and as the principle was—first come, first served; without respect of persons, I directed that they should be put in a neighbouring house, until their turn came. When I proceeded with my surgical apparatus to take care of the new arrivals, I found them in a state of the most violent excitement; abusing each other with the grossest epithets, and very nearly come to fisty cuffs. The French officers were vilifying their countrymen of the Chasseurs—calling them *'sacrés traitres! lâches esclaves d'Angleterre!'* and their opponents were retaliating with equal heat, gesticulation and bitterness. It was altogether a most laughable scene—most genuinely French; and I believe that nothing but the paralysing effects of their wounds restrained them from an actual engage-

---

*I have great pleasure in adding, that this very gallant and valuable officer recovered after this prodigious loss of blood; though he still carried the ball in his lungs. He now commands the 11th Regiment in Lower Canada, and notwithstanding some very severe winter marching to and from New-Brunswick lately, I had the satisfaction of seeing him this very day in good health. (Author.)

ment. When I entered there was a momentary pause; but the quarrel broke out afresh in two minutes. I used all my eloquence to pacify them, but fruitlessly—still the mutual objurgations were bandied about with astonishing volubility and vehemence. At last, perceiving that the case was becoming desperate I seized my instruments, directed the orderly to carry away the tray of plasters and bandages—bade the pugnacious gentlemen good morning, and requested them to fight it out. This calmed them at once; they were then dressed and despatched in separate wagons to Vittoria.

When this tedious and harassing duty was over, and no more wounded were brought in, I proceeded once more to Maya, and found the Divisional Head Quarters again established in that village, and the troops occupying their old posts on the hills. Great was the comfort of meeting my baggage after a long destitution of clean linen, and an intolerable beard of twelve days' growth.

In the course of the month of August we moved with Head Quarters to the classic Pass of Roncesvalles.

At this time the siege of St. Sebastian was going on: at length on a very tempestuous day, the place was stormed, amidst the rival thunder of the sky and the batteries. The storm extended all over the western limb of the Pyrenees, and blew down half the tents of our Division.

We continued at Roncesvalles, until the surrender of Pampeluna left Lord Wellington at liberty to push into France. We then, once more, moved along the mountains to the Pass of Maya; where, on the morning of the 10th November, the Corps of Sir Rowland stood, like greyhounds in the slip, ready for a dash at the position of the enemy in front of Bayonne.

A full hour before day-light, on the morning of the 10th of November, did we wait for the firing of a gun on the extreme left, which was a signal for our advance; whilst high feelings were working in many bosoms.

As soon as the long-expected echoes rolled amongst the mountains, the Column was put in motion and crossed the frontier, whilst a heavy firing was going on to our left. We marched about two leagues, until within cannon shot of the fortified heights above the small stream of the Nivelle, which had the honour of giving its name to the battle. Here we halted in front of a very strong part of the fortified hill, which our Division was to storm;

and as soon as a Brigade of the Sixth Division, immediately to our left, had done their work by attacking a redoubt on the top and taking it, General Byng's Brigade pushed up the steep and abbatied hill at one place, whilst the Light Companies of the Division and the two other Brigades assailed it at other points. When the leading regiment of Byng's Brigade reached the plateau on the top, they looked such a handful that a French Column opposed to them deployed into line and prepared to charge: but, though I saw their officers cheering them on gallantly, they would not move, but kept up an irregular fire, which, being badly aimed, did far less mischief than it ought to have done. When more force came up and the Brigade formed and advanced, the enemy's line wavered, not metaphorically, but visibly and materially; and after two or three oscillations they broke and ran.

There still remained a small field redoubt with two guns in possession of the enemy. These were fought by an Officer of Artillery, a Serjeant and a few men, and being loaded with double charges of grape knocked over our people fast. Lieut. Colonel Leith, 31st—my friend Lieut. Colonel Nicol, 66th, and Ensign Dunn of the same corps, at the head of three or four men, charged this work and carried it in good style. Indeed the three officers took it themselves; for they cleared the ditch with a running leap, and dropped down amongst the garrison, before a man could enter to assist them. As they jumped in, the Artillery Officer and his men jumped out; but not with impunity. Leith, a Hercules in strength and figure, knocked the red-headed officer down with a brick-bat, but his cap saved his skull, and he managed to scramble up and get away. Not so lucky was the Serjeant—he dislocated his shoulder in the leap—was taken prisoner, and I set his arm to rights immediately afterwards.

We lost a good many people in storming this hill. The Light Companies, commanded by Major Ackland of the 57th, suffered severely—every officer was hit, and the Major killed. The death of his pretty little spaniel, that had during the action amused itself by barking at the dust the balls raised as they struck the ground—preceded its master's fall only by a few minutes. I had to lament the loss of two friends in the regiment who were mortally wounded.

Our time was occupied professionally, till late in the evening. When we had done, and were in quest of some refreshment, a well-dressed woman accosted us, apparently in a state of the greatest distraction and distress. She told us she lived in the village of Espelette, immediately under us at the bottom of the hill—that Morillo's Spanish Division had got into the place, and were beginning to burn and plunder, and her husband had run away and left his family, from dread of the Spaniards; and that she had come out alone, trusting in English generosity, to beg for protection. She implored us, therefore, to accompany her home, as our presence would save her and her family from the Spaniards. This poor woman was so importunate, that, after obtaining permission we went to her house. The town was in the greatest alarm and confusion, and part of it on fire; but on this being known a regiment was sent down to extinguish the fire and turn out the Spaniards. A party of plunderers visited our residence, but instantly decamped when they found it in possession of British Officers.

Our family were also labouring under distress of a peculiar severe nature from another cause; and in meeting accidentally with two English Surgeons, Madame Dupré was piously pleased to consider the circumstance as specially ordained by Providence. By a most unlucky fatality, poor Jacqueline, one of her daughters, during the action on the hill, happened to be looking out of the window, listening to the firing, when a grape-shot from a gun in the redoubt last taken, which was turned on the enemy as they ran down to the town—smashed her elbow-joint. Amputation was inevitable and I took off her arm the same evening, and am happy to add that the stump was perfectly well in a fortnight.

It would be a graceful finale to add that Mademoiselle Jacqueline was very pretty. Truth forbids this; but she was amiable and grateful; and after she had recovered the first dreadful shock of such a loss, she presented me with a handsome purse of her own netting as a fee.

Madame Dupré had a good house and was in comfortable circumstances; she treated my friend and myself with great kindness, and made us very comfortable. She had a full cellar, and there was one cask of very rich and clarety *vin du pays*, which she forced me to accept for distribution amongst my brother-officers in camp. Accordingly, next morning I had a *levée* of their servants, with tins and tea-kettles and all kinds of vessels to carry it off.

On the 13th of November, Sir R. Hill made a reconnoissance of the enemy's force at Cambo, a small town on the left bank of the

Nive, which had been partially fortified. When we got within shot, Colonel Nicol and myself happened to be riding together at the head of the Brigade, mixed with the Band of the Buffs, when a ball plunged amongst us, knocking over three or four musicians. In five seconds they all jumped up again, amidst great laughing, for they were all unhurt; and the only sufferer was the big-drum, which was mortally wounded; and its fall upset the two men that carried it – whilst they overthrew the two others.

We stood in line two or three hours exposed to fire. As General Byng was passing on horseback where I chanced to be looking on, *en amateur*, a shell alighted within seven or eight yards of us both. With much coolness he remarked, 'There is no danger – throw yourself off'; shewing me the example. When we had embraced mother earth about two seconds, it burst; and I caught a glimpse of a large fragment describing its parabola over our heads, but at a safe distance.

This was escape the second: I had also a third that day. There was a small house, a little in rear of the centre of our line, where we were attending the few wounded; for we had only four or five, notwithstanding a long cannonade – a brother *medico* and myself were amusing ourselves with a glass, looking out of a window in the upper story, at the French Artillerymen on the rampart of Cambo. When it came to my friend's turn to take a peep, he exclaimed – 'By Jove they are pointing that gun direct at this house – we had better go downstairs.' We descended accordingly, and had scarcely reached the bottom when we heard a crash over our head; and instantly a shower of tiles came down from the roof. The Bombardiers had at last found the range, and had pitched a shell into the very room we had quitted, which killed a poor woman in the house who had brought water to her wounded husband. Thirty or forty officers' horses were picquetted round the house – the noise and the falling of the tiles sent them galloping, with broken bridles, in all directions.

At this time I was witness to a very strange occurrence. The commanding officer of the Buffs, a regiment in General Byng's Brigade, left his corps, then under fire, and came half a mile to the house above mentioned, to inquire after one of his men that had been hit. Unfortunately he met the Brigadier, who gave him a cool look – his personal courage being more than suspected – but said nothing. When the Lieut. Colonel had made the necessary enquiries, and staid as long at the house as he could with any decency, he returned to his regiment. But, in half an hour back he came to the house, and his unlucky stars again threw Byng in his way. This time he was peremptorily ordered to his post, with the withering appellation he deserved, and strictly forbidden to quit it at his peril.

The individual here alluded to, after one or two subsequent demonstrations of cowardice, saw his name in the London Gazette one day; but not in the way of promotion. The Prince Regent, in the name and behalf of George the Third, gave him his gracious permission to go about his business. He and two other *chefs de bataillon* were turned out of the army.

Lord Wellington having resolved to invest Bayonne more closely than he had yet done, and to cut off its communications with St. Jean Pied de Port and the Western Pyrenees, Sir R. Hill crossed the Nive at Cambo, on the 9th December; and on the 10th we found ourselves in a good country, a mile or two from Bayonne.

Byng's Brigade was quartered in and about the village of Vieux Mougerre. The house allotted to me, was that of a substantial farmer, half a mile from the village. As the inhabitants were always glad to have officers quartered on them; thus saving them from the plunder they were taught to expect from the soldiers—the farmer's wife told me she was enchanted to see me in her house. In fact the old lady was overpoweringly civil and complimentary both to myself and my countrymen; assuring me she always loved and respected the English, who were *'une nation superbe'*—so brave, and so good, and so religious. *'Tenez,'* she went on—*'regardez cette église'*—pointing to the cathedral of Bayonne—that magnificent edifice was built by your Black Prince—*'assurément que oui; par votre grand Prince Noir.'* She then told me that every thing in the house was at my disposal, and concluded by inquiring what she would prepare for dinner—recommending particularly—as the best article in the larder—*'une oie magnifique, si grasse et si tendre.'* So the magnificent goose was forthwith ordered to be put on the spit.

Having some professional duty to do, I left my horse in charge of the farmer—the servants and baggage being still in the rear—and went into the village. When my work was over I met, on my way home, a hungry-looking young Ensign of the regiment, on whom I took compassion, and invited him to share my dinner. It was now near sunset, and close on the hour the worthy dame told me the meal would be ready. As we approached the house we heard sounds indicative of something wrong about the establishment—cocks and hens were screaming and cackling—dogs were barking—pigs were grunting—with similar ominous noises, that made us hasten our steps to find out what was the matter. As we entered, the first object we beheld was—O sight of horror! a drunken German soldier of the 60th regiment, bearing away the spit and innocent goose, streaming with its rich juices, in his unhallowed clutch! The frightened farmer had shut himself up in the barn, but the gallant dame had contended bravely, although fruitlessly, against the Philistines. When we entered, she brightened up wonderfully, and just found breath enough to say '*Il y a un autre voleur dans la cave—la cave—la cave!*' The goose-thief bolted out of the back door, spit and all, the instant he descried us, but I soon caught him, whilst my companion dived into the cellar and found the other in the very act of suction at a wine-cock. The disturbed bird was then remanded to its roasting evolutions before the fire, whilst we conducted our prisoners to the Provost Martial, and had the satisfaction of seeing them receive fifty lashes each. Farther and more severe measures had been in contemplation, but we requested that this might be the maximum of punishment; considering the cruel disappointment of the rogues, and that they had got their goose the wrong way.

It is scarcely necessary to add that, after all this, we enjoyed our dinner and some good *vin du pays*. The goose richly deserved the encomiums of its mistress; and I doubt whether a finer or sweeter bird had been cooked since the deliverance of the Capitol.

We were not destined to remain long quiet in our good quarters round Vieux Mougerre. Soult feeling uncomfortable at the closing in of the allied troops, attempted to dash through the investing line with superior force at a favorable point; and thus play over again his game of the Pyrenæan irruption of the last summer. He first attacked the left of the army, on the high road to St. Jean de Luz; but could make no impression during two days hard fighting. He then withdrew all his troops into Bayonne, and on the morning of the 13th December, made a vigorous effort to overwhelm Sir Rowland Hill.

The business was well planned; and had the troops fought out the combinations of their General, we might once more have been obliged to retire behind the Pyrenees. They advanced from the city in most formidable numbers and great apparent confidence, but they found their enemy at all points prepared to receive them; for Sir Rowland Hill perfectly knew their intentions, and had posted his small force in the most judicious manner. Few are aware of the difficulties this noble-minded man had to contend with on the 13th of December; when, isolated by the sudden rise of the Nive, carrying away the bridge of communication with the rest of the Army, threatened by Paris and Pierre Soult in his rear; with his two strongest Regiments, the Buffs and 71st, failing him in the fight, because they were commanded by cowards. He was thus left to contend with fourteen thousand British and Portuguese against thirty-five thousand French, commanded by the intrepid and sagacious Soult.

It was my fortune to witness two prominent incidents in this action, the prompt countermarching of the 71st by Sir Rowland Hill in person when all appeared to be lost; and the leading of a column from the centre by Lieutenant Colonel Currie, his aide-de-camp, to charge down the high road, when he could find no General Officer to whom he could deliver the order. On the return of Colonel Currie from this dashing service, I met him passing a house where the wounded were collected. He pointed to the 6th Division coming down the mount in the rear to our assistance and said, 'There they come,—but, thank God, we have beat the enemy without their assistance.'

One of the two guns taken on this occasion was captured by the Light Company of the 66th Regiment, immediately after a grape shot from the last discharge had desperately wounded Captain Bulstrode in the face. I chanced to be at hand, and gave the necessary assistance immediately. It was an ugly wound; the shot struck his chin, and carried away one side of the jaw up to the joint, burying six teeth in his tongue, which were extracted at the time. He recovered, though with great deformity, and I had the pleasure of dining with him many years after in London.

Our fine little Commander, Sir Rowland, much distinguished himself on this occasion, and was praised for his conduct and arrangements by Lord Wellington, when he arrived from the left in the afternoon, with the 6th Division, as a reinforcement.

Immediately after the action, hospitals were established at Cambo and Espelette, and I was sent to the latter town to take charge. I had about twenty officers and nearly two hundred men under my care for the first three or four days, when a senior officer relieved me in the responsibility, but I continued doing duty at the place. The weather was fine, though cold: I was young and active, and felt delighted in not having an unemployed moment the whole day. As the slight cases recovered and went to the front my patients often sent me a fat turkey, or a goose, or a sucking pig, or some such matter, as a fee, which varied the toughness and monotony of the eternal rations. Amongst the wounded under my charge here was Lieut. Colonel Leith of the 31st, who had been shot through the arm with a musket ball. The ball grazed the brachial artery; but the coats of the artery–like the man they belonged to, were made of good stuff, and not easily torn. The Colonel recovered in a few days; and, as he got the English papers, his quarter was the News-Room of Espelette.

It chanced that a turkey of great merit was sent me one day from Mougerre, which I requested Colonel Leith and two other convalescent officers to partake of. When I went out to my work, after an early breakfast, I gave Antonio very particular directions as to the cooking of the dinner, which he promised faithfully to follow; and I proceeded to my daily laborious task; comforted occasionally, when I had time to think of any thing but my patients, by the pleasant perspective at the close of the day. The hour of dinner was six; and when I returned a quarter before, I found the immaculate Antonio lying prone and dead drunk in the kitchen–the beautiful bird unspitted and unstuffed; and elements of soup, in the shape of ration-beef, lying beside it on the table!

But patience is a panacea for human miseries; and this was one far overtopping the long catalogue in Beresford's book. I repaired to Colonel Leith and told him the calamity that had just happened, and requested the loan of his cook to repair it. The beef was put in the pot and the turkey to the fire incontinently–a fresh batch of English papers had arrived, with which the hungry quartetto amused themselves. *En fin*, about eight o'clock dinner was announced; and notwithstanding the unpromising appearances two hours before, every thing passed off well and happily.

About the end of January 1814, I rejoined my regiment at Mougerre, in good order for some recreation, after a six weeks' fag–which we had in private theatricals, reconnoitring Bayonne, and thinning the Gascon wood-cocks.

The very wet weather we had had lately quite spoiled the roads, so that the advance of the army into the interior was much retarded; at last Sir Rowland's Corps was put in motion on the 13th of February–the Division of General Harispe retiring before us. On the 15th, the enemy made a stand on the strong hill of Garris, near St. Palais. We arrived in front of this position, after a long march, near sunset, and every body expected that the attack would be deferred till the next morning: but Lord Wellington at that time came up; and being apprehensive that Artillery would be mounted on this formidable height next day– ordered it to be assailed immediately.

Four Columns then dashed into the ravine and up the steep side of the hill; which was one blaze of fire from the enemy's skirmishers behind the trees on its face, and the main body along the top. This was, for the greater part, as harmless as common fireworks–the balls going over our fellows' heads; but as it became dusk the effect was strikingly beautiful. Our troops soon reached the summit–scattering the French Division and taking a few hundred prisoners. Fifty or sixty unfortunate wretches concealed themselves in a house at the top until the affair was all over, and our men had piled their arms and were kindling their night fires; when they sallied out in a body, and attempted to escape down the hill. At the first rush our soldiers seized their arms, which were loaded–pursued them with a loud cheer, and shot or knocked down almost every man. They were stripped soon after–for this process takes place in a very short time–and I recollect when the moon rose seeing their plump white corpses scattered over the field. In the morning we were all shocked to see their bodies mutilated of their fair proportions, and all the fleshy and protuberant parts cut clean off down to the bone. How this happened none could say; although a report was current at the time that a certain ingenious regiment of Byng's Brigade, authorised to recruit inside Temple Bar, and pick up all the low talent of London, had metamorphosed the poor defunct's hams into pork, and exchanged them with the Portuguese troops for rum. One of our officers averred that he heard two of the culprits chuckling at the trick.[22]

I happened to be the first surgeon at the top of the hill that evening, and, of course, was in great demand. General Byng carried me immediately to see his aide-de-camp, Captain Clitheroe, who was dreadfully wounded. I found this fine young man with his hand smashed, and a ball through his breast, which had cut a large artery that I could just reach with my finger, and, I believe, I prolonged his life a couple of hours by continued pressure. This young man was much beloved, and his death greatly deplored. His end was serene and calm, and he died in my arms with the resignation and fortitude of a soldier and a christian. He was buried next morning on the hill where he fell with due military honours.

This was altogether as shewy a little piece of fighting as I ever witnessed. The brilliant musketry along the side, and from the crest of the hill–the cheering of our men as they mounted–the continued advance of numerous bugles–the roar of our Artillery reverberating in long echoes from one side to another of the deep ravine at the bottom–all was very fine and grand.

We proceeded the day after the action through St. Palais, and after some sharp skirmishing and fording two or three Pyrenæan tributaries of the Adour, encamped on the other side of the Gave d'Oleron, opposite to Orthes, on the 25th of February. Next morning another officer and myself, in the course of an exploring ramble in quest of eggs or poultry, found an old man badly beaten and bleeding in a farm-house that had been robbed the night before by a marauding party of our soldiers. The temporal artery had been cut by a blow of the robber's bayonet. It was tied up–the matter reported immediately–search made for the criminal; the soldier, having received a cut in the thigh from the wounded man, was soon discovered. Summary justice was the practice in those days; and, after identification of the prisoner, he was hanged in presence of the assembled Division the very next evening on the bough of a tree; and after being suspended forty-five minutes, I was ordered to ascertain whether life was extinct, that the men might not be kept longer in the cold than was necessary.

On the 27th February, we were early under arms. At eleven o'clock an aide-de-camp arrived with directions for Sir R. Hill to ford the Gave above the town of Orthes, and advance round the left of the French position. All this time a heavy cannonade and hard fighting were going on about two miles to our left, on the other side of the river.

Immediately all was in motion. We soon reached the ford, which was covered by some of the enemy's light troops in a thicket on the opposite bank. A couple of guns galloped down, opened on them with grape and soon dislodged them–the grape whistling through the covert like duck-shot. The Division then rushed into the ford–five or six shells dropped amongst us in crossing; but, I believe every one was extinguished in the water without doing any mischief; and in the course of an hour the whole were formed on the right bank and ready to advance.

We moved on very imposingly round their flank; and at length discovered that they had abandoned their position, and were making off with great speed; which the appearance of our Column tended materially to quicken. At the village of Montbrun we joined the Cavalry and the advance of the other English Divisions in pursuit: at this time the whole French Army, despairing of effecting their retreat, if they preserved their formation, had broken irrecoverably, and the face of the country to a great extent was covered with a dense mass of fugitives. All arms were mingled–Artillerymen without their guns–Cavalry without their horses, and Infantry without their arms–were flying pell-mell,–helter-skelter–whilst our Light Artillery were pouring Shrapnell shells amongst them, and thus increasing the general terror and confusion.

We followed the rout till dark: a little before dusk they got into some small degree of order, and made a stand at a village on a strong hill, with a small river in front; and opened with two or three guns. But they retired in the night.

Lieut. Colonel Dodgin, my former refractory patient at Badajoz, now commanded the regiment. Whilst riding at its head over 'a sea of arms'–for upwards of ten thousand stand were flung away–a fine ornamented pioneer axe, with a long handle and glittering head, struck his eye and his fancy. Thinking it might be useful at the night bivouack, he threw it over his shoulder and rode on. At this moment one of Lord Wellington's Aides-de-Camp passed; and on seeing an officer of large stature, and imposing appearance–mounted on a great war-horse, with an immense axe on his shoulder–he stopped and asked his name. When I told him, he inquired farther–'Is that, then, his usual weapon in action?' 'O yes;' was the reply, 'and the Colonel, like Cœur de Lion, often cleaves his man to the chine'. The Aide-de-Camp rode away, primed with a good story for the Commander of the Forces.

When we halted about dusk, in column on the road, a shot from one of the enemy's guns on the hill where they rallied, struck the ground, rose again and knocked over one of the soldiers' wives, who always managed to keep up with the regiment. I ran to her immediately, but found there was only a graze, and slight contusion on the shoulder. At first she was sadly frightened; but when I assured her there was no harm done, she was so delighted that she pulled a fowl out of one enormous pocket, and half a yard of black pudding out of the other, of which she begged my acceptance. I cannot say I pocketted the fee; but we regaled on it at our bivouack that evening.

After three days' pursuit, the French again made a stand on a strong hill, near the town of Aire, on the Adour, and after rather a sharp but short affair, they were driven from their post. They had no guns on the hill, but fired from three or four, placed on the high road, quite over their own position, so as to drop the balls amongst us as we advanced by a narrow causeway, flanked by the Adour, to attack it. I did not observe or hear of any casualty from the round shot; though thirty or forty plunged into a muddy field on one side of the road, and the river on the other, sufficiently near to splash some of our faces. My gallant friend, Col. Dodgin, led the Light Companies of the Division in his usual dashing style, but not with his usual luck. He was hit by a musket ball in the side, and tumbled off his horse.

The ball was fired by a fellow behind a hedge, not twenty yards off. It struck him above the right hip, and was cut out directly opposite, over the left. Yet there was no danger; for it hit a button of his coat, and was thus deflected from its direct course through the abdomen into a curve outside the muscles, but through a deep course of fat.[23] The impression of the two 66 on the button was made most correctly on the ball; proving according to the proverb that it carried its billet with it. The day had been cold and wet, and my friend's defences against the inclemency of the weather may be judged by the circumstance, that the nest which the ball had made for itself, and from which it was cut out, was lined by thirteen plies of cloth.

On the advance from Aire the Lieutenant Colonel requested that I might be permitted to remain to take care of him; which was courteously granted by General Byng. Immediately I got a good quarter for my patient, and established myself under the same roof.

My duty at Aire did not alone consist in attending my patient. We had several other wounded officers who were placed under my charge. A number of French prisoners wounded at Orthes, whose surgeons had deserted them, and a ward in the British Military Hospital were also entrusted to me; so that my hands were pretty full. Dr. McGrigor, Head of the Medical Establishment of the Army in the Peninsula, was then at Aire; and he generally gave his officers plenty of work when humanity and the public service required it; and made them do their work well too.

I may observe here, in passing, that I never had a more painful charge than that of the hospital of French wounded. Whether the state of their wounds was attributable to faulty surgery originally, or to rough conveyance from the field of action, or neglect since their arrival here—or, what is probable, to all combined—the fact was, that nothing could be more deplorable than their condition;—the smaller wounds were foul and sloughing—the men's health very bad—and most of the stumps were what we technically call sugar loaves; with the bone projecting and little union; all of which required re-amputation.

One morning when I was quitting the British Hospital, a cart was driven to the door from the Second Division, then quartered five or six leagues in front, containing a French and an English Dragoon—the latter being the worser case was attended first. This man, Corporal James Buchanan of the 13th Light Dragoons, carried with him a written certificate from his Commanding Officer, stating that he had been attacked the day before by three French Dragoons—whom he fought individually—slaying one outright; putting the second to flight badly wounded, and wounding and capturing the third, who came with him in the cart. Buchanan received fifteen wounds; in the head, face, arms and body: his nose was cut off and one bone of the forearm cut through.

It is needless to add that I paid the tenderest attention to this glorious fellow; patched up a jury-nose for him as well as I could, and, I am happy to say, left him convalescent, and in the best intelligence with his prisoner, who slept in the bed by his side.

On the 2nd of April, my patient being quite recovered, we marched to join the Army. On our way to the neat little walled town of Mirande, a soldier belonging to a detachment we were taking to the front had been guilty of theft with some violence to an inhabitant; and, after due enquiry, was ordered by the Colonel to be punished at the end of the day's march. As soon as the people of Mirande heard this, a deputation of about a dozen of the principal ladies waited on the Colonel in a body, and begged forgiveness for the culprit. They pleaded so eloquently and earnestly, and looked so pretty on this mission of charity, that nobody could refuse their prayer.

The Mayor gave us a billet on the best house in the town, the owner of which, a fine old gentlemanly man, was an ardent Bourbonist. The lady of the mansion was one of the most enthusiastic legitimists I ever met: but there was a tinge of ferocity about her politics that did not comport well with the gentleness of her sex. She shewed me a list of Buonaparte's Marshals which she kept, with black marks opposite the names of those that had died or fallen in battle; and she added that, during the last ten or twelve years, pricking these funereal notices on her chart had been one of her highest enjoyments. She was a firm believer in the illegitimacy of the King of Rome, and told us stories of Marie Louise and Josephine and Napoleon that would some years before have made me blush; but now my visage was already sunburnt into a suffusion far more rosy-brown than agreeable.

We heard next day at Gimont of the Battle of Thoulouse; and the people blamed Soult much–believing that he had no business to expose a great city to the horrors that might result from a defeat in its very suburbs. Every body appeared confident as to the speedy downfall of Napoleon, and Bourbon demonstrations became stronger as we advanced. At length at L'Isle en Jourdain, just as we entered, the Mayor returned from Thoulouse with the astounding news of the deposition of Buonaparte and the restoration of the old family. In five minutes the inhabitants collected in the square, and when the Mayor read from the *Moniteur* the official intelligence, quite a grove of white cockades burst on the sight simultaneously, amidst deafening shouts of '*Vive Louis dix-huit! Vivent les Bourbons! Vivent les Anglais! Vive Lord Vellingtonne!*' and then we all repaired to the Church to hear a grand *Te Deum*. In the evening a Ball on a great scale was given by the Mayoress, to which, of course we were invited, and treated with the most marked friendliness and attention.[24]

We entered Thoulouse amidst universal demonstrations of the most lively joy, and when we reached the great square we witnessed a most extraordinary sight. A fine colossal statue of Napoleon, of white marble, stood on the top of the pediment of the Capitolium—the grandest building in the city, which occupied one side of the square. A strong rope had, that morning, been rove round its neck, and there were two or three hundred people hauling away below with shouts and execrations.

We found workmen busily employed all over the city in substituting '*Royale*' for '*Imperiale*' and obliterating every where the poor persecuted great Ns. The Bees also—Napoleon's emblem— were flying off rapidly, and every external mark of the fallen dynasty fast disappearing.

In the evening we went to the theatre—the play was Henry the Fourth. The demonstrations of Bourbon loyalty and the Anglomania were quite overwhelming. Lord Wellington was present. As soon as he made his appearance in the Royal Box the whole audience stood up—the performance stopped; and actors and spectators joined in three of the loudest peals of acclamation I ever heard. Cries of '*Vive Louis dix-huit! Vivent les Anglais! Vive Lord Vellingtonne! Vive le Roi George!*' were a thousand times repeated. It was all like magic.

This was a week of extraordinary excitement, and unusual festivity at Thoulouse. Balls and *fêtes* followed each other rapidly. Lord Wellington resided in the Palace of the Prêfet, and was attended by a French guard of honour. Still, amidst all this gaiety there was a cloud yet in the military horizon, and a possibility even of some more fighting. Soult, sulky and obstinate, continued with his army at Carcassonne, and refused to send in his adhesion to the Bourbons. It was very generally believed at Thoulouse, that, previous to the battle of the 10th—he had received intelligence of the abdication of Napoleon; but conceiving his great antagonist was at length at fault, and confiding in the strength of his position, and desirous to end with éclat, he had concealed the news, and thus caused a great and wanton effusion of blood. From this false imputation, we have since seen his magnanimous adversary defending him successfully in the House of Lords, and stating that Marshal Soult could not have heard of the abdication of Napoleon when he fought at Thoulouse.

On the 16th of April my patient and I re-joined the regiment at Ville Franche; after a march from Thoulouse, along the Canal of Languedoc, cut by Louis XIV, to connect the Garonne with the Mediterranean. In the vicinity of the city the country is woody, rich, and well cultivated; but as we travelled eastward it became flat, bare and ugly.

The clear morning of the 18th found the whole of Sir Rowland Hill's Corps assembled under arms, near Ville Franche, in a state of considerable impatience to learn the *ultimatum* of the Duke of Dalmatia, which had been peremptorily demanded by the Duke of Wellington. To fight, or not to fight, was the question. After remaining four long hours in this suspense—whilst the eyes of all were strained on the road to Carcassonne, we saw a coach coming along at a rapid rate, escorted by four English, and four French Dragoons. These were cheered as they passed, and we soon learned that the Count de Gazan and one of Lord Wellington's Aides-de-Camp, were in the carriage, charged with the adhesion of Marshal Soult to the Bourbon government. Thus, then, ended our fighting.

On the 27th of April the Duc D'Angoulême entered Thoulouse amidst the unbounded acclamations of the whole city. The streets were lined with the Allied Troops—a cortège of British General Officers, and a very numerous band of mounted gentlemen of the city, escorted him through the streets to the cathedral amidst a royal salute from our Artillery; whilst thousands of bright eyes beamed smiles upon him from the windows, and a whole forest of white handkerchiefs were waving over his head.

We left our pleasant quarters near Thoulouse, on the 3rd of June, to march to Bordeaux; there to embark for England. Our route lay down the left bank of the Garonne; one of the most rich and lovely tracts in France. The marches were short—the inhabitants overwhelmingly civil, and we had a ball every night.

The Portuguese Oporto Brigade, composed of three fine regiments, that had long associated with our second Division, and fought many a well contested field together, accompanied us part of the way. When we arrived at the town of Bezace, where their route turned off to Bayonne, the Officers of Byng's Brigade gave a parting entertainment to the Portuguese Officers. This final *fête* was marked by a remarkable display of cordiality and brotherly affection between the companions in arms. British airs were called for by our friends, and we gave them Portuguese in turn; whilst suitable toasts were cheered in flowing bumpers, until it was time to go to the ball-room. These regiments had secured the esteem and respect of the British soldiers by their gallantry in the field, and general good conduct. Next morning we marched early; and when we came to the cross-roads where we were to separate, the old fellow-campaigners, officers and men, embraced and exchanged affectionate *adieus*: and as we moved in different directions, loud and prolonged cheers answered each other in peals and echoes, until they melted away in the distance.

And there too, excellent and faithful Antonio! there didst thou separate from thy master, and went thy way to thy native Coimbra, to astonish the untravelled simple ones of the Mondego by the relation of thy various adventures. Honestly didst thou always serve me; and though in a moment of weakness thou didst once err, and forget to put the turkey on the spit—this one fault was lost amidst thy general virtue—it was only a spot in the sun. I do believe, my poor knave, that thou didst not soon forget thy master: for of this the tear that fell upon my hand when kissing it at parting, was a pledge!

We reached Bordeaux on the 18th of June, and encamped with the Light Division soon after, on a large heath, four leagues from the city, waiting for ships of war to take us home.

About this period we witnessed another triumphal entry of the Duc D'Angoulême at Bordeaux; which was even more brilliant than at Thoulouse: but there was an unfortunate accident which damped the joy. A British brig of war, moored near the quay, killed one of the crowd with the wadding of a gun, in firing a salute. I was standing on the balcony of the American Hotel, facing the river, when the misfortune happened close to the house. I then heard several cries from the alarmed multitude—'*C'est exprès—C'est exprès*'.

We sailed in the *Rodney* 74—for Cove; and soon after in the *Chatham*, 74, to Spithead, landed at Gosport and marched to Bristol.

6

Leave · Sails for India · Madras · Calcutta · The Ganges · A Tiger Hunt.
Invasion of Nepaul

As soon as I could obtain leave of absence, I proceeded to my
native vale in the North of Ireland, where the three months
soon passed away amidst the kindnesses and warm hospitalities
of a circle of relations and friends. '*Non cuivis contingit adire
Corinthum.*' Every body had not travelled in those days; and a
traveller, particularly a campaigning traveller, was then thought
an acquisition to society. Before I went abroad I had a very
humble opinion of my own merit; but I now rose rapidly in self-
esteem. It may be well believed that I told all my Peninsular
stories to the best advantage—described the battles I had been
in to the Militia Officers—re-amputated shoulders for the Doctors
—detailed the dresses of the Spanish ladies, and expatiated on
their floating movements and pretty lisp, for the edification of
my fair acquaintances; and descanted on the respective merits of
the vineyards of the claret country for the wine bibbers. In short,
when my leave was nearly up, I found myself the centre of a considerable knot, and already expanding into some importance.

In the course of my rambles, angle in hand, it was agreeable to
discover that I had not been forgotten by the good yeomanry of
the vale of Esk. I was frequently coaxed out of a flying advice,
when there happened to be any sickness in the house, by the
flattering exordium—'Oh! shure he's the clever young docthor that
used to be fishing here about, and playing with the childer—Och,
Lord bless him, he's jist come from the wars, and shure its himself can tell us what we're to do to Judy's futt.' After this it was
impossible to refuse.[25]

A renewal of leave was asked and refused. I therefore lost no
time in joining the regiment at Newport in the Isle of Wight.
Soon after, a detachment of eight officers and one hundred men
was ordered to march to Chatham and embark to join the first
battalion in Bengal. I was directed to accompany it.

We embarked on board the *Lord Melville*, Indiaman, in February, but were baffled by contrary winds and calms all the month of March, and lay tumbling about in the Downs until the 3rd of April.

Few things can be more annoying than remaining weather-bound in port with every arrangement for the voyage completed. But, about the middle of March, an event occurred, which dispelled for a while the monotony of our life at the stupid anchorage –Buonaparte again in France! When we heard he had landed, most persons on board thought the attempt was madness, and that he would be instantly apprehended and shot. When, however, news arrived that the Garrison of Grenoble had joined him, matters looked a little more serious; still the general opinion was that the daring invader would be stopped at Lyons, whither the Comte d'Artois and Marshal Macdonald had repaired to organize a loyal force: only one person was credulous–my humble self.

In this state of suspense we left England, and many and various were the arguments *pro* and *con* respecting the result of this astounding expedition–success or failure–the Imperial sceptre once more–or a traitor's grave. During the early part of the voyage, our conversation in the cuddy turned almost exclusively on this absorbing topic: at last, every thing connected with the subject having been pretty well exhausted, it was abandoned, about the time we reached the Line, by common consent; after the Captain, a gentlemanly man named Crabbe, and myself, had made a bet of a Champagne dinner when we reached Calcutta, respecting the issue of Buonaparte's invasion. He betted that Napoleon would not be in Paris except as a prisoner, on the 15th of April. The dinner was to include all the cabin passengers.[26]

We sailed in a fleet of five ships–all Indiamen–our Captain being Commodore. One of the ships–the *Princess Charlotte*–the fastest sailer, was employed as a look-out frigate, to reconnoitre any suspicious strangers, as we were not quite sure that we might not fall in with an American frigate in our course; ignorant, most probably of the Treaty of Ghent that had just been concluded. All the ships had troops on board, and we were determined to make a good fight. We had beautiful weather the whole way; and so fair was the wind, that we had not occasion to wear or tack the whole voyage from the Downs to Madras. We passed our time agreeably–Captain Crabbe had a respectable library, and he civilly invited us all to enjoy ourselves with a book in his commodious cabin when we pleased. Gazing–strolling on deck–reading and chess, occupied the forenoon; and we generally had whist in the evening.

There was but one drawback to our comfort on board–the irregular conduct of Lieut. L[am]b[rech]t of our Corps. This was a talented young man–most agreeable when sober, but half mad when excited by wine. One night when passing Madeira, L[ambrech]t came out of the cuddy tipsy, knocked down the seaman at the wheel and took his place. The Captain was inside; but finding the ship making a wide yaw out of her course, he came running out to see what was the matter; when the new steersman explained–averring that the blockhead he had just ousted knew nothing whatever about his work. This prank was forgiven, and the man got hush-money; but on an exactly similar outrage again occurring Mr. L[ambrech]t was put under close arrest.

This young man was clever and well read; and, it appeared, had been first spoiled by the sentimental and sensual sophistries of the French philosophic school–chiefly of Rousseau. Numerous were the scrapes in which he involved himself during the Peninsular Campaigns by his intemperance; and manifold were the dangers he ran of losing his commission with disgrace. As some persons can sleep at will, L[ambrech]t possessed the power of sobering himself on a great emergency; so that he always managed to avoid any fatal display of incapacity to do his duty. When once on an outlying picket before Bayonne, the night after the Second Division crossed the Nive, he got quite drunk and fell asleep. Immediately after, poor Clitheroe, who was afterwards killed at Garris, arrived at the post, with an order to patrol in a particular direction in front. I happened to be in the hut at the time–the night was dark and wet, and L[ambrech]t so wrapped in drunken sleep that he could not be wakened, and I thought he was lost. All this time Capt. Clitheroe was waiting at the door for the officer in command of the picket, to give him his instructions. After several attempts I roused him at last, by plunging a large pin up to its head in the calf of his leg–when he started up–rubbed his eyes and his leg–cursed the insect that had bit him–went out and received the Aide-de-Camp's orders–took his picket in the proper direction–patrolled where he was desired, and made a very satisfactory report.

Before we left Chatham, L[ambrech]t sallied out of the Mitre

Inn one evening after dinner, with a white-hot poker in his hand. It was Saturday night, and very wet; yet many people were in the streets, and as he proceeded, upsetting everybody he met, winding his formidable weapon—fizzing with the rain—over his head, and spouting German, he looked something like a demon wreathed in fire and smoke.

As we approached the Line we met with the usual number of porpoises, flying fish and sharks. The last being a fish I had not yet enjoyed the pleasure of catching, I baited a hook with a piece of pork, attached this to a chain a foot and a half long, fastened to a strong cord, and promised a shilling for the first intimation when one of these voracious rascals made his appearance; which was generally in the ship's wake, and very early in the morning.

Two mornings after these arrangements, a sailor shook my cot a little after day-light to announce the arrival of the enemy. I started up and ascended to the poop; and there plain enough, was a good sized shark visible, about three feet below the surface, and four or five yards astern. Over went my bait immediately, and I was delighted to perceive that it was not long unnoticed: the shark came up to the pork, reconnoitred it a little with some attention, poked it with his snout; and then—being satisfied that it was sweet, he turned himself half round, opened his huge mouth and sucked it in. I kindly permitted him to indulge in one squeeze of the luscious morsel, and then, just as he was getting into his former sailing order—chuck went the barb into his jaws.

At first he did not appear to comprehend the meaning of this prick; perhaps supposing it was nothing more than a sharp bit of bone in the pork—but when he found the hook piercing deeper and deeper, and 'the iron entering his soul'—down he plunged desperately; but in the mean time the sailors had attached the cord to a coil of rope, and I let him run out as much as he pleased, and then played him like a salmon. By this time half the passengers were up, witnessing the sport. When the shark was fairly tired, I brought him near the surface—a sailor cast a noose adroitly round his body below the pectoral fins—a loud yo-he-oh! was sung out by the captors, and we hoisted the gentleman on deck. He there made great play about our legs; but his tail was soon nicked with an axe—the sailors dragged him forward to the cooking galley—cut him up and ate him.

In the warm latitudes we caught a number of bonitos, from the bowsprit, with a piece of rag resembling a flying-fish, on which they feed. The bonito, notwithstanding its name, is very ugly; and the Portuguese who first named it, could have had little ichthyological taste. Its flesh is very coarse–and only eatable when dressed with some rich sauce, or stewed in wine.

We had fine weather and an unusually smooth sea going round the Cape, and through the Mozambique channel. When we were abreast of the Island of Johanna, we saw a number of canoes waiting to board us, full of the most grotesquely dressed black figures, apparently arrayed in cast-off English naval and military uniforms; shouting to us to lay to and throw them a rope. But the Commodore was deaf to their intreaties–the wind was too fair to stop even for a levee of Admirals and Generals; and thus the Prince of Wales and the Duke of York and Lord Nelson–all hard-working Arab washermen–lost their job.

On the 2nd of July we got amongst a large covey of flying-fish– chased by innumerable dolphins and bonitos; some of which poor unfortunates jumped into the chains, and even on deck, where they were soon secured. They are extremely delicate eating; tasting much like whiting. This morning I caught a very large shark–being the thirteenth–fully twelve feet long, and weighing one hundred and fifty pounds. This monster gave us an hour's play, and I found my hands all blistered afterwards from the running out and hauling the rope–though quite unconscious of hurt at the time.

Whilst rapidly traversing the Indian Ocean, many and various were our conjectures on board concerning the *res gestœ* in Europe; for here there was full scope for speculation. Leaving England as Napoleon reached Lyons, yet, when the 'Bravest of the Brave' was pledged to destroy him, it was hard to say what the event would be. For my own part I entertained little doubt of the general defection of the Army; knowing their invincible attachment to their old master, and the electric effect of the first example: and under this impression betted the dinner, which probably would cost a hundred pounds in expensive Calcutta.

On the 17th July we saw Ceylon on our larboard bow; and soon perceived the peculiar odour of land–notwithstanding the groves of cinnamon and spice, certainly more earthy and warm than fragrant. On the 22nd we anchored in Madras Roads.

And now all was intense anxiety to learn the news from Europe, which would be received here up to a late date by an overland despatch. Soon after dropping anchor we saw a Mussoolah boat approach with a white face in it; and before the owner had time to board us he was hailed from the gangway–'Any Europe news?' 'Great news' was the reply. But he proceeded leisurely up the ladder and stepped on the quarter-deck before he would tell us any more. Then, after shaking hands with Captain Crabbe, he satisfied our eager curiosity in three words–'Buonaparte is reigning in the Thuilleries!'

On the 24th we disembarked; and had the novel excitement previously of passing through the Madras surf. Our course was through three successive tiers of foaming and thundering breakers, often looking down upon us as we sat in the bottom of the deep and elastic Mussoolah boat; the line of the bottom of which, as we ascended and descended the steep and awful hills of surf, was within a very little of being absolutely perpendicular, and as if it was poised on one end. We were flanked on both sides by a fleet of Catamarans; the inmates of which had various shining medals about their necks, as rewards for saving poor fellows like us from the sharks. Allah! Allah! Allah! vociferated the boatmen, as the boat rode over the foaming ridges–Allah! Allah! shouted with equal fear and fervency. At last the flood of the third surf shot us up on the beach; when a hundred Orientals seizing the boat, for fear of the reflux, dragged us out of the reach of the wave, and we jumped out on the soil of Hindoostan.

Here, then, were we fairly landed in this 'Clime of the Sun'. My brother officers and myself were immediately assailed by an army of black and yellow and straw-coloured and mud-coloured and many-coloured natives, in large turbans, fine moustaches, earnest faces, long, white, flowing garments, and naked feet, presenting numerous credentials and certificates with low and graceful salaams; and requesting to have the high honour of being the humblest of our slaves. With some difficulty we made our way through them, but not before choosing one or two each from this importunate crowd. We then got into Palanquins and went to the principal hotel.

Next morning we marched to Poonamalee, a military station fifteeen miles from Madras;[27] the appearance and agremens of which did not prepossess us much in favour of the new country. The barracks were built on a flat; exposed to the heat of a powerful sun—without shade or ventilation: the flies could scarcely have been much worse with Pharaoh, and a sandy plain in front was inhabited by Cobra de Capellos—the most venemous snake in the East. These creatures remained in their holes during the day; but, as soon as it was dark, they sallied out to take a snap at any body's heels that passed. When obliged to pass over this plain during my night visits to the hospital, I was at first very apprehensive of a bite, but I took good care to fortify every thing below the knees with as many pairs of boots as I could move in; and thus defied the snakes, although I sometimes fancied I felt the villains tugging at the leather.

After a fortnight at Poonamalee we were ordered to re-embark in the same ship for Calcutta. We marched at two o'clock in the morning to avoid the heat—enjoyed several delicious drinks of toddy—the cool juice of the cocoa-nut palm—on the road—launched out into the surf, attended by the Catamaran people—cheated the sharks—once more found ourselves comfortably settled in the *Lord Melville*; and after a pleasant voyage reached Calcutta on the 23rd of August.

This Metropolis of the East has a grand and imposing aspect; and the beauty of the fine houses at the western extremity particularly—surrounded by their richly ornamented and luxurious grounds and gardens, is very striking. The mansions are on a large scale, compared with English dwellings at home; and their deep verandahs and balconies, with the white marmorean Chunam with which the walls are covered, give them quite an air of splendour and magnificence.

But to a Griffin (as strangers are called) perhaps the greatest novelty in Calcutta is that huge, grave, Dominie Sampson of birds—the adjutant; stalking slowly and formally through the streets—flying round a corner within a yard of your person, with his enormous bill projecting formidably, and threatening you with impalement if you should come in contact with him—gobbling up large bones of beef, or any other trifle he meets, or, when his meal is over, standing like a statue on the highest pinnacle he can find.

The adjutant is a harmless and useful bird, that performs the duty of a scavenger in India—devouring offal, and punishing snakes—of which he is very fond. His valuable services are so fully appreciated, that the Company have taken him into their

charge and placed his whole fraternity under their protection—
punishing with a heavy fine the murder of one of these birds.
Yet, such is the ingratitude of mankind, that the poor inoffensive
adjutant is persecuted by the most annoying and cruel tricks.
Shank bones of mutton are cleaned out and stuffed with gunpowder, with a slow match applied—then the meat is thrown out
and swallowed, and when the poor wretch is chuckling over his
savoury morsel, it explodes and blows him to atoms.

A more venial trick—and not unamusing, I confess—is to tie
two legs of mutton together with a piece of whip-cord, leaving
an interval of three or four yards—the *jigots* are then tossed out
amongst the adjutants, and soon find their way into the stomachs
of a couple of the most active of the birds. As long as they keep
together it is all very well; but as soon as the cord tightens, both
become alarmed and take wing—mutually astonished at the
phenomenon, no doubt. A laughable tugging match then ensues
in the air—each adjutant striving to mount higher than the other,
till at last they attain a great elevation. When at length the
weaker bird is forced to disgorge his mutton, a new power comes
into play—the force of gravity—and the pendulum leg of mutton
brings the conqueror down to the earth a great deal faster than
he wishes.

These creatures have prodigious powers of deglutition and
digestion. It is a very common thing for one of them to seize
an impertinent crow who is troublesome, when the adjutant wants
to eat his breakfast in quiet, and after turning him right about
face by a skilful *coup de bec*, to send him cawing down his capacious
throat. I recollect at Dinapore, when we shook a bag-fox, and had
an hour's run one morning, some silly servant brought the dead
animal home, and tossed him into the barrack-square amongst
the adjutants, who all came flocking about the poor defunct. One
ravenous fellow would seize him by the brush, another by the leg—
a third by the back—still it would not do—none could manage to
gulp him down. At last one large bird set about the business
scientifically, and took the fox's head in his mouth; which, after
a little straining, was bolted—then, with a great effort he swallowed
the body, till nothing remained but a bit of the tail sticking out
of his beak. At this the others began to pick; till the gormandizer
becoming annoyed at their teasing, flew off with his delicate lunch
to digest it as his leisure.

As I feared at the time that this fact, every circumstance of which had passed under my own eyes, would not be credited at home, I called out two of my brother-officers from their breakfasts, to be corroborating evidence. Still, it must rest on my single authority; as poor L'Estrange left his bones at Sierra Leone, and Harvey is also no longer in the land of the living. But no old Indian will doubt the story.

On reaching Calcutta we found that our regiment had left the Presidency for Dinapore about a fortnight before our arrival. We got quarters in Fort William. At this time the Governor was absent, and every body was complaining of the stupidity of Calcutta. We saw few except our immediate military superiors; and the only large dinner we partook of in the city of palaces, was the bet dinner at Captain Crabbe's house in Chouringhee.

In the middle of September we embarked on the Hoogly–the westernmost and deepest branch of the Ganges, for Dinapore. Another officer and myself engaged a Budgerow of sixteen dandies, as they called boatmen in India–and we all formed a mess, and took a native purveyor with us, who engaged to provide us food on the voyage at a very moderate rate. Three other large detachments for different Indian Regiments accompanied us, and I was appointed superintendent *medico* of the whole. In those Saturnian days, John Company paid his Doctors well. I received so many *annas* each per head, for the individuals under my charge, including myself; and thus was furnished with an additional reason, value about sixpence a-day, for preserving my own health.

Our voyage up the Ganges was quite a pleasure trip. When the wind was fair, we sailed gallantly against the current; but otherwise we were pulled along the shore by our boatmen, who moved in the water like amphibious animals, totally fearless as to the alligators. At these times I was generally out with my gun, ranging a little into the interior; with a couple of servants and a skiff to observe and follow my motions. In the middle of the day I was always on board attending to the sick. We generally halted for the night at some pleasant spot on the bank, ordinarily near some tope or mango grove. Innumerable were the individual teal, widgeon, mallard, *et id genus omne*, that I shot on this voyage; and whenever there were marshes we were sure to find snipes.

But the resplendent wild peacock! What *can* be a nobler sight than a fine cock, with his two yards of tail, flying over your head:

his brilliant plumage nearly dazzling you blind, as the rays of an Indian Sun are reflected from it? And what a sensation when you knock him over.[28] I shot only a few of these magnificent birds, for they are getting scarce in the neighbourhood of the river; and there is an ugly association with them, that has some tendency to spoil one's enjoyment in pursuing them. The peacock jungles are very frequently the haunts of tigers.

During one of my rambles on this voyage, I passed a buffalo bull in a field; but, observing something peculiarly treacherous in his whole appearance, I cocked both barrels, and prepared for mischief; and well it was that I had critically noticed the expression of his savage eye: for I had not advanced from him thirty paces, when he charged me with a roar. I stood firm, and when he came so near that missing him was impossible, he had the benefit of a barrel in each eye. The pain maddened the blinded brute; and ferocious monster as he was, I could scarcely help feeling pity when I saw him roaring with agony and revolving in a bloody circle: and though his infamous conduct scarcely deserved the act of mercy, I put a ball in each barrel and killed him. My two native servants had scampered off very valiantly when they saw the beast attacking me: but when they found him shot, there was no end to the compliments to *saahib* on the occasion.

On these little expeditions, it was amusing to observe the absurd fear the Indian domestic cattle shew of a white man: snorting at his approach—throwing up their noses and running out of his way with all speed. One day when in quest of partridges, I happened to jump into a lane, and there confronted a Hindu riding on one of his gods—a Brahminee Bull, who carried besides two bags of rice. On perceiving my white face, the animal bolted to the right about so suddenly that he unshipped his Indian master, bags of paddy and all, and ran snorting up the lane in a state of great alarm. The Indian, after pulling his bags out of the dirt, ran to catch his deity; whom he abused in the grossest manner his very gross and copious language would permit.

We continued our voyage prosperously and pleasantly. The troops were healthy, notwithstanding the horrid habits of intemperance which the ardent climate and cheap spirits engender. We reached Dinapore on the 2nd November, and I delivered my charge all safe and sound; no casualty having occurred in the detachment since we left the Isle of Wight.

The 66th Regiment marched from Dinapore in the direction of the Nepaul Hills, the very day we arrived. Things were beginning to look warlike in that quarter—the Rajah of Nepaul demurred at ratifying the treaty of peace which had been signed by his Minister: a force was about to be assembled to coerce him, and a camp had been traced out on the frontier. On our arrival we found that the sick, the women and children, heavy baggage, &c., had been left here—I was directed to remain till farther orders, but a hint was given to equip for a campaign.

Thus far into the bowels of the land I had come prosperously, and now was about to contrast Indian with European warfare, and to exchange the pretty valleys of the Pyrenees for the stupendous sublimities of the Himalaya Mountains. My domestic establishment expanded somewhat in the same ratio. I had my Sirdar-bearer, supposed to be honest, *par excellence*; and bound by every honourable tie to let nobody cheat me but himself: nine common bearers for my Palanquin—two Chohkhedars or watch-men—my Dhoby or water-carrier[29]—my Dhurjee or tailor—my Khitmugar—my Mnausalgee, the Syce and his assistant to take care of my horse—three men to look after the bullocks—some others, whose duties I forget: and my incomparable Bastee Rhamm, with resplendent, jet-black moustaches, curling like the horns of his namesake, to superintend my Hookah.

O Antonio, my faithful valet, and thou hard-fisted Jonathan Wild, my trusty groom! often did I regret you, when groaning in the splendid bondage of being lord over twenty and nine be-dizened, and be-muslined, and sashed, and slashed, and slippered, and turbaned attendants.

We marched on the 9th December, with another officer of the regiment, for the camp in the *terraie*, as the belt of level land round the base of the first hills is called. We crossed the Ganges near Dinapore, and at once got into a fertile and populous country. Our marches were only ten miles a-day;[30] the weather was cool and clear. Latitude, about thirty degrees north; and altogether the journey was more a pleasant shooting expedition than a march. We always breakfasted early, and sent on our baggage, with directions to encamp ten miles off, in the most convenient tope the servants could find, and then set about cooking our dinner; whilst we kept a couple of horses and attendants, and digressed from the road whenever we found game. On the

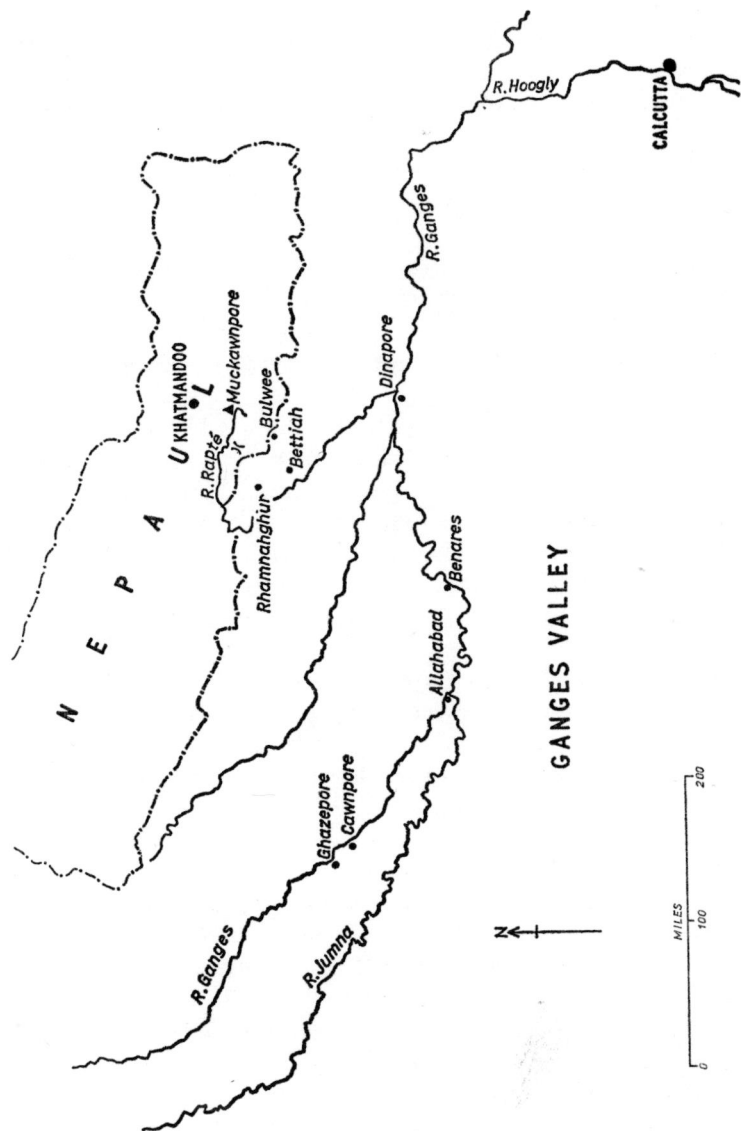

GANGES VALLEY

NEPA U

R.Hoogly

CALCUTTA

KHATMANDOO

Muckawnpore

Bulwee

Bettiah

R.Rapte

Rhamnahghur

Dinapore

R.Ganges

Benares

Allahabad

Ghazepore

Cawnpore

R.Ganges

R.Jumna

N

MILES

0   100   200

111

third day, we had accumulated such a quantity that we were embarrassed with our riches—but, fortunately, meeting some Company's officers, known to my companion, we begged they would assist us in our distress. Our cook set to work, and having bruised the heads of sixty or seventy couple of snipe, they were put into a kettle to make soup, with a few brace of partridges, and a number of ortolans, that we met in flocks every day. I don't know the exact gastronomic name our soup was entitled to, but this I know, that it was exquisitely good. The rest of the game dinner was in harmony.

The next day we had again good sport; having entered a country irrigated by numerous artificial ponds and tanks, to which vast numbers of water-fowl resorted. In the evening we found our tents pitched in a Mango Tope, with turf as smooth as velvet, by the side of a considerable lake. It was near sunset, and we were about to dress for dinner, when I saw a wild peacock emerging from the jungle, fifty yards from the water, and running down to drink opposite our tents. I seized my gun, went down the pond a little way, got across in an old canoe, and then commenced the delicate operation of turning his flank: diving into the jungle, at the expence of some scratches, getting quite in his rear, and cutting him off from his cover. I then advanced until about thirty yards distant; whilst the vain bird, after satisfying his thirst, appeared inclined to pick a quarrel with his image in the clear water. He received one barrel before he took flight, without much apparent injury; for these strong birds are so mailed by their thick feathers that they require large shot, at a short distance, to kill them; and I could hear my charge rattling on his quills, without preventing his getting up vigorously. The reserve artillery, however, brought him down with a broken wing; and even then he nearly escaped into the jungle before I caught him, when he made a desperate fight. I presented this bird to the Mess the day of our arrival in camp. It was buried in moist earth five days, after which the flesh was tender, and of fine flavour.

We found a large encampment near the hamlet of Bulwee; consisting of three British regiments, the 24th, 87th and ours, with twelve or thirteen battalions of Seapoys and Artillery; the whole commanded by Sir David Ochterlony.

To one just arrived, after campaigning in Europe, the novelty and luxury of an Indian camp were extremely pleasing and amusing. There was a large and heterogeneous host of followers—about twenty for every soldier—consisting of the Bazaar people, Coolies, Bangywallas,[31] Jugglers, Nautch girls—officers' and soldiers' servants—tent-people; and attendants on the numerous public elephants, camels and bullocks. We had a good Bazaar, and plenty of provisions; and as one proof of the goodness of our fare, I may mention that at the Mess we had green peas in abundance, that had been carried in baskets on men's shoulders from Dinapore.

Here we remained six weeks, whilst negociations were going on with the Ghoorkahs. Our last campaign against them had been on the whole, unsuccessful; and some failures in attempts on their forts and other untoward affairs had given them confidence. We were now under arms at day-light every morning, but after this parade we had the day to ourselves; and as this was a rich and new country for the sportsman, we had plenty of amusement; fox and jackal hunting and coursing, and abundance of snipe—common and painted—with great variety of waterfowl. A tiger, even, would now and then leave his lair in the jungle, to pay us a visit, and one large fellow had been seen in the neighbourhood of the camp three or four times. At length Dr. Richardson, of the Company's Service, a celebrated tiger-hunter, determined to go in quest of him; and having heard that I was very anxious for an opportunity of getting a shot, he was kind enough to offer me a seat on his elephant.

We started for a ravine, four miles from camp, whither the brute had been recently tracked; mounted on a steady and trained male elephant, with a pair of magnificent tusks, fit to transfix any tiger in the forest. I had my own double gun, and a rifle which my friend lent me.

We were not long in discovering the enemy's retreat; but he slunk away before we could get a shot within proper distance, and we beat about the whole day without success. The same bad luck also attended us on our second expedition; but we were determined to try once more, and skirted the jungle to a great distance without seeing any thing larger than a black partridge. As we were returning in bad spirits at our ill fortune, in passing through a low brake, two miles from camp, the elephant became excited, threw up his trunk and made a dead point. In five minutes afterwards the noble game we were in quest of, gave an angry growl as he emerged from a bush, not ten yards in front of us, and slowly got out of our way. We were both cool, for all our energies had been exerted to preserve presence of mind; so that we fired with certain aim, and in four seconds as many balls struck the tiger. He roared horribly—lashed his sides—turned and attempted to spring at us, but failed, for a fore leg had been broken. Three more balls despatched him; and after pausing until we saw all motion cease, we alighted, cautiously approached, and stood over our fallen enemy.

We entered the camp with our glorious prize. The tiger was a noble male of the very largest size—ten feet four inches from nose to tail. I measured his fore leg near the shoulder, with my pocket handkerchief, and found it exactly the same circumference as my own body under the arms; which is somewhat above medium size. Every muscle of the limb was as defined and as hard as a cord of iron.

The elephants and camels of our little army, were picketted near the part of the camp occupied by our regiment. One refractory brute amongst the former was beginning to shew dangerous symptoms of ferocity, calling for suitable treatment; and severe enough was the discipline he received. They chained him by the four legs to a large tree, which even *his* power could scarcely shake—half-starved him for a week, and every morning they pricked him with half a dozen long bamboos, armed with sharp spikes, about the neck and roots of the ears; when the animal's violent exertions would make the blood spout out frightfully. In this way they brought him to his senses, and he was quiet enough in about ten days.

There chanced to be a female elephant and her calf stationed not far from my tent. I carried the young one a large basin of sweet tea, after breakfast one morning; into which he dipped his trunk and drained the contents in an instant; and, perceiving his mamma looking so wistfully, I procured her one also, which she drank with much gusto. Soon after this introduction we became great friends, and the mother and her son were regular pensioners of my tea-pot: the lady permitting me to take many liberties with her person; such as toying with her delicate ear, scratching her neck, &c., and giving me now and then a hug about the waist with her trunk, which in no instance exceeded the reasonable bounds of a friendly embrace. One morning when she was particularly affectionate, I took a fancy to feel her pulse, and when handling her ear, I groped for an artery at the base, and noted the number of pulsations in a minute; which was twenty four—and I need scarcely add that there was no want of strength.

By the end of January 1816, matters began to assume a more warlike aspect in the camp. Preparations were begun for an invasion of the enemy's sequestered valleys—the sick were sent to the rear—heavy artillery and more troops arrived in camp—the whole force, consisting of seventeen thousand men, was formed into four Divisions—one of which, consisting of our own Regiment, nine hundred strong, and four Seapoy Battalions, was placed under the command of our excellent commanding officer, Colonel Nicol. His column was destined to penetrate into the Nepaul valley by the Bhicknee, or most western Pass, whilst the other columns were to pierce the formidable frontier of mountain and forest, by three other goat-paths, dignified with the name of Passes, simultaneously with ourselves.

On the 4th of February we broke up our camp, and marched westward, skirting the mountain to Rhamnahgur, the residence of a Rajah. All the *terraie* in this neighbourhood appeared well cultivated, and the soil good; whilst the vicinity of the huge snowy mountains maintained a freshness and coolness of climate which was very agreeable. Our mornings were sometimes cold—the thermometer standing at 36° of Fahrenheit, and at mid-day up to 76° or 80°. But the whole country is dreadfully unhealthy in the hot weather.

On the 14th February we arrived opposite the entrance of the Pass, where stood a Hindoo Temple of great sanctity, on a hill called Maahur a Jaggra, which was deserted by the Brahmins on our approach. It was covered with the usual emblems of the worship of the Lingam. Two days were spent in fortifying this strong hill, as a point of importance in preserving our communications with the rear; and three hundred Seapoys and two guns were left as a garrison. These arrangements being made, and our Commissariat stores well up, we prepared for a dash through the belt of forest, and an invasion of the Nepaul territory. We had seen no person—the spies could give us no certain intelligence—except the scream of the parroquet, all was silent in the deep forest around us: and this ominous calm, whilst it impressed the weaker spirits with an undefined dread of something terrible, cheered the bolder with the confidence of certain success.

On the 17th of February, the Column of Colonel Nicol first entered the enemy's territory. After penetrating through five miles of thick jungle, we came to the mouth of the Bhicknee Pass, which we found commencing in the dry bed of a river, about one hundred and fifty yards wide; and very high steep banks, covered with enormous saahl and teak trees, and thick underwood– altogether exceedingly strong and defensible. We, of course, expected opposition here, but saw not a creature, except deer and monkeys: the latter were of a large size, numerous and noisy– running along the tops of the trees on the high banks, parallel with our advance–scolding and gesticulating, and occasionally pelting us with nuts. Like true patriots, they opposed our invasion with all their might.

When we had proceeded five or six miles up the Nullah, it became all at once very narrow, and the day being well advanced, it was deemed prudent to halt and look about us. Accordingly, the baggage soon came up; for in our present position we could not safely leave it far behind the Column, and we pitched our tents as well as we could in the confined water-course, where all was stone, with no earth to hold a peg. Then, having carefully posted treble cordons of pickets in all directions, we proceeded to make our toilet and prepare for dinner.

There was very great desertion amongst the followers of the camp, chiefly the Bazaar people, on this first day's march in an enemy's country, from apprehension of the Ghoorkah Mountaineers, who had acquired a high warlike name amongst the effeminate Asiatics. Our personal servants, however, continued staunch during the whole campaign. The Mess marquee was soon up, and the dinner was put upon the stocks forthwith. And, certes, it was no small enjoyment to sit down in those wild solitudes, not merely to a good, but a luxurious dinner, with our wine cooled artificially, in an absolute, literal 'wilderness of monkeys', chattering high above our heads, and surrounded by beasts of prey: liable too, to be washed off, *en masse*, by any accidental thunder-storm in the mountains. For the river, that now lent us its dry bed for a couch, and was kind enough to trickle between the large stones in a stream scarcely perceptible, but still sufficient to water man and beast, might, in an hour or two, save the Ghoorkahs a world of trouble.

Next day our Nullah fairly ended in a *Cul-de-sac* and after exploring in all directions, the Quarter Master General could find nothing but a faint and doubtful sheep track: yet, this was all the high road that the country furnished; consequently we set to work to enlarge it for the passage of the Artillery. The bearings of our route being known, the pioneers began to hew and burn, clearing their way through the primeval forest, guided only by the compass and the sun. And now the scene was grand—the fire and the axe opening us a path into the enemy's country, and glorious trees, a hundred and fifty feet high, were seen spouting out huge pyramids of flame before us, the beacons of our advance, whilst a touch of the grotesque was added to the sublime by the utter alarm and consternation of the great white-faced baboons with which they were peopled.

Still we saw not a human being, and our Light Companies, that threaded the forest on the flanks of the Column, met with no opposition but the formidable jungle through which they were slowly penetrating. This was strange, considering the nature of the defile we were passing through; and many began to entertain fears that a still stronger pass yet awaited us; and that the Ghoorkahs were preparing certain Caudine forks for Brigadier Nicol, although not deeply acquainted with Roman history.

For four days we proceeded thus through Forest and Nullah, cutting a rough carriage road as we went on, and feeling our way cautiously, but no enemy appeared. The chief inconvenience we experienced was from the round stones in the dry water-courses, which got between the clefts of the hoof and lamed our bullocks. The elephants stood this better; their thick-soled and elastic boots bearing their weight over pebbles as well as any thing else. On the march I sometimes passed my female friend and her son; and although the eye of these animals looks heavy, I fancy I could notice a twinkle of recognition in the old one's physiognomy, conveying a hint how agreeable it would be if I would send her an invitation to tea some evening.

At length it appeared probable that the sameness of our lumbering advance would be relieved by a little fighting, *pour nous désennuyer*, as positive information was received that a strong stockade had been prepared a little way in our front, which the enemy were determined to defend with a large force. Preparations were instantly made to attack it. Flanking detachments were

117

ordered right and left to turn the position, while the Artillery were got ready to batter, and a strong Column was directed to storm. It was pleasing to witness the tone of satisfaction this news diffused through the whole of the Column, native as well as European. Our men prepared their arms, sharpened the points of their bayonets, and examined their flints with great glee; whilst the Seapoys did the same, exulting in the support of so strong and fine a corps, and especially in the batteries of Artillery that accompanied us, in which the Indian troops place a superstitious confidence. But when all was ready, we found that the enemy had decamped precipitately.

As soon as we found that the stockade before us had been abandoned, we pushed on and crossed the highest point of the first range of mountains on the 23rd, after passing through one of the strongest defiles I ever saw, which had been carefully stockaded, and covered with abattis in different places. From the summit we descried a cultivated valley, through which the River Rapté, a clear, winding stream flowed prettily. The inhabitants had all fled on our arrival. Here we found a small mud-fort near the village of Accoah, where we were obliged to halt two days to rest the cattle.

The Rapté is an auriferous stream, and we picked up some particles of gold as big as small shot. The water was very clear, and abounded in fish, somewhat resembling dace, but of an unknown genus. The first evening after our arrival, I caught a couple of dozen as large as herrings with trout-flies. They were sweet and firm, and afforded a little treat to the Mess.

The morning after entering this valley, I happened to enter the tent of my eccentric friend, L[am]b[rech]t, who had annoyed us so much on the voyage out. He was sitting up in bed, with his writing desk on his knees, hard at work; his face much flushed–eyes bloodshot–appearance altogether very wild, and two pistols lying on a camp table beside him. At the first glance, I saw that mischief was impending, but said nothing more than the usual salutations, and sat down. He continued writing for a quarter of an hour, and then addressed me, 'Doctor, I am making my will–I have left you my books and my sabre, as mementoes of our friendship. Do you see those pistols? examine them–well, you find they are loaded–one is destined for Colonel Nicol–a ball from the other will finish my own career–you are shocked–

you will remonstrate in vain, my purpose is irrevocable'.

It was necessary to temporize; so I listened quietly and pretended to enter into the story of his griefs, and even to go farther, and affect some sympathy with them. I learned that the origin of the matter was this. At the battle of Vittoria, when General Byng's Brigade was ordered to lie down behind a small hill, to secure themselves from a heavy cannonade, at the beginning of the action L[ambrech]t sillily jumped up and ran to the top, posting himself on an elevated point—thus drawing fire on himself and those in the rear. When Colonel Nicol observed this he cried out, 'come down Sir, instantly—this needless exposure is an act of madness, not a proof of courage'. These words had rankled in his mind ever since, and now, in his drunken delirium, he was preparing to take a fatal revenge for the insult.

It was of course necessary to take some decided step, but not so easy to fix on what was to be done: after a little reflection, I decided on my course. 'My dear fellow', I said, 'your hand shakes so much this morning, and your eyes are so much inflamed, that you could not hit a church at ten paces—still less a man—your head too, must ache confoundedly after that rascally wine last night—let me feel your pulse—hah—your tongue—foul—fever, by Jove—brain fever! loss of mind soon—perhaps before to-morrow morning—come, come, this will never do—call your servant—a basin instantly—your master must be bled'.

From various circumstances, including former professional services, I had acquired much influence over L[ambrech]t, and I needed it all now, for he was very refractory; but the point was at last carried. The servant brought in a wash-hand basin—I tied up his arm—opened a vein, and had it spouting, *pleno rivo*, as we say, in a minute. I was not very particular as to the number of ounces, within a dozen or so, but when the basin was nearly full my object was accomplished, and the patient fainted. The pistols, sword, razors, &c., were then secured, and himself close watched till the frenzy was over.

On the 25th of February, we moved up the valley of the Rapté; not having yet seen a human being. But on this march we met three or four natives—broad-faced, hardy-looking Tartars. They told us there had been fighting on the right, and one of the central Passes had been stormed. We pushed on as fast as the difficult route would permit, and on the 2nd of March, joined

119

Sir David and the main body of the army, encamped on a plain, at the foot of the mountain of Muckawnpore.

We were much concerned to find that we had come too late to participate in a sharp affair on the mountain, three days before, in which the Ghoorkahs had fought well, but had been beaten with great loss. The enemy had several wooden guns in the action, with iron hoops, and beat-iron balls – one of which had killed the Commander in Chief's Hurkaru [Chief Intelligence officer – editor] close to his side. The Light Company of the 87th had the principal fighting, and had behaved with great gallantry. One of our men had gone up the hill, attached to the 87th, and had done his duty so well, as to cause the commanding officer of that corps, to give him a written certificate of most excellent conduct in the action. I heard him say, when he presented this document to Colonel Nicol, 'I was the only 66th man in the field, Sir; so Sir, I thinks I must fight my best – I peppered three of them any how, Sir, to a cartainty.' It was on this hill that John Shipp, of the 87th, had his celebrated duel with a Ghoorkah Chief.

It was clear that our Commander in Chief was well pleased at our arrival, for he had only one British Regiment at Head Quarters, and the enemy had displayed courage, and a formidable force, and still held the highest and strongest part of the mountain range, where they had built some stockades.

The day after our arrival, fresh operations began. The whole of our Regiment, and a Grenadier Battalion of Seapoys, with four guns on elephants, were ordered up the hill; with directions to push on cautiously along the ridge, and establish ourselves on a commanding point. I accompanied this Brigade. The road up the mountain was only a path – extremely steep; and the Mahouts had great difficulty in forcing on their elephants, which moaned and groaned indignantly at the unwonted labour of this toilsome ascent. When our whole force was collected, we advanced boldly some way to the eastward, until within about eight hundred yards of the enemy's nearest stockade, when we halted, and entrenched ourselves for the night. Pickets were then placed in advance, and on the flanks of our position, in which eight guns were mounted.

My gallant Hookabadar, Bastee Rhamm, a fine, tall soldier-looking man, who was a discharged Grenadier Seapoy, stuck close to my side in going up the hill; wearing his Tulwar, or short sword, and having a couple of my Hookah snakes, folded circularly, on his back, after the fashion of a shield. We had a cold dinner, and afterwards, every officer produced his private stock of brandy, and his cheroot, or cigar. But the incomparable Bastee Rhamm, who gloried in triumphing over all difficulties in the discharge of his vocation, had by some means, carried the Hookah to the top of the mountain; and in a trice, the fragrant tube was prepared, the charcoal balls ignited – the silver mouth-piece, wreathed with folds of snow-white muslin, was put in my hand, with the usual graceful salaam – the *nicotiana* exhaled its aromatic breath – the cool water bubbled – and I enjoyed as perfect a chillum on this wild mountain, as at the Mess Room in Dinapore.

The evening was clear, and we could see the Ghoorkah Chieftains reconnoitring us, or walking about under huge umbrellas, borne by their attendants; although the declination of the sun at that time rendered it quite unnecessary. As night fell, our fellows lined the intrenchment around our guns, with fixed bayonets, and the whole force remained under arms until daylight.

And here, a slight allusion to the beautiful condition and efficiency of the 66th regiment on that occasion, and to its uniform good conduct, may not be unsuitable nor ungraceful, as a small tribute for eight and twenty happy years passed in it. From the time of entering the enemy's country, not even one solitary act of misbehaviour had occurred in the corps – there was absolutely nothing to find fault with – all pressed on with alacrity; obeying all orders, and performing all duties with equal cheerfulness. Thus it has ever been the case with the British Army, generally, in the face of danger; and it is a national trait to be proud of, that the same appalling circumstances on flood or field, that paralyse feebler natures, only serve 'to screw their courage to the sticking place', figuratively and literally.

But, to resume my slight panegyric – when the order came to mount the hill of Muckawnpore, and take the honourable position of leading regiment in the advance, prepared to storm the enemy's stockades in succession – I never saw soldiers in such magnificent fighting order before or since. Even the eight sick in the hospital tent, sharing the fine feeling of their comrades, and under the influence of martial excitement which extinguished illness – left it in a body, unknown to the surgeon, and joined the regiment on the hill – the only irregularity during the campaign. The surgeon was angry, and complained of it to the Commanding Officer, but Colonel Nicol only laughed at him.

It was then, sitting in the redoubt on the topmost point of the mountain of Muckawnpore, surrounded by nine hundred of these noble fellows with fixed bayonets, that I moralized over my Hookah, whilst my brother-officers moved about in animated conversation respecting the scene of blood which the morning might witness.

After two or three chillums amidst such superb associations, I wrapped myself up in my cloak, lay down upon the turf and fell asleep.

Whilst I was comfortably enjoying a sound nap–dreaming, most probably, of amputated arms and legs, or spouting arteries; and when waking visions of glory in the fore-ground, and a perspective of prize money at Khatmandoo, flitted before the fancies of my brother-officers in the trenches, an event occurred that dissipated all our speculations. The Ghoorkah Rajah, frightened at our advance, accepted the terms proposed to him, and signed the treaty; and a Vakeel, bearing the ratified instrument, came in during the night under a flag of truce, and went down to the camp. In passing through our post his attendants repeated in Hindoostanee, the one important word, 'Peace!' which our native servants soon brought to our ears. Immediately all was botheration and dismay–intelligence came up from camp that the war was at an end; and in the morning we received orders to abandon our strong hill and join the Army on the plain.

7

Life in India · Idleness and its consequences · Suttee · Cholera · Ordered to
St. Helena · Mauritius

Thus, then were dissipated into thin air all our anticipations
of a glorious campaign, the capture of the enemy's capital;
and the division amongst the Army of some crores of Rupees.
When the news became generally known, I never witnessed such
a change, nor mortification and disappointment more vividly
painted in human countenances than on the hardy visages of
our men.

My own hopes of prize-money had been faint from the beginning; as I could not perceive any satisfactory data to reason on in
the calculation of much treasure or valuable property to be met
with. The stockades only contained wooden guns, and if there
was any treasure at Khatmandoo they would probably carry it
off into the mountains, and hide it on our approach. From these
considerations, when we were talking over the subject one day at
the Mess, and most of the officers appeared very sanguine in their
expectations—I offered to sell my share of prize-money for a small
sum—fifty rupees—I think. A Field-Officer took me at my word,
and sent me the money the same evening; and thus a very insignificant personage was the only Officer in the Army that
pocketted any prize-money, though he was jeered at the time as
if he had sold his birthright.

On the 8th of March, we began to retrace our steps; and on
the first day's march through the central Pass, we saw the huge
carcasses of five elephants that had been poisoned on the advance.
The Ghoorkahs had infused a plant resembling the Belladonna in
a fine spring at the top of the Pass; and the poor animals, thirsty
and fatigued after the steep ascent, had drunk freely. Here, their
characteristic sagacity was at fault; but these noble creatures
could not suspect such villainy in the lords of the creation. When
the poison began to take effect, their agonies and groans were
frightful; but danger being apprehended from the madness that
pain might cause, it became necessary to destroy them, and they
were shot.

We halted at Bettiah, the residence of a Rajah, where we found a Christian Mission from Goa, established nearly fifty years. The Priest, whose name was Julius Cæsar, was a fine, apostolic-looking man, a Portuguese, apparently learned, and speaking several languages with facility. I found him in the chapel, catechising the native children, who were numerous. He said his congregation consisted of three hundred individuals.

We reached Dinapore on the 28th of March. Here the regiment remained three months. The weather was dreadfully hot; and although we reduced the temperature full twenty degrees, by artificial evaporation from the fragrant grass mats with which our dwellings were surrounded, we could never bring Fahrenheit's Thermometer lower than eighty-eight or ninety degrees. Men were constantly employed in sprinkling water, from the skinful they carried, on the mats; and the first gush of cooled air passing through them into the doors and windows, and carrying with it the freshness and sweet odour of the grass, was very delightful. But the Cuscuss required constant wetting, and the Bheesties were apt to be negligent, and then the temperature would become insupportable. There was no moving out of the house, except for an hour in the morning and evening, and all day within, existence was little better than a succession of gasps and gapes.

Our professional duties were performed very early in the morning, and we were invariably at the hospital by sunrise, and there remained busy enough all the cool time, whilst the other officers were taking their invigorating ride. For, now that the excitement and tension of the last short campaign had been followed by languor and relaxation, mental and corporeal, the sick list swelled out marvellously. Thus, our only chance of getting a morning ride occasionally, was for the Assistant or Surgeon to do the other's duty: and this, at a sickly time, is heavy work—a matter which I very humbly hope the Right Honourable the Secretary at War, for the time being, will take into consideration, previous to the next boon in the Medical Department.

Perhaps one's breakfast is the only meal *eaten* in India—all the rest are sad piddling work, and merely a form. When I returned from my professional duty, there was—*Primo*—my shave—and I take some credit for having virtuously resisted all temptations here to soapy sloth—for I was always my own barber. *Secundo*, my refreshing shower-bath. *Tertio*, a breakfast of the first order of merit; and *Quarto*, my Hookah. For, ever watchful at his post, behind my arm-chair, there stood Bhastee Rhamm, waiting for the close of the meal, to hand 'Doctor Saahib' the incomparable Chillum; and to retire, with the usual low salaam, to a reverential distance, until the nod of approbation from his master should make him happy. Then were the feet thrown carelessly upon the table–the odoriferous smoke was slowly inhaled, and the ample bowl of Mandarin Tea, its morning accompaniment, sipped voluptuously.

After an hour spent thus, the rest of the day, it must be confessed, was heavy in hand. There was no reading attentively without headache–writing involved perspiration to a dissolving extent. Playing backgammon–in addition to the necessity of dry linen every hit or two–burst the tympanum. Playing chess burst the brain. Playing billiards was a labour of Hercules. Thus, were there great difficulties in finding any rational mode of passing the day; and, for want of a better, I thought I might as well fall in love.

There was an English family at Dinapore, with whom I became acquainted. The gentleman commanded a distinguished regiment of Bengal Native Infantry,[32] that had behaved most gallantly in one of the early attacks on Bhurtpore, under Lord Lake–the lady was one of the most pleasing and accomplished women I ever knew. There were two young ladies–one her sister, the other his. The latter, whose name was S—, was the fair object of my affection.

On an impartial retrospect, and after the passion of early years has subsided, and cool judgment has given its verdict respecting the object of it, I am still of the same opinion I was then, that S— Macleod was a very loveable and delightful girl. It is certain that I soon became very fond of her.

My friend, Major M[acleod], was a cultivated and gentlemanly as well as most gallant soldier. He had a very select collection of books, and maintained a handsome establishment. Having been of some professional assistance to one of the family, I gradually became intimate, and at last spent half my time in his house.

Our regiment gave two or three balls on a grand scale at Dinapore, and on the last occasion we covered a large space of green square opposite the Mess-House with marquee-tents, and laid out a very handsome supper-table there, with a long and tasteful avenue, brilliantly lighted, connecting it with the ball-room. When the ball was over, which was about sunrise, I escorted my fair friend's palanquin home, like a trusty Paladin, after passing an enchanting evening; for I can designate it by no fitter term.

The day after our party was the hottest I ever felt, and quite calm; so that we derived little benefit from our fragrant Cuscuss envelopes, which hung uselessly at our doors and windows, without a breath of air to rob them of their moisture. After passing a couple of hours at the Macleods, I went to the Mess to dinner, which was, as usual, a very good one, but no dish was touched, except the Mullagatawny Soup, of which one or two partook. I came home early and went to bed; but the house was too hot for any repose, even after the dancing of the night before. The evening was still as calm as the day had been: thinking, therefore, that my only chance of a nap was in the open air, I made my servants carry out my couch into the square in front of the door, and wrap me round carefully with the mosquito curtains. In this position I soon fell fast asleep.

Unfortunately, this hot night, in which I had chosen to sleep, *al fresco*, and to dream all manner of delightful things, was the breaking up of the monsoon, which is always terminated by a terrific storm. The elements continued to roar away without intermission for four or five hours; and the resplendent lightning, as it illuminated the big drops of rain with the brightest prismatic colours, appeared as playful as if it was the most harmless thing in nature.

The change in the aspect of the vegetable world next morning was most striking—the four months' dust had been washed off the face of the earth—the grass had already begun to shew its tender green—the air was cool, clear and balmy, and the frame felt refreshed as the lungs gulped in the invigorating fluid; and the spirits, long depressed by heat, dust and other discomforts, recovered their elasticity and cheerfulness.

I breakfasted with the Macleods, but S— did not make her appearance. There appeared a *gêné* and singular air about the whole *menage*—especially in the deportment of the host and his wife, much at variance with every thing I had before witnessed in that happy and united family. After breakfast Macleod requested me to walk into the library, and thus addressed me—'My dear fellow, I perceive there has been a sad mistake. We all esteem you highly, and wish for the continuance of your friendship; but,

but–S— has been for some months engaged to be married to a gentleman in Calcutta.'

Crabbe's graphic pen has described the different appearance of external nature under opposite moods of mind, in the case of a lover visiting his mistress, and returning from the interview. I cannot approach within a thousand leagues of his inimitable touches, but I can tell in my own homely way, how miserable I felt that day. As I returned, the air, so deliciously pure in the morning, felt muggy and unrespirable–the heat was intolerable– the mosquitoes atrociously sanguinary and numerous–nothing was as it ought, and every thing as it ought not to be. The palanquin bearers jerked and shook me, as if on purpose. At my evening visit to the hospital, several patients were worse, that should have been better, and had evidently retrograded inten- tionally, as if to spite me. At dinner the punkahs did not move properly–the mullagatawny was cold, and the wine hot; O— was more prosy than usual in his stories, and told one stupid yarn about a refractory Jack-Donkey, that we had all heard a dozen times before. Even Bhastee Rhamm, the *nonpareil* of Hookabadars, failed to please. At last I went to bed, thoroughly disgusted–but even there misfortune continued its persecutions; for two or three vagrant mosquitoes had slipped in when the servant was closing the gauze around me, and it was slap–slap–slap–buzz, buzz, buzz, all night.

In June 1816, the regiment received orders to prepare for a move to Cawnpore, and in the beginning of July we embarked on the Ganges, now full to the brim.

If any person wishes to luxuriate amongst roses, let him repair to Ghazepore, where the whole country, for some hundred or two of square miles, is thickly covered with them. Rose water and the exquisite Attar of roses are, consequently, cheaper here than in any other part of India; though the latter, when genuine, must always be a most expensive article, from the enormous con- sumption of roses in its preparation. It takes a prodigious quantity of the petals to make an ounce of Attar; and to produce a quart bottle, would require, I suppose, a heap about as big as St. Paul's.

We reached the far-famed Benares on the 8th of July, and anchored at the opposite side of the river. This is a large and very populous city, containing, it is said, some half a million of inhabi- tants. The streets are extremely narrow–in fact, nothing more than lanes, about six feet broad, generally. The Brahminee bulls appeared to lead the happiest lives of any creature in this holy city; roaming through the streets as they pleased,—gentle, and sleek, and fat—the domestic gods of the Hindoos. We observed them poking their noses into every confectioner's shop they passed, and always getting a handful of sweets, which they licked up nicely. We saw three disgusting naked Fakirs perambulating the town, attended by a train of devotees and followers—many of whom were women—these fellows would be famous subjects for the Tread-mill.

One of these extraordinary ascetics resided in a hut not far from the place where our Fleet *lagowed*. I went to visit him, and found him a miserable object, scarcely human in appearance, lying on a bed of sharp spikes, with one hand closed, which he had vowed ten or twelve years before, *never* to open. Consequently the nails had pierced through the hand, and stuck out of the back of it, eight or nine inches long; curved, crooked, and sharp, and altogether the most frightful talons imaginable. When I entered the hut I questioned him as to the nature of the crime that had required such terrible expiation—but he made no answer, and when I repeated the question, he scowled forbiddingly and continued silent. I left him gazing listlessly on the Ganges, of which his bed of torture commanded a good view.

As on my former voyage up the Ganges, whenever we mounted the stream slowly, I explored the marshes and jungles with my gun, and had good sport amongst the snipe, partridges, and water fowl—the latter were very abundant.

There is one sad drawback on the pleasure of voyaging up this noble stream—there is one disgusting spectacle which is constantly meeting the eye—human corpses, made buoyant by decomposition, floating down the river; with the odious vultures tearing and disembowelling them as they slowly pass your boat! I know nothing more painful than this sad and humiliating sight. The goddess Ganesa, under the awful authority of the true Deity, outraged by Hindoo crime, casts upon her shores the bodies superstitiously committed to her keeping, charged with pestilence and death. This abominable custom ought and must be forbidden; and the glorious Ganges must no longer be desecrated by millions of dead bodies, and cease to be the great sewer of the accumulated putridity of Bengal.

A certain officer accompanied the Regiment on this voyage, whose education had been not a little neglected; and who was a constant source of amusement from the verbal blunders and malapropisms he sported on all occasions. When he heard a new word, especially a long one, he was sure to repeat it, mutilated of some of its fair proportions. During one severe thunder-storm, I happened to observe that the lightning was particularly vivid—next day this was *flivid*—the electric bolt became a *boulder*, the common military word, defaulter, was murdered, in common with vocables of greater sound, and turned into *defunct*. 'Pray Colonel', enquired Lady Lowe, at St. Helena, 'how do you manage to have so nice a garden at Francis Plain? Do you employ any of the Chinese labourers?' 'No', was the answer, 'we employ nobody but our defuncts.' 'Indeed, Colonel—well, that *is* extraordinary. But, I believe it is very judicious, as *they* ought to know something of the soil.'

This gentleman often asked me to his Budgerow during the voyage. There were a couple of unmarried sisters on board, near relations of the family; and when we anchored at some pleasant spot on the bank, it was customary for the Colonel, the young ladies and myself, to explore the neighbourhood in the cool of the evening.

One calm and clear evening, when the fleet had *lagowed* for the night at a rich Mango tope, with smooth velvet turf underfoot, the sisters, the Colonel and myself, strolled along the beautiful bank—the elder on his arm and the younger on mine. The pairs, however, soon separated, and my companion and I sauntered along, following a path through the trees, until sunset: we then discovered that we were two miles from the boats, and the short twilight of the East soon began to darken apace. Hastening home, we left the circuitous path we had come by and tried a near-cut through a field, but here an unforeseen obstacle interposed. A rivulet, which, higher up we had crossed by a rustic bridge of a log thrown over it, had become wider and deeper as it approached the Ganges, and now required a good running leap. In this dilemma I proposed to go round by the bridge, but my young friend would not hear of it—'You have no idea how active I am—jump first and I'll bet you a pair of gloves I'll follow.' Then, after another remonstrance, and the expression of a hope, as delicately as such an idea could be embodied in words, that her under-garments were sufficiently capacious–I jumped over. Angela then took a running leap–following the leader; but, alas! the petticoats of those days were very circumscribed–the envious muslin clung around, and hampered the active limbs of the unfortunate young lady who, arrested in mid career, uttered a piercing shriek and plumped into the middle of the torrent.

At first I could not help a slight laugh, but I soon perceived it was no laughing matter, as the stream was six or seven feet deep and running with great rapidity, and I knew not well what to do. Throwing myself in, however gallant and chivalrous, would be useless, as I should also be borne away by the strong current. So, telling Angela there was no danger, I ran down the bank, parallel with the floating and screaming Beauty, and waiting for a favourable opportunity to make a snatch. After one or two failures I caught her bonnet, but the riband under the chin gave way, and down the torrent she went, with her loosened hair streaming behind her on the water like a mermaid's. At last, when she had been carried down a hundred yards, I succeeded in seizing a handful of her humid tresses, and brought her safe to land.

Poor lady, she was sadly frightened; and as she clung to me more affectionately than was quite comfortable, considering the state of her clothes, I heard such honied expressions, as 'guardian angel', 'preserver of my life', 'debt of everlasting gratitude', uttered, *sotto voce*; which, however, I was not bound to hear. She deferred the hysterics until we reached the boat, but then we had them in abundance, whilst when she recovered I was such a barbarian as to retire to my Budgerow and enjoy an unrestrained laugh in the odorous society of my Hookah.

Allahabad, a fortified town, at the junction of the Jumna and the Ganges, is a very sacred place with the Hindoos, as most points of confluence of the river tributaries are. When we passed, we saw some thousands of the natives, busy in their penitentiary and sacrificial ablutions; which the Brahmins teach, not only atone for past sin, but purchase uninterrupted ages of happiness.

Suttees, or the voluntary immolation of widows by fire, together with the corpses of their husbands, were not of uncommon occurrence at this time in India. I witnessed one during the voyage on the opposite side of the river, and not far from Allahabad.

This cruel scene took place close to the water's edge, near a huge Banyan tree, whose branches, spreading far and wide, were supported by the vigorous shoots they had sent down into the earth–now grown into strong pillars–like decrepit parents by the piety of their children. It was about ten o'clock at night, and, I suppose, two hundred people were present. The victim was very young–not more than seventeen or eighteen–and though looking a little wild, yet she distributed the flowers and sweetmeats to her friends and relations, with a certain degree of composure; and then mounted the pyre with a firm step, kissed her husband's lips and lay down beside him. Before this time several fruitless attempts had been made by two of my brother-officers and myself to dissuade her from this terrible self-sacrifice–No, no–if she lived she would be an outcast from society–forced to perform the lowest offices–lose her high caste (she was a Brahmin) and be condemned and despised henceforward by all her acquaintances, friends and relatives.

As soon as this unfortunate woman had placed herself beside her husband, a kind of cage made of bamboos was put over them, smeared with ghee, or buffalo-butter, to make it more combustible, and a horrible din of tom toms, gongs and human voices was set up; evidently for the purpose of stifling the poor creature's cries. A quantity of dry wood, leaves, etc., surrounded the funeral pile, and was now set fire to, and blazed up fiercely at once, so as, in all probability to save farther suffering, and suffocate the victim in a few seconds. In a short time the whole was one glowing flame, which, when swayed to one side by the wind, gave the spectators a glimpse of the two blackened objects in the centre. The most abominable apathy pervaded the crowd–scarcely a muscle in any face moved; and when the middle of the bodies was consumed, the woman's own relations pushed the bones of the two skulls and the legs into the fiercest part of the fire with long bamboo poles. It was altogether a dreadful sight–an infernal sacrifice, at the perpetration of which demons might rejoice!

On the 7th of August, we came in sight of Cawnpore, a picturesque military Cantonment, extending five miles along a fine high bank of the Ganges. No barracks being vacant for our reception, we were most unwisely left in our boats, at the opposite side of the river, in a low, marshy neighbourhood, about three weeks. The Ganges having some time before attained its highest elevation, the waters were now subsiding rapidly, and large tracts were exposed to a powerful sun, that were covered with animal and vegetable putrescence. This was represented at the time, and encamping the regiment on a dry plain near the Cantonment was recommended, but in vain. The consequence was—it may be fairly averred—a fatal Remittent Fever broke out, which in four months carried off five officers and 150 men.

During this time, the duties of the medical officers were no sinecure. Each of us had a large hospital, and there was one besides for sick women; which, I may observe in passing, was altogether supported by the munificence of our worthy Commanding Officer, Colonel Nicol. We generally had upwards of two hundred cases of fever daily, and one week, close on three hundred. As the weather became cooler in October, the violence of the disease subsided a little, but it did not cease altogether till January; and then the soldiers were merely the shadows of what they had been: every man, except about half a dozen, having had an attack of fever, and some, two or three times over. It was very melancholy and painful, to see the state to which those noble fellows were reduced by mismanagement, who had so recently mustered nine hundred strong, and in the most glowing vigour of health, on the heights of Muckawnpore.

In these desultory pages it would be out of character to enter into professional details. I shall confine myself to the observation, that as we found in Bengal a strong prejudice running against Dr. Sangrado[33] and his system of depletion, we at first hesitated as to general bleeding to any extent, in our fever cases. Finding, however, that the men died fast, when treated on the authorized system, we abandoned it—prescribed for our patients as we would in Europe, and with striking benefit for the change. Formerly we had lost some twenty-five per cent—now five or six was the amount.

Most of our officers occupied comfortable Bungalows, with gardens, at Cawnpore—I lived in a good house, with a large garden, and kept a gardener and a couple of oxen. The chief business of the latter was to eat, and chew the cud, and, as an amusement, to put their shoulders to the wheel for half an hour a-day, to raise water for irrigating the garden. On my first arrival I found several illegal occupiers of my premises—namely, a large colony of musk-rats, who had built a subterranean city in one of my best beds. These little wretches used to come out of their burrows at night, to make predatory incursions into the house, eating and carrying off what they could, and defiling by their odious and indelible taint, every thing they touched. Incredible as it may appear, it is a fact, that this strong odour is communicated to wine or brandy in sealed bottles, by these creatures merely passing over them—I had a couple of dozen of brandy spoiled thus at Cawnpore: the *modus operandi* I never could make out.

My patience being at last worn out by multiplied nusiances committed by these unsavoury animals—of which the corrupting my Cognac was the climax—I determined to exterminate the whole race. Accordingly I sent to the barracks, and collected all the curs that could be found in the precincts—amounting to three or four dozen. After five or six preliminary fights amongst this heterogeneous pack, and a due administration of the whip, to put them in some decent order, we proceeded to the hunt. First—two Bheesties, or water-carriers, with their pig-skins full of water, were ordered to beat the coverts. Inserting the muzzle of a pipe, attached to the fore-foot of the pig's hide, in one of the central holes of the principal burrow, the Bheestie played away vigorously until he had emptied his skin, when he was relieved by the other; and as the garden well was near, and the bullocks hard at work, water was abundant, and the stream ran uninterruptedly into the subterranean caves of the rats. The tenacious little animals stood the inundation with great courage, which to them must have been nearly as formidable as the Thames bursting into the Tunnel amongst Mr. Brunel's workmen. At last, when the water spread far and wide, and there was no possibility of remaining any longer, they crept out of their holes half drowned, and were all destroyed by the dogs.

There were two or three fine Peepuhl Trees in the garden, which were objects of my special admiration. When I awoke one morning, soon after taking possession, I heard the most horrid noise and screaming close to my window; and on questioning the Sirdar Bearer, who always slept at the threshold, he said it was only the parrots, and he would soon drive them away. Next morning it was repeated; when I started up and saw about a thousand paroquets—active rascals, with red beaks, rich green plumage, and long tails—demolishing the buds and blossoms, and eating and screaming with all their might. The trees were actually loaded with them, and the branches bent down almost to the ground. Notwithstanding my bearer's repugnance to destroy animal life, I made him bring my gun, and sent the contents of two barrels amongst the marauders, which killed fifty or sixty of them. I know not whether this noisy tribe have ever been deemed of any value, except in the oratorical department. Feeling several of those I shot plump and fat, I directed them to be cooked for breakfast, and my Curry turned out a very good dish.

I presume that every body has heard of the feats of Indian Jugglers, and many persons have seen a celebrated magician in London, named Raamaoh Saame, whose beautiful performance with the brass balls before the glass-curtain of the Coburgh Theatre was much admired. When our detachment was quartered at Poonamalee on our first arrival from England, a far-famed Madras Juggler paid us a visit to astonish the Griffins, as they called us Johnny Newcomes, and put a few rupees into the girdle of his long robe. This clever fellow began by swallowing a sword, the point of which I felt in his stomach—ate fire—turned cards into chickens, and chickens into full-grown cocks; and sent eight balls on their travels round his body—moving simultaneously and harmoniously in their different orbits—infallible as the planets—with many other astonishing things.

As the soldiers were staring at him, he caught the eye of one man, in whose countenance there was an air of peculiar surprise. He addressed him immediately in English—'I make you lay one egg here', putting his hand on the soldier's forehead. The man stared and blushed, but at length exclaimed with a shake of the head, 'I'se d— if you can, though.' The officers being desirous to find out how this trick was done, both Juggler and Soldier were stripped naked, and brought into an empty room in which there was full light from a strong sun. The magician then made the man sit down on the floor in the middle of the room; and an ingenuous Yorkshire lad he was, who looked up at the yellow Juggler with a good-natured grin and strong expression of incredulity. The performer than proceeded to fix his eye, and to walk round him slowly and deliberately seven times, repeating some unintelligible gibberish. He then quickened his pace for seven more gyrations—and still increased it for seven additional circles, fascinating his eye, gesticulating and uttering strange sounds as before. At the end of the third series he slapped the man on the forehead with the open palm—when, lo! out started a fine fresh egg! The soldier was so astonished that he ran out of the room, naked as he was, swearing that the Juggler was the devil.

Now, although five of us watched the whole proceeding with minute attention in a full light; and were, besides, sharpened in our observation by the idea of some trickery, none could discover where or how the egg was concealed. That it was genuine there could be no doubt—for we boiled it, and I ate some of it myself, but the frightened fellow who laid it would not taste it.

One morning at Cawnpore, a native asked permission to speak to Saahib. He was admitted, and after a profusion of the most reverential salaams, he told me that from certain indications he was sure there were snakes in Saahib's garden, which he would engage to catch for half a rupee a-piece, being a professed snake-charmer. I closed with his offer immediately, and he said he would come the next morning.

Punctual to his appointment he made his appearance, armed with a long pipe on which he began to play violently, using various grotesque gesticulations, all over the garden. After keeping up this solo for a quarter of an hour, he stopped suddenly before a low bush near an old tree; played two or three bars, *fortissimo*, and then, plunging his hand into the bush, pulled out a large Cobra de Capello, or hooded snake, and put it into a basket slung to his neck. He proceeded in this way for some time, exploring different parts of the garden; and ended by catching two more snakes. Then, after a little more music, the charmer said there were no more in the garden, and claimed the stipulated reward. This, I promised to pay him immediately, if he permitted me to destroy the reptiles, which I knew very well he would not allow. I then examined them and, after some trouble, ascertained that two teeth had been pulled from the jaws of each—no doubt the poison fangs—and the animals, in all probability, had been placed in the very spot where they were found the same morning, by collusion of some of the servants. The magician and his basket were then very unceremoniously expelled—the servants abusing him in the choicest Hindoostanee Billingsgate, for attempting to impose on wise Saahib, who was more learned and sagacious than Suleyman—although some of those very rascals had no doubt entered into the conspiracy against Saahib's sagacity.

I met Cobras on several occasions when out shooting, and twice escaped being bit narrowly enough. One day, when intent on some partridges, I stepped over a Palma Christi plant, and placed my foot almost on the head of a large Cobra just come out of his hole. This trespass he naturally enough resented by erecting his hood, coiling himself up, looking fierce, and preparing for a spring. But, poor fellow, notwithstanding the protection of his own tribe as the symbol of my profession, and the *aegis* the medicinal plant that overshaded his domicile afforded, I was obliged, in self-defence, to shoot him. He was large of his kind—being seven feet long.

The snake-charmers in India, who make these creatures dance to music, effect their object, I believe, in a way, and from motives on the part of the snake, that are imperfectly understood. Notwithstanding popular belief, as old as the time of Alexander the Great, and deemed worthy of notice amongst the wonders of India by Arrian the Historian, I suspect that snakes have no 'music in their soul', and are not to be charmed—notwithstanding appearances to the contrary—by 'concord of sweet sounds.' On a careful analysis, I fear the poetry of the matter is reducible to a very unromantic and simple element. The snake, previously deprived of its death-fangs, is kept coiled up in a basket with two or three others, equally harmless; and when one is wanted for an exhibition, the Juggler seizes him by the neck, hauls him out of the basket and throws him rudely on the ground. This raises the reptile's choler—which I fancy, is not a difficult matter—it hisses, bristles out its hood and erects its head. The charmer, playing away on his noisy pipe, confronts the enraged creature, as if about to tread on it; but adroitly moves about beyond the reach of its spring. Thus fixing and fascinating the animal's eye, he keeps describing a half-circle—perpetually in motion, menacing the snake, and obliging it to move as he moves—in momentary expectation that he will approach within its reach, and prepared to dart on him, if he does—which never happens. This quick oscillation of the creature in pure anger and self-defence—perhaps in disgust at the barbarous music—is attributed by the spectators to its fondness for the very sounds it cordially hates.

In the beginning of January 1817, we received the unexpected and unwelcome intelligence that our regiment was soon to proceed to Calcutta and embark for St. Helena, where Napoleon was detained a prisoner of war by the English Government. As at this time arrangements were making for a grand campaign against the Phindarrie hordes, and stirring times were approaching, we were not at all pleased with the prospect of leaving the country.

Besides, the idea of changing our luxurious Indian living for the mackarel and yams of that barren Islet was by no means agreeable to say nothing of the state of constraint and vigilance to which we should be subject; but the Horse Guards had said the word and there was no remedy.

Our relations of mutual friendship had not been broken off by the vanishing of any prospect of nearer connexion; and my friend Macleod and myself had corresponded regularly since the regiment left Dinapore. He now resided in Allahabad, and was Commandant of that Fortress. As soon as he learned that we were coming down the river, he sent me a warm invitation to stay a week or ten days with him in passing, which I accepted, and started on a fortnight's leave to Allahabad.

I found this amiable family well; and was not a little surprised to meet S— still unmarried. She was in distress; for some unfavourable disclosures had been made respecting the character of her lover, and his honour was suspected relative to certain gambling transactions, in which he had been engaged at Calcutta. Besides all this, he had been dangerously ill; and was now cruising about in a pilot schooner off the Sunderbunds, by medical advice. I was received with the most affectionate cordiality by every member of the family.

I spent a fortnight at Allahabad—a golden time. The whole family, from some over-estimate they had formed of certain professional services I had done one of them, considered themselves under obligations, when in truth, I was the obliged party. They therefore, one and all, exerted themselves to crowd into this final visit, before we should part for a long separation, every *agrément* and pleasure possible—morning and evening drives on beautiful roads—dinners, dances, music, Waverley Novels—then in full blow, and brought from Calcutta by *dawk*, or post. In short, whatever of agreeableness and enjoyment the kindest solicitude of refined minds could suggest, and ample means afford, were concentrated in that exquisite visit.

I told them of the Suttee I had witnessed in the neighbourhood, and learned that three more of these horrid sacrifices had occurred near the town lately. In fact, human life seemed of small value there; for instances of voluntary drowning, as an atonement for sin, were common enough—particularly at the precise point of junction of the rivers, which was eminently sacred. Old bed-ridden people were constantly brought to the shore of the Ganges, their mouths were stuffed with the river-mud, and there they were left to perish. At one of the Suttees the ladies had fruitlessly endeavoured to prevent the widow from submitting to the dreadful decree of selfish and sanguinary Brahmins, of whose income these sacrifices used to form a large part.

In the course of my intercourse with the Major, I saw and learned a good deal of the character of the Indian Seapoy, but chiefly of the native soldier of Bengal. It is altogether, a fine one. The Bengal Seapoy is distinguished for temperance, docility, fidelity to his officers, and a large share of courage. The corps which my friend commanded had fought most bravely at the storm of Bhurtpore, and vied with the King's regiments in their desperate attempts to overcome insurmountable obstacles on that fatal occasion. He and two of his grenadiers had succeeded, after a murderous struggle, in reaching nearly the top of the Breach, when one of the brave fellows was shot, and the Major was knocked down by a stone dropped on his head, and rolled to the bottom. There he lay insensible, and must have been soon despatched, but for the other grenadier, who watched over him, and bore him out of the ditch in his arms—receiving a severe wound from a matchlock ball, as he carried him off. This noble fellow was, most deservedly, made a Havildar on his recovery; and, following up this good conduct, had been recently promoted to the rank of Jemimdar—equivalent to our Lieutenant. He was pointed out to me when I was at Allahabad, and I never saw a finer looking man. My gallant friend assured me that he felt as certain of the attachment and devotion of his regiment as of his own family.

In corps like his, whose recruiting had been carefully conducted, and into which low-caste Hindoos and Musselmans were refused admittance, there exists a high sense of honour, or *esprit de corps*. Nor do the high-caste Moslems and Hindoos quarrel in the same regiments; for it is a point of importance to mix them: but they conduct themselves much the same as Protestants and Catholics in the British Army. They have separate messes, and respect each other's particular customs; and thus they generally go on harmoniously together under the salutary restraint of strict discipline; confiding implicitly in their officers and in the Company's Government.

The day before my departure, my friend drove me to see an enormous Banyan tree in the neighbourhood, that covered between two and three acres of ground. The age nobody could tell; but it was supposed to be a thousand years old.

A great change had taken place in the river since we last sailed on it–the water had fallen about thirty feet; and large tracts over which we had passed were now covered with luxuriant crops of rice and other grain. The high banks along which we coasted when the wind was contrary, being composed of loose alluvial materials, used to come tumbling about our ears rather alarmingly–often threatening to swamp our boat.

At Benares, I paid a visit to the Fakir of the spiky hand. There he was, exactly as before–in the same attitude–wrapped in pride, sulky and silent, and gazing on the sun and the river. I spoke to him in his own language, but he would not condescend to answer.

At Dinapore, on this voyage, the career of my eccentric friend, L—t, was closed. Being apprehensive of meeting his creditors at Calcutta, he desired his servant, the evening of our arrival, to put a bottle of brandy on the table and leave the cabin of the boat. He then commenced drinking and smoking, and singing German songs; whilst all the other Officers were at a Ball given by the 24th Regiment. Having finished his brandy he drew his sword, attacked the boatmen and his native servants, then, having cleared the boat, he waved his weapon several times over his head, spouted something to the Moon, that was shining at the time, and jumped into the Ganges. The river ran deep and rapid, and his body was never found.

Head Quarters of the Regiment, with three hundred men, embarked at Calcutta on the 2nd April 1817, in the ship *Dorah*, for St. Helena. Colonel Nicol, our excellent Commanding Officer, made every thing as agreeable as possible during the voyage; which was sufficiently pleasant and diversified by several little incidents–one of which was of a startling nature. Whilst at breakfast on the 20th April, we had a sudden alarm of fire–a thick smoke was seen ascending near the forecastle, and that awful word rang through the ship. The Captain made a spring over the table clearing everything like a hunter, without touching a tea cup and ran forward, whilst the Colonel in less than a minute had two lines of soldiers, with fire-buckets, formed from the gangways. There was no confusion: and an abundant supply of water being secured, the fire was extinguished in five minutes.

We had the Regimental Band on board, which played every fine evening, and then a little dance on the quarter-deck would follow. This is a most salutary amusement on board ship, where exercise is so much needed; and here, at least, Petrarch's anathema can scarcely hold–'*Choroea circulus cujus centrum Diabolus.*' On board the good ship *Dorah*, we had a much more attractive centre figure–the blooming goddess Hygeia.

Having run short of water from the leaking of our water-casks, we put into the Isle of France for a supply. Here we found Port Louis, the capital, slowly recovering from a dreadful fire that had half destroyed it the year before. Sir Robert Farquhar, the Governor, was exerting himself to promote the rebuilding of the place; but every thing about the town shewed the severity of the calamity, and the great distress that had been the result.

The appearance of this Island on approaching the shore is very pleasing–the mountains in the centre rise boldly, and are crowned by fantastic and picturesque pinnacles; whilst the extent of verdure and wood surrounding the neat looking villas is agreeable to the eye and gives promise of comfortable shade.

They told us that when the Mauritius came into our hands in 1811, the state of society was deplorable; nothing was thought of but smuggling and privateering–agricultural pursuits were quite neglected–morality was at a low ebb amongst the Colonists–marriage was considered a silly restraint universally–divorces to be had for a song, and the atheistical catechisms of the French worst æra still in the few schools on the Island. The most ultra Jacobin principles prevailed, and with these anti-social tenets was found the usual accompaniment–a cordial hatred of Great Britain. A great improvement in all these things was represented to have taken place.

Two or three days after our arrival, a party was formed to visit the Tomb of Paul and Virginia. I acknowledge that I was then simple enough to believe in the actual existence of this charming couple; and it was, therefore, with pain I learned that the story was all fiction.* We drove to the farm where a small obelisk had been erected by the proprietor as a good speculation, and were received with great politeness and civility–paying for the same.

* The novel *Paul et Virginie* by Bernadin St. Pierre (1737–1814). Published 1787. A best seller in its day. (Editor.)

The race of Slaves here were large and muscular, and some amongst them fine specimens of Herculean proportions. They were chiefly from Madagascar. Many of them are most active in the water, and admirable divers. One morning in going ashore, we found a party of Blacks employed by the Harbour-Master in weighing a large anchor, from which some ship had recently parted in a gale; and as we approached, one enormous negro, with a rope in his hand, dived with a spring from the edge of the Harbour-Master's boat: I timed his performance. A minute passed and all was quiet—another—still he did not appear, and we began to fear he was drowned, and begged the rope might be pulled and the poor fellow hauled up. But the officer only laughed at us, and in twenty seconds more up came Mr. Blacky puffing and blowing like a Grampus.

Having completed our watering, we left the Isle of France with a fair breeze, coasted the Isle of Bourbon, with its pretty-looking capital, St. Denis—its white trellised houses, beautiful foliage, and terrific surf: and for the next fortnight dashed through the Indian Ocean at a famous rate.

I felt often a strange enjoyment in watching the ship's course through the water from one of the quarter-boats, when every body but the watch was asleep; and sometimes have sat there occupied in all imaginable reveries half the night. When tired of gazing at the bright sheathing of the vessel, gliding hissingly through the phosphorescent brine, I turned my fatigued eyes to the sky, and beheld multitudes of strange stars, soon to sink in the south, and which, probably, I would never see again, it was natural to indulge in speculations on the illimitable vastness of the Universe—the surpassing glories of the Heavens—the unimaginable power and wisdom of the great Creator—and, in humiliating contrast, the littleness of man. And truly, it is in a ship, at night, in the midst of the wide ocean, that we can best appreciate our own insignificance compared with the stupendous grandeur of Creation. Happy are those who turn such humiliating ideas to a salutary account.

We now drew near the Cape. On the 17th June, long. 24, 18, E. lat. 35, 20, S. we sounded, and found bottom at seventy fathoms—the water perceptibly discoloured, and multitudes of pintado birds, and Mother Carey's chickens, with a few albatrosses in our wake. We passed the Table Mountain with a fresh and fair breeze, got into the South-East Trade, and rolled down before it to St. Helena.

One night as we approached our destination, we felt a shock as if we had struck the bottom, which jingled our tea-cups and caused some alarm. This was accounted for immediately after, for a whale emerged close to the side of the ship, and began to blow hurriedly and violently, as if in great alarm. We had seen half a dozen near us in the course of the evening; and it appeared that the vessel had come right against one individual, probably in his first sleep, and roused him from his soft slumbers by a rough nudge in the ribs. We did not stop to set his bones to rights, but proceeded on our course, and made St. Helena by daylight on the 5th of July. We anchored off James's Town at eight o'clock in the morning.

8

St. Helena · Officers of the 66th received by Napoleon · His conversation with
them

I N COMMON, probably with many other persons, I had formed
a very erroneous opinion of the Island of St. Helena. From
reading of the Company's ships touching there on their way home
for water and refreshments, I had associated shade and verdure
with St. Helena; and classed it with Juan Fernandez, and other
delectable spots, dotted here and there in the midst of immense
tracts of ocean, for beneficent purposes, by the hand of Nature.
It was therefore, with no small disappointment I beheld the
ugliest and most dismal rock conceivable, of rugged and abrupt
surface, rising like an enormous black wart from the face of the
deep. Not a blade of grass or trace of vegetation could be perceived from the ship, as we sailed round to get to leeward of the
Island, until we came to our anchorage, when James's Town, the
metropolis, and only town, was first descried; sunk in a deep ravine
between two steep mountains—with its white church—English-
looking houses, bristling rocks and batteries, and two or three
dozen of trees.

These objects derived value and relief from the surrounding
desolation; but on a little more extended acquaintance with our
new abode, we found other pleasing points in St. Helena—the
rugged husk contained some kernel, and we afterwards discovered
several really beautiful and romantic spots; but, on the whole,
the aspect of our future residence was at first very unprepossessing.

We found our Second Battalion and the 53rd quartered here,
and great were the rejoicings on a small scale, of old friends from
the east and the north, at the meeting. My gallant old Badajoz
patient commanded the Second Battalion—now about to be
broken up. He and his officers, asked the '*Qui Hiis*', just arrived,
to dinner, at which the coincidence-hunters were delighted to
find the party of the exact number of the regiment.

Regimental baggage is an article apt to increase in a marvellous
way in any country; but in the luxurious land whence we came, it
had swollen beyond all reasonable compass. I had nineteen or

twenty trunks, boxes, packages and portmanteaus—some with two locks—consequently my bunch of keys was no trifle. My valet de chambre at this time, was a little tipsifying Milesian, named Patrick Kelly, five feet nothing in height—full of humour, and never at a loss for an answer—two out of three of his responses involving a blunder, and every word richly lined with brogue. Nevertheless, although small in stature, he was a very valiant little chap, and had brought down many a bigger man in the Peninsula. His address when taking my plate for vegetables at the Mess dinner, always excited general cachinnation—'My Master will trouble you for a murphy, if you plase, Sir.'

As this facetious person was standing in the fore-chains when we were coming down to our anchorage, gazing on the black rocks past which the ship was brushing, and engaged in the useful occupation of twirling the ring containing my keys, on his hand, *pour passer le temps*, the sapient Mr. Patrick chanced to give too much *momentum* to one of the revolutions; and the centrifugal power beating the centripetal hollow, off the whole bunch went into the sea! Now, it is a fact well known, and not merely a joke of Joe Miller, that the astonished little fellow did actually exclaim 'Stop the ship!' but the ship would not stop, and he was obliged to content himself with an irreverent exclamation, and 'one long, lingering look' into the blue water; and then he ran aft to tell me the calamity. My piscatorial abilities were here at fault—the bunch of keys sank two hundred fathoms deep—unless it was intercepted by some hungry fish—the two or three and twenty locks required to be picked—and in the ignoble office of superintending a smith in this operation, was passed my first day in St. Helena.

Shortly after our arrival, one wing of the regiment was marched to Deadwood Barracks; only half a mile from Longwood, the residence of Napoleon. I considered myself fortunate in having medical charge here—being thus placed in the close vicinity of our illustrious Prisoner.

He, of course, was the great object of curiosity and interest to all on the Island—more especially the people lately arrived; and innumerable were the enquiries made, and discordant the answers received, respecting his habits, and health, and the way he passed his time. Strong and well armed were the batteries of Telescopes on all points commanding good views of Longwood—and ardent and sustained was the gaze for the first few days after our arrival—yet little was to be seen; and after becoming familiar with every visible object around the old house, and every tile on top of it, and fatiguing their eyes and eyestrings to little purpose, the glasses were at length put in their cases.

At Mess in the evening, every officer had his own story as to Buonaparte's private life. Some said he lay in bed all day, dictating memoirs of his life—others averred that he got up punctually to breakfast at nine o'clock, made a satisfactory meal and drank his bottle of light Claret. From one quarter it appeared that he played at Chess or Billiards half the forenoon, and read French Novels the remainder—from another that he passed all his mornings at Marshal Bertrand's. Some wiseacres shook their heads and insisted that he was dying of a decline—others maintained boldly that he was in excellent health and growing very fat. In two points, only, all accounts concurred—that he maintained Imperial state with his Suite, and was on the worst terms with Sir Hudson Lowe, the Governor.[34]

The second morning after establishing ourselves at Deadwood, I took my gun and directed my steps to Flag-Staff Hill, a conical mountain rising on one side boldly from the sea—about two miles from the barracks. My way led me round the Race-Course, which had been traced for a mile and a half along a semi-circular sweep at the top of our elevated plateau. This was covered with coarse grass and wild gooseberry bushes, under whose roots thousands of little mice burrowed, and popped in and out as I passed, in all confidence—luckily for them no kites or hawks being in the Island. The only birds I saw were a flock of white sea-gulls, that would rise perpendicularly from the surface of the ocean beneath, and disport themselves in graceful circles round the peak of the mountain. These were particularly silly gulls, and so tame that I could not shoot them. One of them came within a yard of my head, and put down his little black feet as if he was going to alight on my straw hat; and I believe if I had not put my hand up and attempted to catch him, he would actually have made a lodgement. But, although he failed in his attempt, he touched the magic chain of association, and visions of early scenes came flitting across my memory. My poor uncle, and my cousin, and Simon Stylites, and the fish-pond and the bowery garden—ending alas, in the shrouded imagery of death!

Dolefully did we look at each other, 'with hungry eyes', at our first Mess dinner; for a sad, sad change had taken place in our fare: then we began to appreciate the bathos from an Indian to a St. Helena table. In the first place we had oily soup made of Cape sheep, which all sprout out in huge fat tails, twenty pounds weight, and cannot nourish any other mutton—then there was the staple of the Island—Mackarel at top—Mackarel at bottom—Mackarel at one side as a Curry—at another as a Stew. Next, we had Albacore Steaks, like coarse Pork Chops, and hempy Ration Beef stripped off the thin-clothed ribs of Benguela bullocks, and some other abominations. In fact, the only thing eatable at table, were the Yams and the King's Own.*

But, although this is a true copy of our first Bill of Fare, it must not be concealed, (yet, the fact will never have much influence on the destinies of nations), that our table improved afterwards very much.

The first excitement of being in the immediate neighbourhood of Napoleon having subsided, and himself and every thing about him being invisible, we began to find that our new abode was likely to be very *ennuissant*, and our time very heavy in hand. To be sure we saw black balls hoisted, indicating that ships were in sight; which was the case almost every day in the year—the Island being in the direct high road from India: we observed signals flying, and communicating from one hill to another, and R.O.B. telegraphed daily about two o'clock from the post near our Barracks to Plantation-House, the Governor's residence, meaning, 'All is right at Longwood.' We also had the advantage of descrying ships, from our high position, nearly thirty leagues off—like motes on the edge of the horizon; and of watching the cruizers attached to the station, hovering about the rock to windward and leeward. Vessels, too, when they could find or make any decent excuse, would touch at the Island to get a chance of a glimpse at Buonaparte, and to carry home with them all the gossip they could collect. One very common trick of the Masters, was to start their watercasks on the run from the Cape; invent some plausible fib of a leak or something else to tell the windward cruizer, and thus get permission to stop two or three days for a fresh supply.

About a month after our arrival—both Battalions being now

* Contemporary slang for Army Rations of salt beef and pork. (Editor.)

incorporated, the Regiment, about twelve hundred strong, was inspected by Sir Hudson Lowe, and when this was over we had a sham fight. I observed Napoleon sitting on a bench at Longwood, watching the manoeuvres through a glass. Our puny mimicry of war must have appeared as utterly puerile and insignificant to him. They might have spared the warrior of a hundred fields the mortification of contrasting the child's play of which he was now an unwilling spectator, with the triumphs of Austerlitz or Jena. Afterwards we were all introduced, and dined at Plantation-House. Two other officers and myself got beds. The style was good—the wines first-rate, and although the Governor appeared somewhat reserved, and a little absent at times—Lady Lowe kept the conversation from flagging. Nobody seemed disposed to like Sir Hudson, but we were all delighted with his wife. Lady Lowe was not a good figure, but she had a fine face, laughing eyes, much talking talent, a fair and beautiful neck; and lovely arms. In short, she presided at her own table with much grace and brilliancy, and was altogether a very captivating woman.

The Governor appeared to be much occupied with the cares and duties of his important and responsible office; and looked very like a person who would not let his prisoner escape, if he could help it. His countenance was unpleasing, and from first impressions, I entertained an opinion of him far from favourable. If, therefore, notwithstanding this prepossession, my testimony should incline to the other side, I can truly state that the change took place from the weight of evidence, and in consequence of what came under by own observation in St. Helena. Poor man, he has since that time encountered a storm of obloquy and reproach enough to bow any person to the earth. Yet I firmly believe that the talent he exerted in unravelling the intricate plotting constantly going on at Longwood, and the firmness in tearing it to pieces, with the unceasing vigilance he displayed in the discharge of his arduous duties, made him more enemies than any hastiness of temper, uncourteousness of demeanour, and severity in his measures, of which the world believed him guilty.

On the 8th of August, I was playing Backgammon with my old patient and friend Colonel Dodgin, when one of the Longwood servants, Napoleon's Piqueur, rode up in a violent hurry, requesting me to go to Marshal Bertrand's immediately, as one of the children had met with a serious accident, and Dr. O'Meara,

Buonaparte's Physician, had gone to James's Town. I galloped there in a few minutes, and found that the eldest boy, Napoleon, had fallen on a flint and cut his forehead a good deal. The injury was not of much consequence, but the sight of the blood naturally caused some alarm in the family. After putting the little patient to rights, and settling him comfortably in bed, I sat half an hour with the Marshal and Countess Bertrand. He was quiet and pleasing in manner; very unostentatious, conversible and well informed. Madame Bertrand had rich remains of what must have been once, the mien, figure and face of an Empress—she spoke English with equal fluency as French. They had then three children—two boys and a girl; the most rosy, playful and attractive creatures in the world.

Next day Dr. O'Meara called, and politely thanked me for my professional services. His address and manner were agreeable and gentlemanly. Soon after this time he was admitted as an honorary member of our Mess; and unquestionably, as far as I ever witnessed or heard, his deportment there was that of a gentleman. Perhaps his conversation, sometimes, became more animated in defence of Napoleon than was prudent or proper under existing circumstances; but the subject was never introduced wantonly or offensively by Dr. O'Meara.

All our officers being very desirous of seeing our celebrated neighbour, a negociation was set on foot to gratify our wish. The fact of Buonaparte and the Governor being on such bad terms, was an obstacle in the way, but not quite insurmountable. At last the second in Command, Sir George Bingham, made an arrangement with Marshal Bertrand, that we should have the honour of an introduction to the Great Man.

On the afternoon of the 1st of September 1817, the officers of our regiment, with Sir George Bingham and Colonel Nicol at their head, repaired to Longwood. We called at Marshal Bertrand's house, fifty or sixty yards from the residence of Napoleon, to pick up the Marshal, who accompanied us to the billiard-room, where we found Counts Montholon and Gourgaud. After waiting five or six minutes, the folding doors of the anti-chamber were thrown open—we entered, formed a ring round the room, according to seniority, and in about a minute Napoleon walked into the circle.

He was dressed in a plain dark green uniform coat, without epaulettes or any thing equivalent, but with a large star on the breast, which had an eagle in the centre. The buttons were gold, with the device of a mounted dragoon, in high relief. He had on white breeches with silk stockings, and oval gold buckles in his shoes—with a small opera hat under his arm. Napoleon's first appearance was far from imposing—the stature was short and thick—head sunk into his shoulders—his face fat, with large folds under the chin—the limbs appeared to be stout, but well proportioned—complexion olive—expression sinister, and rather scowling. The features instantly reminded us of the prints of him we had seen. On the whole, his general look was more that of an obese Spanish or Portuguese Friar than the Hero of modern times.

Buonaparte walked round the room, with an attempt (as it seemed) at the old dignity, and addressed a few words to most of the officers. Colonel Nicol was first introduced by Sir George Bingham—he and Marshal Bertrand acting as interpreters. The following conversation then took place; which I copy, as well as the whole proceedings on this memorable occasion, from minutes noted down immediately after the interview:

NAPOLEON 'Your regiment has lately arrived from India—coming from that rich country, you should wear gold and not silver.[35] How many years does it take to acclimatize a regiment of Europeans?'

COLONEL NICOL 'Two or three years—a few die the first year—more the second, but the mortality is much reduced the third.'

'Did your officers save much money in India?'

'No; the expense of living is too great.'

'How many servants did you keep there?'

'I had at one time between thirty and forty—I think, thirty-nine.'

'Do you think a regiment is efficient after twenty years' service in India?'

'Yes; it is fed by recruits from home.'

'What kind of troops are the Seapoys?'

'Those in the British Service, are excellent troops.'

'How many battalions of Seapoys of equal strength, would you engage with the 66th?'

'Do you mean battalions with British Officers, or without them?'

'Both the one and the other.'

'Seapoy regiments with British Officers, are good and steady soldiers. I should not like great disparity of force with them, though, I might manage to defeat four or five battalions belonging to the Native Powers, and I am pretty sure we could.'

'Very good—you are a fine fellow. (*Un brave homme*.')

'How many officers have you in your Mess?'

'We have sixteen at Deadwood.'

'You sit very late at the Mess I hear—often till midnight.'

'O yes; when we have a few good fellows there, we don't stir sometimes till cock-crow.'

'But the officers get tipsy then, don't they?' (then in English—'*drunk—drunk—eh?*')

'O no, no—they don't get drunk.'

'Your men, I perceive, walk about very much in the sun, and without their caps. That's wrong.'

'It is, and we do all we can to prevent it.'

'Have you not a Catholic Officer in the Regiment?'

'Yes,' (with a nod at Lieut. McCarthy, who stood nearly opposite at the other side of the circle.)

'He has been to Rio Janeiro lately, I hear.'

'Yes, and is just returned.'

'He went there to get absolution for his peccadillos, I suppose?' (Repeated—'*Absolution, n'est ce pas?*')

(Answered by a laugh from Colonel Nicol, and a blush on the honest and naturally rubicund physiognomy of the officer in question.)

Napoleon then turned to Lieut. Colonel Lascelles.

'What countryman are you?'

'An Englishman.'

'From what part of England?'

'From Yorkshire.'

'Were you born in the city of York?'

'No.'

He then passed to the next Senior Officer, Lieut. Colonel Dodgin, c.b., who had several clasps and medals on his breast. He was, besides, a remarkably fine military-looking man, and when walking with me in London, had been more than once mistaken for the Duke of York. Napoleon looked at him with some complacency, and took hold with his fingers of the most glittering of the batch of distinctions, which happened to be the Vittoria medal; but as soon as he read 'that word of fear', he dropped it instantly, and rather abruptly. It was no mere fancy of mine, but a matter of plain fact, observed and spoken of at the time by us all, that his gesture was exactly that of a person letting fall something unexpectedly and disagreeably hot. He then said:

'You have decorations, I see. Where did you serve?'

'In Egypt and the Peninsula.'

'Were you at Salamanca or Thoulouse?'

'No.'

'Was your Regiment at Talavera?'

'Yes.'

'Were you ever wounded?'

'Yes; twice.'

'Was your name sent home as an officer who had distinguished himself?'

(When Colonel Dodgin hesitated, Captain Baird answered for him—'Yes, three times.')

Buonaparte next addressed Captain Baird:

'You are a Captain of Grenadiers?'

'Yes.'

'How many years have you been in the service?'

'Nearly twenty.'

'And still only a Captain.'

'Even so.'

Next, Captain Jordan passed the ordeal. He was married to a handsome St. Helena lady whom he had met in India, and whose father's house was not more than a mile from Longwood.

'You are married?'

'Yes.'

'Your wife is pretty, I hear. How many children have you?'

'Two.'

Then Captain Dunne:

'You have been in India?'

'How long have you served?'

'Fourteen years.'

Napoleon then glanced at the next officer, Captain E[llis], a Cambridgeshire man, of most uncouth and forbidding exterior and physiognomy—in fact, an evident descendant of the Colony of Barbarians settled in that County by a Roman Emperor—but not being pleased with the Vandal, he passed by without addressing him, and accosted his neighbour, Captain L'Estrange, a worthy little fellow, of very dark complexion.

'Have you served in India?'

'Yes.'

'How long have you served?'

'Fourteen years—two in India.'

(There seemed to be some mistake made here by the Interpreters, in confounding the entire services of this officer with the time passed in India.)

'How is it your complexion is so dark? Were you sick in India?'

'No.'

'Do you drink?' (and then, translating the French—'*drink? drink?*')

(Answered by a smile.)

'Which do you think the best Town? Calcutta or James's Town?'

(Repeated, and attempted to be translated—'*Veech you tink de best town?*')

'Calcutta.'

Next in the circle stood Captain Duncan:

'How long have you served?'

'Upwards of twenty years.'

'You have been in India?'

'Yes.'

'Were you ever in action?'

'Yes.'

'And ever wounded?'

'No.'

'Then you are a lucky fellow.'

Buonaparte then addressed Mr. Heir, the Surgeon:

'You are the Surgeon of the Regiment?'

'Yes.'

'Do you hold any other Commission?'

(This question was answered by Sir George Bingham.)

'This gentleman is the Surgeon Major;' (not unhappily, considering that my excellent *amigo*, Heir, was about six feet and a half high,) and then there was here some confusion, and the Interpreters, Sir G. Bingham and the Marshal, were a little at fault; confounding Surgeon Major and Serjeant Major—Sir George not being perfect in French, and Marshal Bertrand very defective in his English. At length Napoleon said:

'Lord Wellington promoted several of his Surgeon Majors, I have heard.'

Sir George Bingham–'Pardon, *Sire*,' (for this Imperial recognition, which had never been sanctioned by the British Government, was evidently a lapsus of the moment,) 'Pardon, it was the *Serjeant* Majors–several of whom got Commissions during the Peninsular War.'

To Mr. Heir:

'You had a great many sick in India?'

'Yes–it is not a healthy climate.'

'Many liver-complaints?'

'Yes.'

'Do you prescribe calomel largely?'

'Yes.'

Next in order, was Lieutenant Moffatt.

'What countryman are you?'

'An Irishman.'

'Are you a Catholic or a Protestant?'

(With marked and indignant emphasis,) 'A Protestant.'

Buonaparte now moved somewhat quicker than before, round the circle, passing by some of the officers without speaking to them, after individual introduction, and addressing merely a word as to length of service to one or two others. When he arrived at the point where I stood, Marshal Bertrand made me a bow of recognition; on which the great man stopped, and the Marshal formally introduced me as the English Physician that had recently attended his eldest son, Napoleon's little favourite, and namesake. He then looked at me with a slight expression of complacency, and said:

'You have served in India?'

'Yes.'

'You had much professional duty there?'

'A good deal certainly.'

'Were diseases of the liver very common in India?'

'Yes; they occur there more frequently than in colder climates.'

'Your soldiers drink an enormous quantity of brandy in India?'

'They are much too fond of spirits–arrack is cheap there, and the climate makes them thirsty.'

'Do you bleed and give large doses of calomel there, as the English Doctors do here?'

'I believe the practice is similar.'

'Are you, too, a devotee of the lancet? Ah, God defend me from it! (*Ah, Dieu m'en garde!*')

'In my opinion it is our most potent weapon.'

'To kill or cure? Eh, M. le Docteur?'

'It is our duty to cure.'

Then Ensign Wardell.

'You are a young man. How long have you served?'

'Seven years.'

'You entered the service very young then?'

'Yes; but I have served in the Navy.'

'You were a Midshipman?'

'Yes.'

One or two more were asked one question, only as to length of service, and the round was completed. He then addressed Colonel Nicol a second time—

'So the Seapoys are good troops?'

'Yes; they are excellent soldiers—respectful, sober and obedient.'

'But, yet, you would fight five or six battalions of them with your own regiment?'

'Not Seapoys with British Officers—I should not like to engage two such battalions.'

A few sentences were then exchanged between Napoleon, Marshal Bertrand and Sir George Bingham; and we all bowed and retired.

As we walked home to Deadwood, and calmly reviewed what had passed; and compared the appearance, manner and conversation of Buonaparte with our preconceived ideas, prepossessions and expectations, the general feeling and result was disappointment—but this might have been reasonably anticipated. Without reference to the usual sobering effect of vicinity and contact, in dissipating the gilded halos with which a sanguine fancy invests distant and remarkable objects, the interview with Napoleon had dissolved a glory, *par excellence*. A fascinating prestige which we had cherished all our lives, then vanished like gossamer in the sun. The great Emperor Napoleon, the Hero of modern times, had merged in an unsightly and obese individual; and we looked in vain for that overwhelming power of eye and force of expression which we had been taught to expect by a delusive imagination.

At our Mess-dinner the same evening, our illustrious neighbour had evidently fallen off by one half from our notions concerning him, of the day before. Of course our conversation was exclusively occupied by the great event of the day, which would form a sort of epoch in our lives. Various and amusing enough was the confidential chat over our wine that evening. Some were much dissatisfied at the answers they had given, and wished the interview could be re-acted, that they might behave better. One or two honest fellows acknowledged a loss of all presence of mind on the occasion. We had some mirth at poor L'Estrange's expense, about the '*drink? drink?*' and the fuddling propensity of which he was so unceremoniously accused by Buonaparte; though the charge was quite unfounded. Besides, we were puzzled to understand by what peculiar mode of reasoning the Emperor had established the whimsical connection between intemperance of this sort, and a dark complexion; and the more particularly as the induction would bear hard against himself.

Colonel Nicol's reply to Napoleon's question about the Seapoys was deservedly admired as happy and correct. The interrogation was, in all probability, a trap; and the querist thought that in the Colonel's desire to puff his own corps, he might choose to elevate its character at the expense of disparaging the Seapoys. For it was well known that Buonaparte generally spoke slightingly of our Indian Army; and any depreciation of the excellent troops that compose it could scarcely be unacceptable to him. Besides the peculiar dislike he might entertain for that army, as a vast, though distant bulwark of British power, there was a peculiar and strong association formed in his mind between it and a distinguished individual, for whom he never had reason to cherish much affection. He, himself, was believed to be the writer of an article in the *Moniteur*, about the time of Massena's retreat from the lines before Lisbon, full of virulent abuse of England, and the English Army; in which Lord Wellington was opprobriously called 'only a Seapoy General.'

My brother-officers quizzed Moffat about the emphatic, 'I am a Protestant': nor did McCarthy's 'absolution' at Rio, escape comment. They were also a little severe on me—mis-applying the question of Napoleon, as to the soldiers drinking in India, to myself. However, as 'my withers were unwrung', and conscience clear in that matter, I could afford to join in the laugh. There was more point in their jokes about the Lancet, and they unanimously adopted Buonaparte's exclamation, '*Ah, Dieu m'en garde!*' as a capital *môt* deserving of all remembrance.

The abruptness with which Napoleon dropped Col. Dodgin's Vittoria Medal, became the subject of much conversation at the Mess. Yet was the gesture natural enough; for the recollection of the sad consequences of that decisive engagement, must have caused a pang. Poor man! how changed now his condition, surrounded in captivity by men bearing on their breasts, the badges of triumphs over his armies, from the period of his brilliant Levees at the Thuilleries, in the midst of a circle of the Heroes of Marengo and Austerlitz! I have, both at the time and subsequently, collated the respective statements of the officers with each other, as to the exact conversation with Napoleon, and compared them with my own Minutes, made the same day. There were a few unimportant discrepancies in their recollections of what had passed; but the detail in the text, is, I believe, as faithful an account as possible, under the circumstances of such an interview, and without a professed Reporter.

Notwithstanding the ruggedness of the surface of our Island, a Race-Course had been traced out at Deadwood; and we had our Spring and Autumn Meetings: but, being South of the Equator, the Spring Races took place in September, and the Autumn in April. There was scarcely an English horse in the Island at first; but the Cape breed, with a cross of the Arab, were showy and compact, though small animals, possessing much speed for a short distance, but, of course, destitute of the more game qualities of the high-bred English Racer.

During the first day's sport after our arrival, an awkward circumstance occurred on the Course. A certain half-mad and drunken Piqueur of Napoleon, named Archambault, took it into his head to gallop within the ropes, when the Course was cleared and the horses coming up. For this transgression he was pursued by one of the Stewards and horse-whipped out of the forbidden limits. This gentleman knew not that the offender belonged to the Longwood Establishment, or he would, no doubt, have spared his whip; particularly as Napoleon at the time was sitting on a bench outside his residence, looking at the crowd through a glass; and probably interpreted the accidental chastisement his servant received into a premeditated insult to the Master.

But we did Napoleon injustice by the supposition. Mr. O'Meara told me the next day that he had distinctly witnessed everything that passed, and had been very angry when he saw Archambault galloping alone along the Course, and was pleased to see him chastised; and that he had called him to his presence, and expended on him a few '*F— bêtes*' and '*sacré cochons*' afterwards.

We had Pheasants, Partridges and wild Peacocks in St. Helena; which, with wild Goats on an almost inaccessible and barren mountain promontory, called 'the Barn', constituted our game. Owing to the peculiar conformation of the surface, and the steep rocky ridges on the upper parts of the Island, shooting was very fatiguing–the birds after a shot or two, had only to fly a hundred yards across a ravine, impassable to a pedestrian, and the sportsman would be obliged to go two or three miles round before he could get another shot. The Pheasants and Partridges were strictly preserved–the Peacocks were very wild, and inhabited the highest and roughest points and pinnacles. One noble cock led me a dance one day in the hot sun, of fourteen or fifteen miles, and, after all, got off with the trifling loss of three or four of his quills.

On the night of the 21st September, a little after I had fallen asleep, I was awaked by a strange motion of the bed, and jumped up immediately, for I recognized at once the well-known vibration of an Earthquake. The bed-posts danced against the floor, and the glass and the delf jingled in the cupboard; but an instant's reflection shewed me there was no danger in the little frame-work wooden barrack I occupied: however, as the room was ceiled, and the falling of the lime into my eyes would not be pleasant, it was as well to walk out of the house. The shock lasted ten seconds; for its duration was timed by one of our officers, Captain Baird, who was sitting with some friends round his table, and had the curiosity and presence of mind to take out his watch and calculate the time it continued.

On the high ground where we lived, and so favourably circumstanced as to the nature of our domiciles, there was no danger to be apprehended–the Island might shake away as it pleased without doing any harm to our wooden cribs; and the only thing to be feared, was the sudden subsidence of the whole rock into the depths of ocean, from whence it had evidently sprung up. But the case was very different in the valley; and we anticipated the most terrible consequences from the loosened rocks tumbling down the steep sides of the mountains on James's Town, and waited for accounts from thence with much anxiety. Fortunately our fears turned out groundless; yet, how nothing started from the mountains, is a problem I could never solve, for the shock was rude enough in the town; shaking the houses well and setting the Church bell ringing ominously and violently.

In the latter end of 1817 two of my brother-officers, Davy and McDougell and myself, arranged one night at the Mess that we would go to fish at day-light the next morning, off the rocks at the south-west of the Island. The weather was fine and the morning broke calm and clear. I arose at the appointed hour; but, soon after, a fit of unaccountable drowsiness came on, and although I have always been punctilious in keeping appointments, and one of my friends tapped at the window, I declined accompanying him, and again composed myself to sleep.

I got up at the usual hour, and after breakfast and the performance of my Hospital duties, rode down to James's Town. A little after dismounting, a soldier came running from the signal post with a slip of paper in his hand. It was a telegraph from Deadwood, ordering me back instantly—my two friends had been suddenly washed off the rock, where they were sitting fishing in all apparent security, twenty feet above the water, two minutes before. Parties were going in search of their bodies, and I was directed to accompany them, in the faint hope of resuscitation.

But, poor fellows! they were never found. McDougell, had been recently married to a St. Helena lady—his companion, generous and warm-hearted Davy, knowing that he could not swim, and seeing the end of a fishing rod within his own grasp, which the servant, who sat higher on the rocks and escaped the wave, had stretched out to him—cried out 'seize it McDougell, I can swim.' McDougell did grasp the rod, but in the agitation of the moment he seized it too violently—the slender top gave way, and he sank to rise no more. Davy then suddenly and unaccountably disappeared, and it was believed he had been seized by a shark. The Men of War of the station had boats out several days in quest of the bodies, but no vestige of them was ever discovered.

The officers of the Navy and Army lived very amicably together at St. Helena, although the circumstances of our financial condition in the garrison could scarcely fail of exciting some slight soreness and envy in the minds of our friends afloat. We were on the allowances of the Indian Establishment, and our pay more than doubled theirs. Parties of our people were frequently dining on board the *Conqueror*, 74, the Flag ship; and afterwards, though not so often, on board the *Vigo*, 74, her successor, and we very often had the pleasure of seeing our naval friends at the Mess; whilst the United Service met two or three times a week at Plantation House: for, severe as the judgment of the world has been against Sir Hudson Lowe, his enemies could never impeach the liberal hospitality of his table.

On the 25th October, we had the novelty of the arrival of two ships of war from India—the *Melville*, 74, and the *Iphigenia* frigate—new Teak-built ships from the stocks of Juttshughee Bummaunjhee, the Parsee ship-builder at Bombay—with the timbers of another 74 on board. Two or three military officers of rank, who came by this opportunity, wished very much to wait on Napoleon; but the personage had now become exceedingly morose and disinclined to receive visitors. Consequently they failed in their object.

I had at this time a very pretty chesnut horse, mixed Cape and Arab, named Whiskey, very quiet and active, and who could beat any thing for the centre half mile of the course, which was down hill; but failed at both ends. Nevertheless, he won me several matches down the steep part, when I had discovered his forte. Mr. Whiskey had one weakness—he shied a little at objects which he could not comprehend; and one of his incomprehensibles was a cask or barrel of any description—particularly in the act of progression. This was not a fault strictly speaking, but a physical misfortune, dependant on a defect in the shape of his eye. At this time a supply of water for the troops at Deadwood was brought in casks from the side of a mountain, named Diana's peak, and rolled along the road, close to the perpendicular side of the Punch Bowl, by fatigue parties of soldiers. Many an amusing little encounter Whiskey and his master had with these barrels. My steed's imagination appeared to be as Quixotic on approaching them as the Knight's of the rueful countenance, and disported itself in similar amplifications as his. The road was narrow; ran close to the very brim of the immense cavity, and there was no fence nor parapet. When I met a train of barrels, and the horse began to prick up his ears and look frightened, I used to incline Whiskey to the Punch Bowl—as was but natural—until finding himself on the very edge, and being fully as anxious to avoid going down as his rider, he was in the habit of choosing the lesser of the two evils—dashing desperately at the water casks, and clearing them with a spring, a yard higher than was necessary, one after the other.

When going down to James's Town one morning, I met General K—r, who had arrived in the *Melville*, riding very cautiously along the edge of the precipice. He was mounted on a fiery, hard-mouthed, unmanageable brute, belonging to Mr. Balcombe, called Emperor; and appeared in great trepidation and perplexity – casting now and then an anxious glance down into the hollow, as if measuring its depth, and the steepness of its sides. We stopped to exchange salutations, when the General accosted me – 'Pray do you ride a quiet horse, Doctor?' 'Very.' 'Then you will do me a particular favour if you will exchange with me for the day, for I am sure this savage animal will land me in the Punch Bowl before I get to Deadwood' – 'Certainly, General, with much pleasure.' So I gave him Whiskey and mounted Emperor.

There was a return fatigue party rolling before them about twenty empty casks, that I knew the Brigadier must meet; and I supposed I should see an amusing little rencounter when they came in contact; to enjoy which I dismounted and led my horse to an eminence commanding the road. As soon as the General and Whiskey approached the first cask, the horse pricked up his ears, fidgetted and swerved against the bank, and the rider having un-wittingly touched him with the spur, the gallant animal cleared the whole series of barrels in his usual high stile, making about twenty consecutive leaps without halting, amidst the cheers of the soldiers –

> 'And every soul cried out – "well done!"
> As loud as he could bawl.'

How the astonished Brigadier managed to stick to the horse, with his arms round his neck and his feet all abroad – is a point I could never satisfactorily make out.

There was a neat little Theatre in James's Town, and the Garrison and Navy furnished a respectable corps of Amateurs. The manager, principal performer, scene painter and factotum, was a worthy officer of the Commissariat, named Ibbetson. In the beginning of November, Henry the Fourth was got up, chiefly to shew off my old patient and commanding officer, Colonel Dodgin, as Falstaff, and a famous Falstaff he made with little stuffing. The play took so well that it was encored to a bumper house no less than three times.

9

Quarrels and scandals · Dr. O'Meara and Sir Hudson Lowe · Attempt at bribery

IN the month of February 1818, Buonaparte's Maître d' Hôtel, Cypriani, a faithful servant, who had followed all the vicissitudes of his fortune, from the time he was a Lieutenant of Artillery in 1794, was attacked with inflammation of the bowels. The symptoms having assumed a dangerous character, Mr. O'Meara requested me to see him. Accordingly, having obtained the Governor's permission, I went to Longwood and continued to attend the patient until his death, which took place on the 26th of February.

This poor man suffered much pain previous to the setting in of mortification of the intestines. I had known him before, and often had long conversations with him when we chanced to meet in our evening walks. Although Buonaparte's devoted servant, he was one of the most violent republican Jacobins I ever met, and a person of a class that I imagined had almost ceased to exist in France under the Imperial rule. M. Cypriani was very ferocious in his anti-religious sentiments; and although Voltaire was his Evangelist, and he had always a volume of his works in his pocket, he was no admirer of the tolerant principles of his great favourite, but declared 'war to the knife' against all Priests, all Kings–all Emperors (except his master) and all religions. The horrid wish expressed by some hero of the Reign of Terror, whom I forget– that 'the last of the Kings might be strangled by the bowels of the last of Priests', tickled his fancy mightily, and he often told me he heartily concurred in it.

M. Cypriani was buried in the Protestant burying-ground, by a Protestant Clergyman; and it certainly required an ugly stretch of conscience to call him a dear brother in the Christian Faith, and to entertain a sure and certain hope of his resurrection to eternal life: for the poor man laughed at Christianity and the Resurrection, and joined heartily in the wish of the Ferney Philosopher, as well as admired his formidable attempts, *'pour écraser l'infame'* –the Christian Religion.

161

But, leaving these serious matters, I am obliged to tell that in the course of my attendance at Longwood, I was not a little surprised to find that Napoleon had never visited his devoted servant during his last illness. No doubt but this piece of Imperial condescension would have been highly gratifying to the patient; yet it is a fact that no visit ever took place, although the sick man's chamber was under the Emperor's roof, and not twenty feet distant from his bath. I have reason to believe, however, that during the last evening of Cypriani's malady, and when he was in a state of delirious insensibility, his master proposed to see him, but was dissuaded by Mr. O'Meara, on the ground that the patient would not then be in a state to recognise the Emperor. With no small degree of absurd *charlatanerie*–if I may be forgiven for using the word with reference to such a man–Napoleon, on that occasion expressed an opinion that his presence might re-animate the expiring efforts of nature, as it had, he said, under desperate circumstances, retrieved the almost fatal disorder of his Army at Marengo, and some other of his battle-fields.

Some time after Cypriani's death, Mr. O'Meara called on me at Deadwood, with a smiling countenance, to tell me he was the bearer of good news, on which he offered me his congratulations. The Emperor it appeared had consulted him as to the propriety of giving a fee or a present to the English Physician, who had attended his servant; and the result was that a present had been preferred. Mr. O'Meara added that Napoleon had condescended to enquire the name of the English Doctor, and whether he was married or single; and that the business had ended in an order having been given for a Breakfast Service of Plate to be sent for to Rundell and Bridges, Fleet-street, London.

This was all very pleasing information, and it was not unnatural for me to felicitate myself on the prospect of such a present, coming from such a quarter. Unfortunately the sequel proved, that, as there are many 'slips between the cup and the lip', so an accident may occur sometimes between the teapot and the cup.

A few days after this communication, Mr. O'Meara again called; but this time his countenance had no such riant expression as on the former occasion. A difficulty had occurred. A statute had passed in England lately, constituting the acceptance of any gift from Napoleon, or any of his Suite in St. Helena, a criminal act. It was therefore necessary, previous to any farther step, to ascertain how I felt disposed, and whether I would consent to accept the Emperor's present clandestinely, and without the knowledge of the Governor. This, it was now the object of Mr. O'Meara's visit to ascertain—the Emperor, he assured me, having an invincible repugnance to hold any communication whatever with Sir Hudson Lowe; or, as he expressed it, to permit any gift from himself to be contaminated by passing through the hands of '*Cain*', as was his favourite nick-name for the Governor.

I took a little time to consult with my friends; more, indeed, as a thing usual in such cases, than from any doubt as to what was proper to be done. Two hours after, Mr. O'Meara returned to Longwood, with the information that all must be above board, and nothing done illegally or clandestinely. I heard no more of my plate.

The thing was plain enough—a palpable attempt at a bribe, to enlist even so humble an individual as myself, '*l'homme d'Empereur*', and to bind him down to future obedience by making him first commit himself in a wrong action.

This did not altogether rest on Mr. O'Meara's assertion, as, afterwards in returning from St. Helena, General Montholon assured me that the present was *bonà fide*, intended for me, and would have been sent if the above mentioned difficulty had not come in the way.

About this period, Sir Hudson Lowe and Mr. O'Meara, after various desultory skirmishes, at last engaged in regular battle. Mr. O'Meara was an honorary member of our Mess, and used to dine with us two or three times a week. As I said before, his conduct at the Mess, and every where else, I believe, was that of a gentleman of agreeable manners and conversation. When the quarrel, of which I have just spoken, took place, the Governor expressed his wish that Mr. O'Meara should not be permitted to continue a member of the Mess, as he had heard and believed, that the Doctor repeated our convivial and confidential conversation to Napoleon. At this time my friend, Colonel Nicol, had gone on leave of absence to England, and another officer, whose name I do not mention, commanded the regiment. Without consulting the members of the Mess, he sent an intimation to Mr. O'Meara that his society was no longer desired by the regiment: which pretty strong hint the Doctor disregarded—came to dinner that very day, and afterwards appealed to the officers as to the propriety of his conduct whilst mixing with them. They could only state with truth, that he had comported himself always in a gentlemanly manner.[36] Dr. O'Meara was, soon after, confined within the bounds of Longwood, and in a few days sent to England.

Now, as I have no object but to tell the truth, notwithstanding that it was highly incorrect, and a breach of social confidence to repeat our table talk at Longwood, I conceive that Sir Hudson Lowe should not have directed our Mess to expel Mr. O'Meara. We ought not to have been implicated in the quarrel, so long as Mr. O'Meara conducted himself amongst us *comme il faut*, and nothing affecting his character as an officer and a gentleman, could be substantiated against him.

With regard to Mr. O'Meara himself, I have no doubt, and I think no reasonable doubt can be entertained, that he suffered himself to be cajoled and fascinated–I will not say corrupted, into the admirer, adherent, agent and tool of Napoleon.

Mr. O'Meara was dismissed from the British Service for having officially stated, or insinuated that Sir Hudson Lowe had suborned him to poison Buonaparte, or sounded him respecting such a crime, nine or ten months before he made the communication to government. The Secretary of the Admiralty said–'You have either fabricated this most grave accusation, or it is a true bill. If it is false, you are unworthy to remain for a moment in the service–if, on the other hand, the horrid and improbable charge is true, you have grossly violated your duty in concealing such an atrocity so long.' Now I do not perceive any way of escape from this dilemma.

That a young Major General, appointed to one of the most important and lucrative commands in the gift of the Crown, should have lost sight of his own interest so far as to desire to shorten the existence of the Life of his Lease, carries absurdity on the face of it, even putting out of sight any moral consideration of the question. If, as I believe was the case, Mr. O'Meara wilfully misconceived some peevish expression of the Governor, in a moment of irritation at some *tracasserie* going on at Longwood, and construed it into this horrid design, or desire–then, after brooding over it nine or ten months, made it the subject of an official charge–I dispassionately think his conduct was vile, and that he richly merited dismissal from the service.

In March and April 1818, the weather became very wet at

Deadwood and all the high lands of the Island; and the duties of the soldiers in carrying materials for the new house about to be erected at Longwood, and digging its foundations, being severe and laborious, bowel complaints broke out and became frequent amongst the men. As the season improved the sickness wore off.

From an accident that happened to the Surgeon of the regiment, on account of which he went to England, soon after our arrival in St. Helena, I, as senior Assistant, took medical charge of the regiment, and kept it nearly three years. I mention this merely to shew that I had good opportunities of becoming acquainted with the climate of the Island, and of judging respecting its character, as well as the nature of any endemic disease. I append a note to substantiate this assertion.[37]

EXTRACT

from General Order of Lieut. General Sir Hudson Lowe, K.C.B. dated St. Helena, 23rd May, 1821

The Lieut. General desires Col. Nicol will also express to Assistant Surgeon Henry, the high sense entertained of his very meritorious services in this Island.

In consequence of the accident that befel the Surgeon of the regiment, soon after his arrival here, the duties of Surgeon have fallen during a long period on Mr. Henry, and the Lieut. General is happy to acknowledge the able and satisfactory manner in which these duties, as well as every other call of his profession, have been attended to by him.

(*Signed*) T. Reade [Lt. Col. Sir Thomas Reade, C.B.]
Asst. Adjutant General

For a tropical climate, only fifteen degrees from the Line, St. Helena is certainly a healthy Island—if not the most healthy of this description in the world. During one period of twelve months, we did not lose one man by disease, out of five hundred of the 66th, quartered at Deadwood. In 1817, 18 and 19, the thermometer then kept at the hospital there, ranged from fifty-five to seventy degrees of Fahrenheit, with the exception of two calm days, when it rose to eighty degrees. It was about twelve degrees higher in James's Town. The south-east Trade Wind, coming over an immense surface of ocean, cools the rock, and wafts over it every morning a cloudy awning which mitigates the strong sun.

Notwithstanding the assertions of Napoleon's adherents–who had an interest in painting the place in as dark colours as they could–I must maintain that we had, strictly speaking, no endemic disease in the Island. Human life, certainly, did not extend to the same length as in cooler regions; though some organs appeared to be privileged there–the lungs, for instance, and their peculiar diseases were rare. The upper parts were decidedly the most healthy; and we often sent our regimental convalescents from James's Town to Deadwood, for cooler and better air. The clouds moved so steadily and regularly with the Trade Wind that there appeared to be no time for atmospherical accumulations of electricity, and we never had any thunder or lightning. No instance of hydrophobia had been known in St. Helena.

Napoleon was much disgusted at Mr. O'Meara being sent to England, as was natural enough, and shut himself up entirely at Longwood; never stirring out, except to visit Marshal Bertrand's family. He could, if he had so chosen, ride eight or nine miles unattended, except by his own suite, at the period I speak of. There was much difficulty in providing him with a medical attendant. The Longwood people wished to have Mr. Stokoe, the Surgeon of the *Conqueror*; who accordingly repaired to Longwood, with positive orders from the Governor and Admiral to withhold his signature from any bulletin respecting Napoleon's health, which they anticipated would be presented him to sign, on his first duty at Longwood, without first submitting it to their inspection. These orders Mr. Stokoe disobeyed, and was also sent home under arrest; but soon after remanded to St. Helena for trial. Dr. Baxter, Deputy Inspector of Hospitals, was then directed to act; but Buonaparte indignantly refused to see him, coupling the refusal with an unworthy insinuation, that he distrusted any medical man in the confidence of Sir Hudson Lowe–in other words, that he apprehended poison.

Notwithstanding this rebuff, the Governor ordered Dr. Verling, of the Royal Artillery, to take up his abode at Longwood, in a part of the building separated from the western end, which was occupied by Napoleon; to be at hand in case of any emergency. Dr. Verling is an esteemed friend of mine; and I know that he was well qualified in every respect for the duty on which he was employed; being a clever and well educated man, of gentlemanly and prepossessing manners, and long military experience. After he had been four or five months resident at Longwood, overtures were one day submitted to his consideration by Count Montholon, of a very delicate nature, and after some preliminary matter, a formal proposal was made to him of a sum of money equivalent to the principal, of which his British pay was the interest, if he would agree, *sub rosa*, to be the friend of Napoleon, or, as Montholon expressed it, '*l'homme d'Empereur.*' This was indignantly rejected, and the fact reported immediately to Sir Hudson Lowe; accompanied by a request from Dr. Verling, to be relieved from a post where he was subject to such an insult. The Governor, however, would not accede to my friend's request, and Dr. Verling remained at Longwood till the arrival of Dr. Antommarchi.

When this gentleman arrived in St. Helena, the Governor himself brought him to my hospital at Deadwood, and introduced him, requesting at the same time that I would permit him to visit it as often as he pleased; and, generally, that I would give him all the information of a professional nature he might desire, to make him acquainted with the climate, peculiarities, prevailing diseases and general topography of the Island. Of course, I complied with, or rather expressed a wish, to comply with the Governor's wish; for after his first visit the Doctor never did me the honour of coming to the hospital again.

The year 1818 passed away without any thing else particularly deserving of remark. After communications had been opened regularly with Rio Janeiro on one side, and Benguela on the African coast on the other, our Mess improved considerably. We got large bullocks from Africa, which, after a few weeks good feeding, yielded tolerable beef; whilst Rio furnished us French claret at a reasonable rate, that was well suited to the climate, and relieved the bad, earthy Cape wine, the ordinary beverage at the Mess. Tolerable malt liquor was made in James's Town— we found out various kinds of fish—amongst the rest a delicious little Schomber, called the 'Old Wife'; and Turtle would drop in from Ascension occasionally– sometimes of prodigious size. Notwithstanding this improvement in our living, the superior quality of every thing used at Longwood at this time, was notorious. The Purveyor for that establishment found means always to monopolize the best meat, and his daily cart conveying provisions to Longwood often underwent the envious scrutiny of our officers as

they met it in the course of their rides—and the peevish exclamation—'We can't get any like that for the Mess,' was generally
the result. Captain Hunn, of the Navy, uterine brother to Mr.
Canning, after a cruize round the Island with him in his fine brig,
made me a present of a noble fellow—the father of Turtles—as the
Easterns would say—that weighed eight hundred pounds. I distributed the rich flesh amongst my friends for three days; and the
shell afterwards made the roof of a small hut at Francis Plain, in
which a soldier of the regiment and his wife resided.

About this time an order was issued by the Governor permitting fifty persons, selected by Marshal Bertrand, to visit at his
house without any formal leave, as was necessary before. This
list included several of the Garrison, and myself amongst the
number; and I often availed myself of the right of *entrée* to call
on the Bertrands, and enjoy the amusing and animated conversation of the Countess. One day after a long chat, when in
particularly good humour, she said—'Come here Doctor, come
here—I am going to pay you the highest possible compliment—I
shall measure your height by the standard of the Emperor's
stature.' So saying she led me to a white door, and pointed out
two pencil lines, one of which she had drawn as the height of
Napoleon, when he stood with his back to the door—and the other
he had made when she took his place. It was a comfort, when
considering the immense disproportion in our intellectual stature,
to know that I beat him by two inches in the physical. Madame
Bertrand, who was very tall, also beat him by an inch. She playfully remarked, when pencilling my height above the other two
marks—'There, Doctor—yours is a proud position—standing above
the tallest lady in the Island, and the greatest man in the world.'
Of course the reply was, that my enviable situation was due to
the kind condescension of the finest woman in both. A lady will
forgive a bull for a compliment.

Another day, when visiting at Longwood, I found Madame
Bertrand in a very different mood. It appeared that her two white
kids, great pets of the children—particularly of Hortense, her
beautiful little girl—having unfortunately trespassed on the Emperor's little Chinese garden, were slain by his own hand. The *on
dit* was that he had become very irascible lately from the circumstance of a bullock belonging to the East India Company having
broken into this private spot. On this invasion of the 'sacred

territory', (poor man—his France was now reduced to narrow limits,) he called lustily for a gun, and wounded the intruder severely. Not long after the innocent kids jumped over the boundary; and a fit of the Corsican again coming on Napoleon—he shot them both.

When Mr. O'Meara quitted the Island, he represented the state of Buonaparte's health as very bad, and pronounced him to be labouring under a severe and dangerous disease of the liver, for which he was then taking medicine. Montholon even asserted in his letter to Sir Hudson Lowe, that in removing the physician from his patient, when this course of medicine was commencing, 'a great crime was committed.' Yet the fact is, there is the strongest reason to believe that at this time the Emperor was in his usual health, and had not even touched medicine, to which he always had the greatest objection. Every body knew that Buonaparte was quite a sceptic respecting the utility of physic, and trusted only to abstinence to set him right, when out of order. He had often told Las Cases and others, that man was a machine intended to last a certain time, and he would never permit the hand of a doctor to wind him up. But it now suited his views to make it be believed that he entertained every confidence in Galenicals, and was become all at once the best patient in the world.

After Mr. O'Meara's departure, when Napoleon was said to be so dangerously ill, time wore on, a year elapsed, but no change took place; whereas, if real Hepatic disease had existed at that time, the self-imposed confinement of the patient, and the refusal to avail himself of the proffered services of a skilful physician residing under the same roof, were circumstances calculated to increase and develop the mischief. Reasoning in this way, we came at length to the conclusion that the malady spoken of had no existence, and was merely simulated for political purposes, and to keep alive the flagging interest in Europe for an illustrious captive pining away in hopeless captivity.

In the beginning of 1819 the 20th Regiment came out from England, and soon after relieved us at Deadwood; when our Head Quarters were moved to James's Town.

We found the town a much less agreeable quarter than the highlands. The air was hot and confined—the sun became overwhelmingly powerful, sometimes, in the middle of the day; and the radiation of heat from the smooth surfaces of the lava rocks on the precipices jutting over the houses, was annoying and almost insupportable. The clouds, that cooled us in the higher regions and often gave us more of their contents than was agreeable, appeared to be nearly dissolved and dried up by the hot air shooting high from our ravine, and only occasionally yielded a mizzling rain.

The hottest spot in the town was the Officer's Guard-House, situated near the landing place, under an enormous projection of black rock. His occupation, like that of his brethren on Guard in every part of the world, and in all services during peace, was sufficiently monotonous—still, there was a good view of the Bay from his window, and moving objects in and about it were not wanting to give employment to his telescope. A boat from the Flag Ship would push off with an officer on board—a cruizer would drop in after her week's watch round the Island, or a merchant vessel brush round Buttermilk Point to take up her berth at the anchorage—a gigantic surf would sometimes pitch the spray into the Guard-Room windows; or a fleet of Flying Fish dash into the Bay, pursued by Albacore, Bonitos and Dolphins. Occasionally a Shark would be visible close to the surface, with his large dorsal fin sticking out of the water.

Some of these voracious monsters round the Island were of prodigious size: the capture of one this summer caused quite a sensation in our little society.

A bombardier of the Royal Artillery, posted at a battery near Lemon Valley, got drunk, fell from the rocks into the sea, and was drowned. Careful search was made for the body, but without success. A week after a large shark was seen astern of the Flag Ship, at anchor at James's Town, and after some difficulty from his great size, was caught in the usual way. They were obliged to fasten two nooses of rope round the monster before they could hoist him on deck. When the sailors had hauled the fish in triumph to the forecastle, and were cutting it open, the first object that presented in the maw was the blue sleeve of the Artilleryman's jacket, which was found nearly entire, and contained some fragments of bones—all that remained of the poor wretch. The shark's head was purchased by the Company to which the man belonged, and the capacious jaws were hung up to dry over the gate of the barracks at Ladder Hill. Two or three times when riding in, I have lifted it off the nail, and put my head, cocked hat and all, into the prodigious mouth; although it had been shrunk very much in size by exposure to the sun.

The Flying-Fish abound in the Bay near the shore, and the little boys catch them off the rocks with crooked pins. As I said before, they are nice and delicate eating, much resembling Whiting in taste. Some are very large, and we one day saw an urchin haul one out of the water that was twenty inches long, with its ex-tremely beautiful and delicate wings—the pectoral fins—of great size, and the most exquisite workmanship.

During our time the East India Company employed about six hundred Chinese labourers in St. Helena. Before we arrived they had always lived in peace and harmony, and cultivated their long tails, and picked up their rice together with chopsticks, (an evolution difficult to the uninitiated) at their meals in great good friendship. But in 1818, a religious feud broke out amongst the Chinamen which separated them into two hostile parties—totally broke up and disorganized their society, and was attended with actual fisty-cuffs and even bloodshed.

It seemed that the orthodox followers of Confucius, or Yu, as they called him, far outnumbered the disciples of Fo; but the Budhists—somewhat after the fashion of dissenters generally—made up by greater zeal and activity what they wanted in numbers. Besides, they had the great Fung-Mun-Rhin-Ko-Chinn, as a Leader and Chief—a venerable straw-coloured, pig-eyed prophet, with a tail five feet long. Such was the virulence of the con-troversy that the whole of these people were one day arming themselves with pistols and various weapons, and preparing for a pitched battle, so as to make it necessary to call out our Grenadier Company to disarm them, and quell the disturbance.

A Chinese was hanged for murder in James's Town in 1819. The Bonze or Priest who attended him in the gallows—a tree near the barracks—went through a great many religious ceremonies before the criminal was turned off. The whole concluded with placing a letter written on a wafer on his tongue, which he was directed to swallow at the last moment. This, it appeared, was a recommendation of the soul of the culprit to the care of the High Priest of some very sacred Temple in China, by which it would pass on its way to the other world. The temporal effect of this mystic ceremony was to lull the apprehensions of the poor man, who never moved, but seemed quite passive and resigned during the whole proceedings. A group of our officers occupied a good position near the tree, and could see that the last act of the man was to swallow the wafer.

Gentlemen of the medical profession meet with strange treatment in China, according to general report; and when unsuccessful in their practice, are subjected to the *lex talionis*, and made to suffer for the death of their patients. Few of us, I take it, would enter in practice under these conditions. The Emperor Kien Long's system was much more rational; for His Majesty only stopped the regular salary of his physicians when his health got out of order, and restored it when he recovered. There were one or two possible abuses of this plan, however, which might bear hard on the Imperial Doctors–Kien Long might indulge too freely over his cups, and mulct their pay every time he had a morning headache–or the Emperor might now and then sham sickness to save his purse. On the whole, the European practice is more convenient.

The labourers of St. Helena were on one occasion preparing to act on the Draconic principle of life for life, with reference to one of their number who was sick. This was a weakly old man of seventy, who had the misfortune to labour under Popliteal Aneurism; which is an enlargement of the principal artery of the leg, and if not cured will burst suddenly and destroy life. The cure consists in exposing the artery in the thigh, and tying it with a string above the diseased part. After a consultation with another medical man and myself the operation was decided on, and very well performed by a little hump-backed Doctor in the Company's Service, who had charge of the Chinese. At this advanced age, when the circulation is apt to get languid, recovery after the operation is somewhat doubtful. Fortunately the old man did well–and lucky was the cure for the Doctor; as it came out afterwards, that three hundred of the labourers had engaged in a conspiracy, and bound themselves by oath to assassinate him if the patient died.

We had three Commissioners in Saint Helena; from Austria, France, and Russia, viz: Baron Sturmer, Le Marquis de Montchenu, and Count Balmaine. These gentlemen were never recognized by Napoleon, who would not see or hold any intercourse with them. Perceiving after a short time, that the illustrious

Captive was quite safe in the vigilant custody of Sir Hudson Lowe, their station became altogether a sinecure—they enjoyed themselves as they might, and gave themselves no concern about him.

The Baron was a very pleasing, gentlemanly person, with a pretty Parisian wife, but no family, to their great regret. The Count was also a gentlemanly man, but somewhat eccentric—nevertheless very social and amusing.

Foreigners laugh at our English modesty and delicacy—particularly in love matters. We generally choose seclusion and privacy when making tender avowals, and shrink from obtruding any of the little manœuvres of *la belle passion* on the gaze of a third party. Effect and display and éclat are, however, so necessary to social enjoyment on the Continent, that even a *tête-à-tête* with one's Mistress requires a certain *quantum* of publicity to give it the proper zest. When Count Balmaine was making love to Miss Johnstone, Lady Lowe's daughter, we used to meet him at dinner at Plantation House, and when the gentlemen left their wine to join the ladies in the drawing room, the Count, another officer of our regiment and myself, generally retired together. On seeing Miss Johnstone sitting between her mother and Lady Bingham, the enraptured Commissioner would give his arm to each of us and saunter in front of the ladies—nudging us every minute or two, gazing on the betrothed, and pointing out her various charms, *en connoisseur*, with the greatest enthusiasm, 'Look my dear friend—*O ciel!* what a neck—*Dieu d'Amour!* what an exquisite bust—what a profile—what an expression—what an *ensemble* of charms!' Of course, as in duty bound we could only acquiesce—'Look at that attitude,' he would resume—'how delightfully easy—how graceful.' 'Happy Count' we would reply—'happy Count, with such a prospect—you will be *furieusement jaloux*—you will let nobody speak to your wife—*n'est ce pas vrai?*' 'O que non—*pas du tout je vous jure*—but see, Lady Bingham rises—*il faut me nicher—il faut me nicher—Adieu.*'

Count Balmaine married the lady after a long courtship. She was young and handsome, and the gentleman neither the one nor the other. There was a gay wedding at Plantation House, and great mirth and enjoyment. At dawn the next morning a disconsolate individual was noticed wandering alone through the grounds, and the gossip of the Island amused itself for a week with various stories of some trick that had been played; and of shut doors and barricaded bed-chambers. But whatever truth there might be in these reports, it is certain that I met the Count and his fair Bride riding out three days after, happy and glorious – that I felicitated the parties and got cake and gloves.

Napoleon was much in the habit of saying that the Marquis de Montchenu was the greatest fool in France. He was one of the oldest of the French Nobility, and had been Page of Honour to Louis the Fifteenth, and in attendance on that Monarch the night he died. The Marquis had emigrated, but returned to France on the first Restoration – followed the fortunes of Louis the Eighteenth to Ghent – came back with the King, and was rewarded by the appointment of Commissioner to St. Helena.

The Marquis de Montchenu was much addicted to the pleasures of the table – more, however, in a solid than a liquid state – in fact he was a *gourmand*; and it required little medical sagacity to foresee that an inactive life with such habits, and in the climate of James's Town, where he resided, must be followed by bad consequences. Accordingly, although warned repeatedly, having still followed the same course, he was taken ill in the beginning of 1820, and requested a professional visit.

I found him sitting without his coat, and with his waistcoat open, puffing and perspiring with the heat, and busily employed in hunting for his Complaint in a French Translation of Buchan's Domestic Medicine, which was lying open before him on the table. He wanted me to assist him in the search; but having no wish for a consultation in that quarter, he was told that either Dr. Buchan or myself must be discarded. Seeing me very positive, the book was thrown into the drawer, and the patient was put under treatment, very similar to that forced upon Sancho Panza, Governor of the Island of Barataria, by Dr. Pedro Snatchaway.

I attended the Marquis for several months, and finding his recovery was slow in the valley, he was recommended change of air to the higher part of the island. As soon as Sir Hudson Lowe heard this he invited him to Plantation House, and I rode there to see him two or three times a week, until his health became perfectly established. As I had had a good deal of trouble and many hot rides in the course of his illness, and did not conceive myself called upon to attend him on any score of duty, charity or friendship, I had a right to expect, if not a handsome fee, at least an acknowledgement of my services in the shape of a trinket, however inconsiderable in value. But the excellent Marquis, who prided himself on being a good scholar—that is to say, on writing French grammatically and orthographically—a quality by no means common even among persons of the highest rank in France—no doubt considered that he gave me something a great deal more valuable; for on leaving the Island he sent me the following note, which is so good that I shall give it an honourable place in my humble history:

Ce 21 mai 1821

Monsieur le Docteur

je ne sais pas si j'aurai le plaisir de vous voir avant votre embarquement, pour vous renouveller tous mes remercimens des soins que vous avez bien voulu prendre de moi pendant ma maladie. ils m'ont été bien utiles, ainsi mon estime, ma reconnoissance, et mon eternel attachement font ils si bien graves dans mon cœur qu'ils sont ineffaçables.

C'est pénetre de ces sentimens que j'ai
l'honneur d'être, Monsieur le Docteur
Votre humble et
tres reconnaissant serviteur
(Signed) MONTCHENU

Vous devez voir par
mon ecriture que j'ai
toujours mes tremblemens
A M. le Docteur Henry

Who would exchange such a letter for a Gold Snuff Box?

10

A rapacious Brigadier humbugged · Death of Napoleon · The post mortem.
The route for England · Dolphin fishing

S IR GEORGE BINGHAM, an officer much and deservedly liked,
had gone to England in 1819, and was succeeded by a
man of a very different character–of narrow mind and sordid
disposition; in short, an unamiable combination of miser and
martinet.[38] He quarrelled with our Commanding Officer, because
he could not get unlimited fatigue parties from the regiment to
work on his grounds, gratis; and in consequence annoyed us all
as much as he could–harassed the corps with drills and field-days,
and availed himself of any trifling irregularity to insult it in
General Orders.

This officer resided near our Head Quarters at Francis Plain,
where he farmed some acres of land from a poor octogenarian
widow; which he cultivated *à la* Cincinnatus; but he beat the old
Roman hollow in fattening his own cattle and making money of
his mutton. Poor Mrs. P— thought at first she had found the
nonpareil of tenants, for she received every week nice presents
from the General–a dish of sweet-breads, a neat little roasting
rib of beef, or a leg of lamb; but she soon had reason to change
her opinion, when she saw every article charged at the highest
rate, and deducted from the rent. Major H—, the Brigade Major,
was also taken in like the old lady. He found on his table one day
after coming in from riding, a kind note, accompanied by a quarter
of mutton, which he ate in due time, with all the relish that unsuspecting credulity and fine flavour could confer–but was
horrified by a memorandum of its price before the end of the
month.

Now, not having the fear of the Commander in Chief before
his eyes, the writer determined to expose and raise a laugh at
the Brigadier for all these shabby proceedings. Accordingly, a
number of placards were secretly printed and stuck up one night
all over the town. One of these was sent to Plantation-House,
another to the Flag Ship–each Regimental Mess in the Island
got one, and the General himself had the pleasure of finding

one next morning on his breakfast table. The notices were as follows:

ADVERTISEMENT

The public are respectfully informed that Brigadier General— will kill a fat bullock at his house on Wednesday the 10th instant, and three fat sheep on the Friday after. Beef, from 11d. to 1s. per pound according to the piece. Mutton—Hind Quarter, 1s.1d.—Fore ditto 11d. The General farther gives notice that Tripe is to be had at a reasonable price, and Geese are grazed on his grounds at one penny a-head per week—the Ganders to pay double.

By Command

The reader who can enjoy a joke, may judge of the sensation these placards excited next day in the limited circle of St. Helena, where —'s stinginess was notorious. The risible muscles of the community certainly had no sinecure for four-and-twenty hours. Even the Governor laughed, but the Brigadier stormed, and Commanding Officers were directed to assemble their officers, and take every step to find out the audacious wag. It was with the gravest complacency that I listened to the lecture Colonel Nicol gave us on the occasion. Measures to ensure secrecy had been carefully taken, however, and the author of the libel was never discovered. It may be added that the unseemly practices against which it was levelled were effectually stopped, and Cincinnatus thence-forward only cultivated his cabbages and live stock for his own table.

The beginning of 1821 passed away with little change in our Island affairs; but in February it began to be known that Napoleon was seriously ill; and, in addition to his bodily sufferings, had lately undergone much mental distress from certain reports of the infidelity of the Empress Maria Louisa, that had found their way to Longwood. He complained of constant pain at the pit of the stomach, with sickness and total loss of appetite; and suffered great agony from two or three emetics in succession, which his surgeon, Antommarchi, prescribed. At length he declined all medicine, and flung the last potion that was offered out of the window.

Signor Antommarchi had been a pupil of the celebrated Mascagni, at Florence, and was a good anatomist, but not remarkable for a profound knowledge of the other therapeutic sciences. There is good reason for believing that the Emperor never had any confidence in him. General Montholon told me that on the arrival of Signors Bonavista, Vignali and Antommarchi, at Longwood, they respectively underwent the keen scruitiny of Napoleon. The two latter gentlemen were Corsicans; and, according to my informant, Cardinal Fesch, who conceived the Emperor's countrymen would be agreeable to him, had made a great mistake in sending them, as he could not endure them. However, this may be, Bonavista, who was a South American Bishop and a learned man, passed the ordeal creditably; as did the Abbé Vignali, though a man of far indifferent attainments. But the Doctor being an inferior Chemist, broke down when undergoing an examination in that science, of which Napoleon had picked up some of the elemental principles. Montholon farther stated that on this occasion the Emperor waxed very wroth and ordered Antommarchi out of his presence, with the courteous mittimus–'*Va-t-en–bête!*' The poor Doctor came immediately to Montholon to complain of the treatment he had received, saying he was *un homme perdu*. He was told not to despair, and assured that the fit of passion would soon be over. Montholon farther advised him to solicit an interview the next day, acknowledge his imperfect education and deficiency in Chemistry–throw himself on the mercy of Napoleon, and promise to improve himself, if his Master would condescend to lend him some of the Chemical books in the Longwood Library. The story goes on to say that this plan succeeded; but I doubt the fact of his ever having acquired any considerable part of the Emperor's good opinion, as Antommarchi was the only individual of his suite at St. Helena who was not mentioned in his Will, though afterwards pensioned by the family.

The state and ceremony which the Great Man still maintained amongst his dependants at Longwood were sometimes carried to a ridiculous extent. No one was ever allowed to be covered in his presence in the garden or about the Longwood premises, we were informed; nor even in his blandest mood, when conversing in great good humour with his suite, was any of the highest rank–even the Grand Marshal Bertrand–permitted to be seated. Up to the last hour of consciousness this etiquette was preserved, and Antommarchi more than once alluded to this in conversation with me on our voyage home; declaring that he had been often exhausted to the verge of fainting, by preserving a standing posture during his long attendances in the dying chamber of Napoleon for the two or three last days.

In March matters began to look serious at Longwood; and towards the end of the month, Buonaparte, having now become very weak and being in great pain, consented that an English medical gentleman should be sent for. In consequence, Dr. Arnott, Surgeon of the 20th Regiment, then quartered at Deadwood, was requested to attend.

From the first, Napoleon appeared to be aware of the nature of his malady; referring it to disease of the stomach, of which his father died, and with which the Princess Borghese was threatened. There is much ground for believing in the hereditary transmission of a tendency to stomachic ulceration in his family: for exclusive of himself and his father, the Princess Borghese and his other sister Caroline, formerly Queen of Naples, are stated to have died of this complaint. His own feelings appeared to confirm this idea, and Arnott assured me at the time that his patient would often put his hand on the pit of his stomach and exclaim—'*Ah! mon Pylore—mon Pylore!*'

The 4th of May was an unusually stormy day in St. Helena, where the wind not only always blows from the same quarter, but is also for the most part of uniform strength. At two o'clock in the morning an officer of ours, who had slept at Plantation-House the night before, came galloping to my door, bare-headed, and only half-dressed, with a summons for me to go instantly to the Governor's—his youngest child being taken suddenly and dangerously ill. Messengers had also been despatched to James's Town, and night-signals made by telegraph for farther medical assistance.

I found the little patient—an infant of eight months—apparently gasping its last under a terrible attack of Croup; and the peculiarly distressing sound of the spasmodic and stridulous breathing audible over half the house. It was plain that without prompt relief the poor child would be lost. 'The child must instantly be bled,' I said. 'Good G—, Sir,' said Sir Hudson, 'bleed an infant of this age!' 'Yes,' was the reply—'else the child will be dead in ten minutes.' 'But, Doctor, you won't be able to find a vein.' 'We'll try.' So the little sufferer's arm was bandaged—a tiny vein opened, and when three ounces of blood had flowed, the breathing became comparatively quiet and easy; and after some medicine had been given, the child fell into a sound sleep. In this state it was when the other medical men arrived.

During my residence in St. Helena opportunities of observing minutely the character of Sir Hudson Lowe were not wanting; and I believe nobody could fill all the ordinary relations of domestic life and of society better than this much calumniated man. He was, to my certain knowledge, a kind husband and father, and I believe an excellent Magistrate and Civil Governor. He obtained the consent of the Slave Proprietors in the Island, with some difficulty, to abolish Slavery prospectively in 1818, without receiving any compensation; and carried the humane instructions of the British Government into effect on this delicate question with much address and talent. The abolition was dated with grace and propriety from Christmas Day; after which doubly auspicious day for the blacks, no slave could be *born* in the Island, and the supply by importation had long been stopped. Perhaps this cautious and judicious disenthralment would have been a good model to follow in the great change that has lately been effected in the West Indies, and might have prevented some of the evils that have already ensued—and more that are yet to result from a sweeping and premature emancipation.

The morning of the 5th of May continued very blustery and stormy, and, according to the old notion already alluded to, the conflict of the elements was symbolical of the violent struggle of a master-spirit with the last enemy that was then going on at Longwood; for Buonaparte was dying.

I remained at Plantation-House with my little convalescent patient. The Governor went early to Longwood, staid there the whole day, and did not return until all was over. The important event of the day was naturally the chief topic of conversation in the evening, as Sir Hudson took a hurried dinner previous to writing his despatches; and in bare justice to an ill-used man, I can testify that notwithstanding the bitter passages between the great Departed and himself, the Governor spoke of him in a respectful, feeling, and every way proper manner. Major Gorreguer, I think, observed that the deceased was the most formidable enemy England ever had; and the writer, that Providence appeared to have taken that favoured Country under its special guardianship, and covered the Island for many centuries with a shield of adamant, against which all hostile Potentates, from Philip of Spain to Napoleon, had shivered themselves to pieces. 'Well, gentlemen,' said the Governor, 'he *was* England's greatest enemy, and mine too; but I forgive him every thing. On the death of a Great Man like him, we should only feel deep concern and regret.'

The body was examined in the presence of Bertrand and Montholon, one or two officers of the Governor's Staff, and all the Medical Officers of the garrison, with some of the Navy, and Antommarchi, Surgeon to the deceased. Sir Walter Scott's account of the persons present on this occasion is not accurate, as two or three gentlemen who attended are omitted in his history. The principal medical officer, Dr. Shortt, Physician to the Forces, directed the Writer to minute down the appearances and to write the bulletin which was afterwards published; although his name was not appended to that document, because he was then only Assistant Surgeon, and the Governor had directed that no officer under the rank of Surgeon should sign the bulletin.[39]

Death had marvellously improved the appearance of Napoleon, and every one exclaimed when the face was exposed, 'How very beautiful'; for all present acknowledge they had never seen a finer or more regular and placid countenance. The beauty of the delicate Italian features was of the highest kind; whilst the exquisite serenity of their expression was in the most striking contrast with the recollection of his great actions, impetuous character and turbulent life.

As during his eventful career there was much of the mysterious and inscrutable about him, so, even after death Buonaparte's inanimate remains continued a puzzle and a mystery; for notwithstanding his great sufferings and the usual emaciating effects of the malady that destroyed him, the body was found enormously fat. The frame was as unsusceptible of material disintegration as the spirit had been indomitable. Over the Sternum, or breast-bone, which is generally only thinly covered, there was a coat of fat an inch and a half thick; and on the Abdomen two inches – whilst the Omentum, Kidneys and Heart were loaded with fat. The last organ was remarkably small and the muscle flabby, in contradiction to our ideal associations, and in proof of the seeming paradox, that it is possible to be a very great man with a very little Heart.

Much anxiety was felt at the time to ascertain the disease of which Buonaparte died. Mr O'Meara had represented the Liver as the faulty organ, and this had been echoed by Antommarchi; though, as was said before, the illustrious sufferer himself, with better judgment, referred the mischief to the Stomach as its seat and source: and he was perfectly right, as the event proved. This organ was found most extensively disorganized; in fact it was ulcerated all over like a honey-comb. The focus of the disease was exactly the spot pointed out by Napoleon–the Pylorus, or lower end where the Intestines begin. At this place I put my finger into a hole made by an ulcer that had eaten through the Stomach, but which was stopped by a slight adhesion to the adjacent Liver. After all, the Liver was found free from disease, and every organ sound except the Stomach.

Several peculiarities were noticed about the body. He appeared at some time to have had an issue opened in the arm, and there was a slight mark like a wound in the leg; but which might have been caused by a suppurating boil. The chest was not ample, and there was something of feminine delicacy in the roundness of the arms and the smallness of the hands and feet.*

The head was large in proportion to the body; with a fine, massy, capacious forehead. In other respects there were no remarkable developments for the gratification of the Phrenologists.

The diseased state of the Stomach was palpably and demonstrably the cause of death, and how Napoleon could have existed for any time with such an organ was wonderful, for there was not an inch of it sound.

Antommarchi was about to put his name to the bulletin with the English Medical gentlemen, when he was called aside by Bertrand and Montholon, and after this conference declined signing. The reason was, no doubt, that such proceeding on his part would contradict the diagnosis of Mr. O'Meara as to disease of the Liver. With the object of supporting O'Meara, and also of throwing odium on the British Government, a new insular disease, called 'Gastro-Hepatitis', was found out for the nonce,

* *Partes viriles exiguitatis insignis, sicut pueri, videbantur.* (Author's footnote)

The author's delicacy in putting into Latin his observation that Napoleon's 'private parts were seen to be noticeably small, like a boy's' was presumably done so as not to shock his female readers, who would not be expected to understand Latin. Today perhaps some male readers will not be insulted at being provided with a translation into English. (Editor)

of which Buonaparte died. Now, I will broadly assert that we had
no such disease, nor any other endemic in St. Helena. We had
some rare instances of Hepatitis, or inflammation of the Liver,
amongst the soldiers, when much exposed to the sun in the valley
of James's Town, but not one twentieth part of the number we
used to have in India. At night, too, from wet and exposure the
men would catch Diarrhœas; as under similar circumstances they
would any where else, with Pulmonary complaints, besides; from
which we were remarkably exempt. But, as was before observed,
that cannot be an unhealthy climate where a twelvemonth passes
without a death amongst 500 men—as was once the case at Deadwood—and where during five years, and with an average of about
forty officers, we did not lose one by disease.

The body of the deceased Emperor lay in state all the 7th of
May in full military costume, during which time almost every
respectable person in the Island paid Longwood a visit. On the
morning of the 8th, all the Garrison off duty, the Governor and
Admiral, with their Staff—a great number of Naval Officers, and
Foreign Commissioners—many ladies and gentlemen, and half the
population of St. Helena attended the funeral.

When the Hearse bearing the body came to a point whence
there was only a foot-path down to the grave, the Coffin was removed from it and carried to the willow-trees at the bottom, on
the shoulders of twelve Grenadiers of the 20th, and twelve of the
66th Regiments. Two Protestant Clergymen attended as well as
the Abbé Vignali, but only the latter officiated. After the funeral
service the body was deposited in the grave—the Heart being
sealed up in a silver vessel full of Alcohol and put in the Coffin.
A signal was then made and three salvos of fifteen guns, and three
volleys of musketry from a line of three regiments—repeated
grandly in a succession of fine echoes from the hills and ravines—
sounded the requiem of NAPOLEON BUONAPARTE!

Two days after the final obsequies, an officer of the 66th and
myself were taking our favourite ride towards Sandy Bay Ridge,
when we met the Bertrands and General Montholon going to
Plantation-House, and turned to accompany them as far as the
gate. Madame Bertrand informed me that their object in visiting
the Governor, was to convey to him the Emperor's last request
that the past might be forgotten, and that a reconciliation should
take place between the parties. Such was their story; and we found

afterwards that Sir Hudson Lowe, although doubting its truth, acted on the supposition that such had been the dying wish of Napoleon. The tale was too evidently got up from interested motives, and too inconsistent with the inveterate hostility Buonaparte had manifested towards the Governor to the last, to be very credible. The man who could, in the near approach of death, deliberately pension the assassin of his great enemy in his Will, was not very likely to act so amiably. However, the story answered its purpose—peace was made between the Suite of Napoleon and Sir Hudson and Lady Lowe—the party lunched at Plantation House, and dined there the day after, when the *élite* of the Island, the Garrison and the Fleet, were asked to meet them; and several subsequent large parties were made for them, both in the country and at the Governor's residence in town.

The Island appeared relieved from an incubus by the death of Napoleon, and that disagreeable state of watchfulness, restraint and coercion, under which all had felt themselves so long, was at once relaxed. The sentries were withdrawn from the numerous commanding points about the rock—the cruizers ceased to interfere with strange vessels—the fishermen resumed their labours without police surveillance; and the *taboo* was every where taken off. Yet St. Helena, on the whole, had been much benefitted by the presence of Buonaparte—great sums of money had been disbursed by the Garrison and the Fleet; an improved tone had been communicated to the insular society—the blot of Slavery removed—agriculture stimulated; and the wretched goat-paths turned into good roads by military labour—to say nothing of prospective advantages from future visitors, attracted to the rock by the celebrity it had now obtained.

When about to quit St. Helena, some of the foreigners were found to be considerably in debt to the shop-keepers in James's Town, and one of the highest rank amongst them owed no less a sum than between nine hundred and one thousand pounds. Payment being delayed, legal measures were threatened, and all was consternation at Longwood. In this dilemma, application was made to the Governor, who handsomely guaranteed payment of the debt; thus removing the principal difficulty in the way of their embarkation. I have heard that the amount was paid soon after their arrival in Europe, and I should expect nothing else from the high character of the distinguished debtor. This generous behaviour of the Governor, together with other acts of kindness to the exiles after Napoleon's death, notwithstanding the abuse they had all, publicly and privately, showered upon his character, shew that Sir Hudson Lowe was a very different man from what he was represented by his enemies at the time, and what the world still believes him to be.

And now that the strong Garrison was no longer required, preparations were made to send some of the troops to England. The 66th was directed to prepare for embarkation, after a high compliment in General Orders from the Governor—contradicting in the most ludicrous manner some splenetic Brigade effusion of our worthy Brigadier, the mutton-monger, of the day before. The French people, too, were to be disposed of; and the *Camel*, a good ship of five hundred tons, commanded by a Master in the Navy, was got ready for their accommodation. Mr. Ibbettson, the Commissary, laid in an excellent stock, and Head Quarters of the 66th, two Companies and the Regimental Band, were sent on board, with the writer to take care of them. On the 21st of May, after dining with a farewell party at the Castle, the Suite of Napoleon came down to the wharf in the Governor's carriages, accompanied by himself, his Staff, and a large *cortège* of respectable persons. A barge from the Flag Ship was in waiting, which immediately brought them to the *Camel*, attended by Colonel Nicol. In the course of a couple of hours the baggage and stock were safely on board; and the same evening we weighed anchor and sailed for England.

The Suite of the deceased Emperor consisted of Marshal and Countess Bertrand and their four children, Napoleon, Henri, Artus and Hortense—Count Montholon, Dr. Antommarchi, the Abbé Vignali—Marchand, Buonaparte's principal and favourite valet—besides four or five other servants. The Bertrands, Montholon, the Priest and the Doctor, messed with the Captain and our four officers. Marchand presided at a good servants' table.

The run of six hundred miles from St. Helena to Ascension is plain sailing, and the wind always as fair as possible. The sea-sickness soon wore off our friends—the Band played all the evening—our fare was good—the weather fine, and our voyage thus commenced auspiciously. But, when we approached the Line, we lost our refreshing breeze, and were tossed about helpless by the swell in the mirror-like ocean. I had no enjoyment, except in looking out for Sharks, and killed fourteen of these monsters during this voyage.

The young Bertrands were remarkably fine, good-looking children—Napoleon and Henri, handsome and sprightly boys—Hortense, a very lovely little girl of eleven—but the youngest, Artus, a sweet fellow of three years old, was a great pickle. He had learned several naughty words from the soldiers about the Longwood stables, and these he would often apply to his Mamma, when she refused him any thing he asked at dinner, after a fashion that was laughable enough. There was a large white Newfoundland dog on board, that had been given to Madame Bertrand by one of our officers. This noble animal was Artus's horse, and carried his little master regularly for an hour or two every morning and evening along the quarter-deck; and, indeed, Cæsar appeared to enjoy the promenade fully as much as Artus; allowing his long silky hair to be pulled about, and all kinds of tricks played on him with the most philosophic good humour possible. It was very pretty and interesting to witness the perfect harmony between the petulant child and this fine dog; and great was the pity that we had no Landseer on board to sketch them. As the weather became warm, the pitch that exuded from the seams of the deck marred the beauty of Cæsar's sleek sides sadly, covering them with black, unsightly lines, so that the servant who attended Artus was obliged to provide the dog with a saddle, to save the little gentleman's white trowsers.

When Artus saw me catching the first Shark with a piece of pork, he insisted on trying his hand at the same amusement. As every whim of the child was instantly gratified, a tiny bit of pork was put on a hook, fastened to a line, which he always carried when taking his ride on Cæsar, and took into his little cot every night. Few children could have been more petted and spoiled; and if he has not turned out a self-willed and passionate young man, it certainly was not for the want of careful cultivation of these amiable qualities.

Hortense was a general favourite—quite amiable, sweet tempered and lively, and extremely handsome—giving promise of becoming a magnificent woman. She has been married, it is said, to an American gentleman of good fortune and character; who will not be displeased, I hope, to hear such good reports of the girlhood of his wife, nor to be informed that I possess a beautiful lock of her hair, which was one day cut off in a frolic on board ship.

Our conversation often turned on the events in St. Helena. Madame Bertrand was very frank and communicative generally—now that reserve was no longer necessary—and acknowledged that the Longwood people had found no difficulty in maintaining a clandestine correspondence throughout with their agents in London. She told us, to our surprise, that two British Officers of the Garrison had been the chief agents in contravening the regulations of Government, and in forwarding letters and parcels to England. General Montholon made himself very agreeable; being clever, courteous, and most gentlemanly—besides being an admirable *raconteur*. It is true that he was occasionally a little hyperbolic, and some marvellous stories he told of his exploits with the French Army in Spain, and certain scandalous anecdotes concerning the private history of the ladies of the Thuilleries under the Imperial regime, required to be listened to, *cum grano salis.*

I believe that Marshal Bertrand was the most honest and honourable man of the Longwood Establishment—perhaps of the whole Court of Napoleon; and on all other subjects than those immediately referring to the Emperor himself, of unimpeachable veracity. But falsification, deliberate and systematic, had been so firmly and thickly wound round the Imperial portals, that every person privileged with the *entrée* became, voluntarily or involuntarily, involved in its meshes. Marshal Bertrand has made unfounded assertions respecting Captain Blakeney, of the 66th, contained in a letter to Count Las Cases, and published in the Eighth Volume of that gentleman's Journal. There are also several exaggerations, and some positive mis-statements, which he was, no doubt, commanded to promulgate—such as, snares laid for the Emperor to insult him when riding—affronts intended for him by the sentries, &c., &c. There never could exist in any British soldier's breast, a wish or thought of insulting Napoleon—the desire and the act would be to respect the fallen greatness of his unhappy condition.

During one very interesting conversation with Marshal Bertrand respecting the Battle of Waterloo, and the last advance of the *Moyenne Guarde* up the slope of the English position in the evening, I presumed to state my opinion that on that great occasion Napoleon had been wanting to his own illustrious name as much as to the French Army, in failing to lead them on to the attack. 'Why, M. Le Marechal,' it was asked, 'why did not the Emperor, in this very agony of his fate, act over again the heroism of Arcola or Lodi? When he knew that all was now at stake–his last reserve brought up, and the Prussians clustering thickly on his right; but that one daring burst through the English centre might in an instant change the aspect of the whole battle, and perhaps enable the Emperor to break up the Coalition and dictate Peace at Brussels. When he must have been aware that his presence at the head of this chosen Column would inspire the men with a burning enthusiasm scarcely to be resisted, O, why did he abandon them from an ignoble apprehension of personal danger? How differently would we speak of him at this moment, had he then perished at their head! It was become absolutely necessary for his own character then to dare the worst, for the world had begun to doubt his personal intrepidity in action.'

To this appeal, made under the influence of strong feelings, the Marshal replied that the Staff around Napoleon had seized the bridle of his horse, led him aside, and prevented him by force from heading the Guards when mounting the position. To this it was replied–'This is a poor subterfuge, M. Le Marechal–which of you would have dared to stop him, if the will to go on 'had impelled him? No–no. When you saw him blenching, and perceived that the violence would not be unacceptable, you forced your Chief into shelter, and kept him there, whilst Fate was mowing down his last hopes on the slope of the English position! Yes, M. Le Marechal–you know in your soul that Napoleon–however a plausible sophistry may try to excuse him–was then wanting to himself, to his devoted Army, and to France.'

This was the truth, and the honest heart of Bertrand felt its force. I even saw a tear gather in his eye; but, true to his Master, he defended him to the last.

After stagnating for five or six days under the Line, and seeing nothing but the sun and the sea–covered with the empty bottles that had been thrown overboard; which undulated on the calm surface around us much longer than we wished–we at last got a gentle air, which freshened into a steady breeze, and bore us along in high spirits. During the greater part of the voyage the writer enjoyed a delicious shower-bath in the mizen-chains every morning before any body was up. A couple of sailors, having each a bucket and a long cord, got into the rigging over his head, and poured water on him from the height he wished—sometimes as far up as the yard-arm—which was the *altissimum*. Dr. Antommarchi tried the same experiment one morning; but being of delicate frame the shock was too great and half killed him, so as to require two or three tumblers of Champaigne to set his blood once more in motion.

One day when going very smoothly through the water, we fell in with a shoal of Dolphins, which immediately attached themselves to the ship, and gambolled about the quarters and stern very playfully and picturesquely. I tied a couple of Salmon-hooks on a line of whipcord, and commenced fishing with a small bit of pork fat. The shoal formed a wedge of forty-five fish; for occasionally they would swim in such close and quiet order under one of the quarter-boats, that we could count them with great ease in the bright sunshine. One large fellow, who appeared to be the commodore, was conspicuous at the apex of the triangle, swimming along leisurely with the ship—then only going three or four knots an hour. I singled him out for my prize, and dropped the bait close to his nose. On seeing the white object descending through the clear water, two or three fish made for it; but when they perceived their leader shew a wish to gorge the tempting morsel, they dutifully retired. The commodore then seized the pork, and when he was well hooked he was hoisted up from the head of the squadron—to their great astonishment, no doubt. He was a fine shaped and very large Dolphin, weighing thirty-four pounds.

Let not the sentimental reader be utterly shocked at the sad and unromantic sequel. Alas, the barbarous truth, how painful soever may be its avowal, must be told. Instead of watching the beautiful play of colour in the rich golden skin, which is developed as life leaves these classic fishes—the poor commodore was handed over to the black cook, and ordered forthwith to be converted into chops; for it was dinner time. The fish turned out excellent, with much salmon flavour.

There were many opinions on board as to the reception which the Suite of Napoleon would meet on their arrival in England; and some even doubted whether they would be permitted to land. Madame Bertrand herself anticipated rough and rude treatment, but her husband's good sense, which was always conspicuous, induced him to laugh at her fears. The Writer never had the shadow of a doubt in the matter, and often represented to the desponding lady that fidelity, such as theirs to their fallen Master, would, probably, be better appreciated and more highly esteemed in England than any where else: for if any attribute pre-eminently distinguished the great people she was now about to visit, it was generosity. The English nation would not stop a moment to consider—as might be done elsewhere,—whether, in attaching themselves to Napoleon and following his fortunes in the hours of his distress, they had not adopted the most prudent course which their proscribed state and desperate circumstances admitted. The English would solely view them, after alleviating and sharing their Emperor's exile and sufferings, as martyrs of high and chivalrous devotion to him. They would be respected by all parties in England for it would be the wish of all to compensate now in some degree for the necessary severity of the measures in St. Helena, by acts of kindness to the friends and followers of Napoleon, when that great Disturber of the world had ceased to exist.

Near the Azores we met a very heavy gale, which rose suddenly and very nearly threw the ship on her beam ends; blowing every stitch of canvass to ribands, except a new foresail, in five minutes. The dead lights had not been put in the stern windows soon enough, consequently one terrific wave beat in through the cabin, and set poor Madame Bertrand and her family afloat in all directions, to the imminent risk of one or two of the children's lives. Bertrand, the Captain, our Colonel and myself, remained on deck, whilst my brother officers, happy rogues, were asleep in their cots—Montholon was paralysed by sickness—Antommarchi and the Priest were dreadfully frightened; and the latter in particular. Poor man, he must have thought it was all over—so piteous were his ejaculations, and so fervent his Latin prayers.

Our breakfast the next morning, after the gale, was uncomfortable enough; for there was still much swell, and the stomachic agitations of most of the passengers rose and fell in unison. Sea sickness, however, being an 'ill of life', which neither Captain Webb, Colonel Nicol nor myself was 'heir to', we sat down to the meal as usual; and at length had it all to ourselves.

The cabin of Madame Bertrand was a sad scene in the morning; but the mops and swabs and brooms being set to work, and every assistance afforded, the half-drowned inmates began gradually to revive; and we even heard a giggle from Hortense at the remembrance of the calamities of the night, before our breakfast was over.

We made the Land's End on the 29th July, and after a couple of days' delightful sailing along the coast of England—which looked a hundred fold more fertile and attractive than ever—contrasted with the black desolation of the Rock we had just left, we anchored at Spithead on the evening of 31st July 1821.

11

Garrison duty in England and Ireland · George IV · Lord Strafford's debt ·
Lord Enniskellin on riot control · Rudeness of Lord Palmerston

W E arrived at Spithead at the time George the Fourth was
at Portsmouth on his cruize to Ireland. As soon as that
courteous Prince heard that the Suite of Napoleon had reached
England, he despatched two Noblemen of the Court to the *Camel*
to make enquiries as to the health of the Countess Bertrand; a
piece of Royal condescension that made a great impression on
that Lady, and tended much to dissipate her fears of an unkind
reception. Still she was apprehensive of rudeness from the lower
classes, if permission to land were granted. Madame Bertrand
observed that she had often heard that the King of England was
the very first gentleman in the world, and she was now convinced
of the fact. So much value lies in a bit of civility.

Oysters had just begun to make their appearance when our
good ship dropped her anchor, and we were next morning surrounded by several shore boats with these delectable little fishes—
besides fruit, eggs, milk, fresh bread and butter, and other edibles
likely to find favour after a long voyage. Consequently, I am sorry
to be obliged to disclose the fact that at breakfast we had a scene
of indiscriminating and somewhat hazardous voracity; for scarcely
any animal but an adjutant or an ostrich could have escaped subsequent inconvenience from so large and heterogeneous a meal.
Oysters were prime favourites with all the foreigners, and were
first attacked—then all other eatables in rotation or combination—
and *such* combination. First, oysters *soli*—then oysters and goose-
berries—strawberries and poached eggs—beef-steaks and cherries—
mutton cutlets and red currants—black soles and green apples—
with fresh rolls, new potatoes, &c., &c. were devoured by all—
children included—and as for Artus, he ate like a little cormorant.
The result was more inconvenient to the parties than its details
would be agreeable to the reader.

About one o'clock the Writer availed himself of the return of
the Health Officer's boat to go to Rhyde; intending to spend the
day with a friend at Newport. The place we had left was not

celebrated for its tailors, consequently we had deferred getting plain clothes until our arrival in England, and he now went ashore in uniform. This rather *outré* costume in a Rhyde boat gave rise to an odd enough circumstance.

George the Fourth in his Yacht, attended by a couple of Frigates and a Tender, besides several private Yachts, had come out of Portsmouth as we stepped into the boat; and was now making a sweep round the Roads towards the Needles on his way down the Channel. From a wish to get as near a peep as we could of His Majesty, our boat was steered for the Royal Yacht, whose course we were now crossing. At this time the vessel was not more than two hundred yards from us, and we saw the King, dressed in his blue jacket, white trowsers and foraging cap, reconnoitring us through a spy-glass. As our boat still kept its course towards the Yacht, and the Writer's red coat and cocked hat were conspicuous and rather puzzling objects (ugly and anomalous as the Surgeon's dress then was), and the vessel was leaving us fast, the civil persons on board backed the foresail and lay to. Probably they wished to examine the non-descript in the boat more narrowly, or imagined that something had been forgotten at Portsmouth, which we were now hasting to bring on board – or that despatches had just arrived from town. From whatever cause it originated, we felt very much obliged to Sir Charles Paget or His Majesty, for it gave us a clear view of all on board. We passed close astern, taking off our hats, which was gracefully returned; and it may be added that few persons can thus say with truth, that they stopped the course of a King of England, sailing in his own ship, under his own Royal Standard, and on his own waters.

The Isle of Wight appeared a Paradise after St. Helena; and the drive from Rhyde to Newport delightful. When walking after dinner with some ladies through a flowery field, the Writer threw himself down on the velvet grass and clover, from sheer enjoyment once more of the English soil, and rolled over like a horse or an ox.

Far from receiving them with coolness or incivility at Portsmouth, and refusing them permission to land, intimation was given the French people, that whenever it would suit their convenience, the Admiral's Barge should await their pleasure to bring them ashore. This was accompanied with an invitation to dinner. Eleven o'clock in the morning of the 3rd of August was the hour fixed on; and at Madame Bertrand's request the Writer agreed to dress himself in red and accompany the party, as a kind of protection from the apprehended rudeness of the mob—a chimera which still haunted her imagination.

At the appointed hour, the Barge was in waiting and the whole party went ashore. The Fortifications were covered with a very large crowd of spectators, and when we landed—as had been predicted to Madame Bertrand—a most respectful silence was observed, and the foreigners appeared, as they deserved to be, the objects of interest and respect.

It was necessary to go to the Alien Office to pass through certain formularies of enrolment, &c. When we landed at the Point, carriages were in waiting, but the party preferred walking. The Countess took the Writer's arm—the Marshal gave his to Hortense, whilst Montholon conducted two of the boys, and Antommarchi and Vignali brought up the rear. The Priest must have imbibed strange notions of English ferocity, for he was in as great a fright as if about to be roasted in some Cannibal Island. He stuck so close to the Writer's skirts, that his panting breath was felt moist on the neck, whilst the toes of his boots were very inconvenient to the hinder part of the white trowsers.

After the business at the Alien Office had been concluded we all repaired to the Crown Inn, when the Admiral, Commandant, and principal people of the town waited on the exiles, and every civility possible was paid them.

Marshal Bertrand and Count Montholon dined with the Admiral. The Writer remained for the day at the Crown with the Countess, and in the evening we took the children out for a walk on the ramparts. The little people expressed great surprise at the redness of people's faces in England. As we were returning up the High-street, a well dressed, foreign-looking gentleman passed us slowly; stopping for an instant to clap Napoleon on the back, and addressing him—'*Mon petit ami sois toujours fidèle comme ton père*'. Next morning the Writer bade the whole party (now reinforced by the arrival of Mr. O'Meara from London) good bye, and returned to the *Camel*.

The ship weighed anchor for the Nore the next morning early, and a delightful sail we had up Channel in company with some hundreds of vessels; all of which we passed with ease. When off Dover the Flag, half-mast high, shewed us the Queen was dead; which few on board regretted, as she had become the tool of faction and was likely to do mischief. Finally, we left our good ship, and arrived in Chatham on the 13th of August.

Who does not instantly run up to town on setting foot in England after a long absence, and what Cynic can there be who will not then enjoy its pleasures? A friend and myself got a week's leave and started the morning after our arrival. At this time the controversy about the Queen was the great topic in England: a lady, the only other passenger, entered warmly into it, and abused the King lustily for the whole stage of ten miles. She called him a tyrant, an adulterer, a glutton, a whole host of bad names; and concluded by expressing the wish he might be drowned and feed the fishes on his way to Ireland. We did not interrupt her for an hour; but then gently informed her she had talked all this treason a little imprudently in the presence of total strangers, who happened to be Officers in His Majesty's Service. The poor lady was much frightened, and continued mute as a mouse all the remainder of the day.

We arrived in London the day of the Queen's Funeral, when serious riots, with loss of life, had occurred, and much more serious mischief was apprehended. The day was dark, with mizzling rain; and from many long faces we met, it seemed as if people were apprehensive of some great calamity. But the day passed; and next morning the mighty tides of human beings rolled eastward and westward through the vast city as quietly and as regularly as before.

The regiment was ordered, soon after, to Sunderland. In passing through Lincoln a couple of the officers ascended the Bell-Tower of the beautiful Cathedral on a windy day. We found a prodigious vibration at the top, and during one strong gust, as we were preparing to retrace our steps, there was no small ground for apprehension that great Tom might take a fancy to accompany us down stairs. To those Cognoscenti who make it their business to hunt after new sensations, we would recommend a visit of this kind as a probable source of novel excitement.

There is not much, except coals, to be seen at Sunderland. The iron bridge over the Wear, however, is a fine object—its span large—the structure gracefully light, and the elevation and position, striking.

One is reminded of Paley at Bishop Wearmouth, of which place he was Rector. The Writer often traced this eminent man in his trouting excursions along the banks of the Wear, half-way to Durham; and heard many stories from the old country people, of the good Doctor's affability on these occasions. By all accounts, Dr. Paley was a better philosopher than fisherman, and more skilful in persuading his delighted readers to follow the line of his induction, than remarkable for success with the illogical trouts in any other line.

We had a dreadful gale from the south-east when quartered at Sunderland, and three or four vessels were driven ashore close to the town. The sea ran frightfully high, and the piers of the harbour and line of coast were covered with thick masses of spectators, anxiously watching some ships in the offing that were making for port. The Life-Boat was got out in the very crisis of the storm, and we had the delight of seeing the gallant fellows that manned her, impelling their craft in the most admirable manner through the surf, and picking off half a dozen men from a brig that had been driven on the rocks a little while before, and was now going to pieces.

Soon after this happy escape, a ship was seen a mile distant, making for the harbour, which has a very narrow entrance. Down she came before the wind, under a close-reefed topsail—her hull and half her rigging now and then hidden from sight by some monstrous intervening wave. As she approached we could perceive either that she was steered unskilfully, or obeyed her helm very badly, and the sailors on the pier began to be alarmed lest she should broach to, before she made her port. On she came, however, labouring and pitching dreadfully in the terrific sea; whilst the assembled crowd, holding on their hats and bathed in the spray and rain, watched her progress most anxiously. When the vessel came close to the mouth of the harbour, a tremendous wave, as if determined that the prey should not escape, burst over the stern, and by its irresistible force sheered her in a direction straight for the head of the southern pier, against which, if she struck, she must be dashed to pieces. 'Up helm! Up helm!' shouted a thousand voices, silencing for a moment the roaring of the storm; and we saw three or four sailors obeying the injunction with the force of desperation. Providentially her fatal course was changed, only in the very nick of time; for she actually brushed the pier-head, but passed harmless into the quiet water of the harbour amidst loud huzzas from the multitude.

Ten modern years produce wonderful changes in this whirling world of ours, and it is not easy to keep up with the progress of society, even at home, 'with all appliances and means to boot', how much more difficult to march with any liberal science, away from England and Europe. To endeavour to save his distance in the race of therapeutic knowledge, and to rub off the rust contracted during a ten years' absence, the Writer obtained six months leave, with the intention of passing that period in London and Paris, enjoying himself amidst the medical schools, and making 'dainty comparisons' between the impressions of his juvenile years and the more reflective judgment arising from experience and advancing life.

Nature, ever wise and beneficent, intended there should be no idle people in the world, but that occupation and enjoyment should go hand in hand, mutually enhancing each other. Even the laziest people must find or make some employment; and the gross Yorkshire boor, whose *beau ideal* of happiness with £1000 a-year, was to have nothing to do but '*eeat fat beeacon*', found it necessary to add – '*and swing upon a geate*'. Business is as necessary food to the mental constitution as animal pabulum to the corporeal; and when we add a little harmless pleasure occasionally, to season toil and give it a zest – like green pease to our roast beef – we ensure a healthy condition. Acting on some such notion as this, the Writer during this winter devoted five days in the week to medical observation and study – the sixth altogether to miscellaneous sight seeing and theatrical enjoyment, and the seventh to its own peculiar objects.

The mornings of the London pleasure days were spent at the British Museum, the Exhibitions at Somerset House, one or two private collections of works of *vertu*, and the Picture Galleries of Lords Stafford and Grosvenor, to which he had the entrée. In these the Writer found great enjoyment – not unmixed with a shock to his anatomical perceptions occasionally, on seeing a manifest fracture in the limb of some *chef-d'oeuvre* of a great Master, from incorrect drawing. One day he well recollects he saw Rogers, who was a frequent visitor, frowning at a magnificent Titian Venus in the Stafford Collection, and afterwards endeavoured to trace the cause of such misplaced expression on that pale but placid brow. The Poet's displeasure was well founded, for the Goddess had her right arm broken just above the elbow; yet was looking unconscious or reckless of her misfortune, and smiling with celestial magnanimity.

The Writer joined the regiment in May 1822, at Hull, on the move for its old quarter, Sunderland. During the summer the Duke of Sussex came to Lambton Castle on a visit; and, a day or two after his arrival there was a grand procession down the Wear to Sunderland, with much display of flags, pretty boats and well dressed women – the whole winding up with great eating, drinking, toasting and speechifying. The Duke praised the fine bridge and eulogized his liberal Host, and Mr. Lambton bowed and returned the compliment in neat terms. This gentleman lived in good style, and at the Newcastle Races this year, he sported the handsomest equipage in the field – his four beautiful blood bays in harness, and two mounted by out-riders, harmonizing in colour and shape to a hair.

This summer our worthy old Peninsular Brigadier, Sir John Byng, now Lord Strafford, who commanded the northern district, inspected the 66th at Sunderland. At the Mess dinner, after asking me to take wine, he said–'Doctor, I regret to see you still in the same rank as when we were acquainted in the Peninsula'–to which the reply was, 'you are very good, Sir John, but I assure you, you cannot regret it *much* more than I do; at the same time– if you will excuse the *tu quoque*–I don't perceive that you have got a step since yourself.' This was a slight *gaucherie* on the part of the good Brigadier; for nobody likes to be reminded that his name has an Ass prefixed to it in the Army List.[40]

Lord Strafford is a clever man and a first-rate officer – clearheaded and cool in action, and brave as a lion, as several of us had more than once witnessed during the Peninsular Campaigns, and as has been since demonstrated at Waterloo: yet, notwithstanding these good qualities, and doubtless many others – there is one small shade, His Lordship owes the Writer a sack of oats, with compound interest, since the spring of 1814.

The case stands thus. On the heights of Garris, near St. Palais, there was, as has been mentioned already, a brilliant little affair, and we took a few hundred prisoners – many of whom were wounded. Next day on our advance, these poor people were left in the charge of a very young and inexperienced medical officer. Two days afterwards Sir John Byng said he had misgivings as to the care of these unfortunates, as he had no confidence in the young Doctor who attended them–'So Mr. Henry, I request as a favour of you that you will ride back to Garris–you have a good horse and can soon overtake us–see all the wounded dressed and sent carefully to the rear, then join the Brigade as fast as you can, and I will direct Edwards the Commissary, to issue you a bag of oats in consideration of this extra work.' The Writer executed his mission with despatch; returned and reported himself to the General–but–*coetera desunt*–his horse got no oats.

It is but justice to this distinguished officer–who I hope will pardon my little badinage–to say, that when I dunned him at the mess, he kindly gave both man and horse an invitation to his head quarters at Pontefract, where we might pay ourselves in kind, or any other manner we pleased, but which I could not accept.

In the middle of March we received the route for Liverpool; there to embark for Ireland. The weather was very cold and in-clement at this time, and in the course of one long and circuitous march to avoid Durham, where an election for a Member of Parliament was going on, the men were up to their knees in snow and sleet half the way. In consequence, almost every man caught a severe cold; and many contracted bad chest inflammations; dangerous at the time, and in some instances productive of evil consequences in the shape of subsequent consumptive complaints.

It is not alone in combatting their enemies in the field that British Soldiers risk their lives. Here we had four hundred men at once knocked up by the elements in obedience to a municipal regulation, and under the visionary apprehension of interference with the freedom of election.[41]

Dr. Granville in his Russian Travels, tells a story of a German Physician in St. Petersburgh, who treated his military patients in the Hospital of the Russian Guards, in a compendious manner. At the hour of his morning visit he had them arranged in line, and proceeded from right to left–'*Un, deux, trois, quatre, cinq, six*–saignés–*sept, huit, neuf, dix, onze, douze*–purgés–*treize, quatorze, quinze*, &c. émétique.' Whether this practice was suc-cessful or not does not appear–at any rate it was regular; and to a certain extent the Writer adopted it on this occasion. When we reached Leeds the whole regiment began to cough, as if from one common impulse; and on examination the great majority were found feverish, with pain of chest and impeded respiration. The Writer collected all the sick in the large yard of the Inn where the officers messed, and having opened a dozen veins at once, he bled them nearly to a man. This was repeated in some of the worst cases at the end of the next day's march; and having procured carts for those who could not march, we took them all with us convalescent to Liverpool. Now, in this instance Dr. Sangrado fearlessly asserts 'that he did the State some service'–though unfortunately they don't 'know it'.

We stayed a couple of days at Liverpool, admiring the rising grandeur of that great commercial emporium; and were then put on board some miserable schooners, and had a very disagreeable passage to Dublin.

The transition from English wealth, comfort, cleanliness and neatness, to Irish beggary, slovenliness and filth, is very painful to a stranger, but much more to a rational and observant Irishman. Although by no means disposed to join in the vulgar outcry against the Saxon domination, nor to place the existing poverty and misery of Ireland entirely to the English account; yet I fear that England is now suffering, in the constant embarrassment of her relations with the sister Island, for her own former criminal neglect in one weighty matter.

England found Ireland the scene of cruel civil wars between barbarous rival Chieftains, and made an easy conquest of the Island. The Pope blessed the enterprise and liberally gave over the country to the British Crown; and the first grateful act of England, afterwards, was to assist his Holiness in establishing there the Papal supremacy, and in suppressing the ancient and simpler form of Christianity that had before prevailed.

But, farther–when the Reformation was spread through England, and the Protestant Church was firmly established in the times of Elizabeth and James the First, the English Government took the worst possible way to extend its benefits to the Sister Island. The English Ministers proscribed, according to the general custom of the age; and thus made it a point of honour for the natives to adhere to the Roman Catholic Religion. After three centuries of coercion, the plan was changed; but it was too late. In a word, England might have made the whole of Ireland what the North now is, had she set about it in a spirit of mild wisdom and the purest primitive Christianity–studied the language and customs of the people–sent exemplary Missionaries, like Bishop Bedell, amongst them, and ruled them with impartial justice. She chose to use force in propagating a Faith that disclaims and abhors it, and in the just retribution of a superintending Providence, the turbulence and pauperism of Ireland are now paralyzing her arm and eating into her heart.

But I must quit these grave matters, and proceed with the 66th to Cavan. This is a poor town, but we found the neighbourhood most respectable and hospitable, and many comfortable houses within an hour's ride of the place–amongst which we were disposed to place Castle Saunderson in the first rank; and the visits of ten days or a fortnight under old Colonel Saunderson's roof, are recorded in golden letters in my memory. This gentleman was advanced in years and of infirm health; the kindness of his disposition therefore, induced him to attach a professional character to these visits; although the numerous *agremens* the house afforded, far more than compensated any little services I might be able to render him. First and foremost, there was an excellent Library, in which I luxuriated–often wishing for a Briarean power to read fifty books at once–then all the Periodicals of note; with the backs of the chairs and the fender covered with drying newspapers before the blazing turf fire when we came down to breakfast. Next a pack of hounds–then a billiard table–then fishing in the lake–and a preserve of hares, woodcocks, and snipe, in their seasons.–Lastly, some pleasant people always in the house; with good wines, excellent *pottheen*, and a good table.

I recollect with great gusto, but at the same time a melancholy feeling, my last visit to Castle Saunderson, accompanied by a valued friend of some thirty years' standing–Colonel Goldie. The worthy host was a little deaf, and so was his son, Captain Bassett Saunderson, of the 44th. It so chanced that more than any of the party, Colonel Goldie and I found out the pitch of sound that suited the Governor's auditory nerve; and one of us was generally placed at the table on his good ear side–but bad was the best. Although this position was not particularly agreeable–being the medium of communication between the master of the house and the company at table; and the office no sinecure–yet I liked the old man so much, that the fatigue of my post, as confidential minister on these occasions, was not at all regarded. Colonel Saunderson and his deaf son used, when I sat between them, to complain mutually of each other's bawling. 'Well, I *do* wish Bassett would speak a little lower–he thinks I can't hear a bit'–

and, 'Certainly I should make out the Governor better if he reduced his voice by an octave–why, I declare he'll split the little
nerve I have left.'

The Colonel had several times offered me a fee on leaving his
house, which I always declined, from a feeling that I could not
decently pocket his money after the good things I had enjoyed
under his roof. The last morning I left Castle Saunderson my
horse was at the door, to ride down to the bottom of the avenue
to await the mail-coach, when the old gentleman accompanied me
into the hall. In shaking my hand I felt a bundle of bank notes
pressed into it, which I returned to his, and he thrust them again
in mine; and thus we bandied them about for half a minute. At
last, when he shut both hands against them, I dropped them at
his feet–mounted and cantered off. Now, I happened to be
particularly poor at that precise time; and such is the weakness
of human nature–or, begging its pardon,–mine, that before I
reached the high-road I began to be sorry that I had not the notes
snugly filling up the ugly hollows in my pockets. However, I gulped
down the regret, jumped into the coach, and went off to Enniskillen.

All the world knows how common rows, as they are termed, but
in plain truth absolute battles, are at Irish fairs, and how briskly
the shillelahs jump from one head to another. All the world knows
this; but only a select few have any notion of the cause why so
few heads are broken, or lives lost, on these occasions. A friend
of mine thus explains it.

Beneficent Nature has kindly accommodated animals in all
countries to the necessities of climate, or other imperious external
circumstances. She turns wool into hair within the Tropics, and
hair into wool, besides making a present of an additional blanket,
towards the Poles. She provides white dresses and cloaks for
creatures that require such covering, to screen them from notice
that might end in their destruction, and for other good reasons.
It would be hard, therefore, if she were not correspondingly indulgent to the necessities of the Hibernians, since to the inhabitants of hyperborean regions she is so lavish in her gifts.
Accordingly, we find the important physiological fact demonstrated by Cuvier in his last great work, now printing, intituled,
'Recherches Physiologiques Nationaux', that the Crania of Irishmen, or at least of three hundred and eleven which he had
examined and carefully compared with others, are nearly double

as thick as those of the Celtic tribes generally, and excel those of the other European races in a somewhat larger proportion. It is remarkable that this is more noticeable about the Frontal and Parietal bones, and particularly along the course of the Sagittal suture, than any where else. Nature has thus, in beautiful accordance with her operations in hyperbrumal countries, fortified and defended the skulls of her favourites of the 'first Flower of the Earth', and enabled them to stand, without serious inconvenience, the manifold beatings and belabourings to which she foresaw they would be liable.

We had the pleasure of witnessing one very respectable fight on a fair day at Enniskillen, about three o'clock, when the whiskey was beginning to develop the pugnacious qualities of the crowd. It was very confined in its origin, being only a simple duel between two men with shillelahs at the door of a public-house, but the quarrel extended like wild-fire, and soon pervaded the whole multitude. Thump! crack! crack! whack! thwack! crack! went the sticks on the heads and shoulders of His Majesty's liege subjects; but in consequence of the beautiful endowment discovered by Cuvier, the thwacks and the thumps produced no more effect than a racket-ball against the wall of the Court. In the very height of the battle we saw a stout man, riding on a strong Punch, threading his way amidst the infernal tumult, regardless of the din of oaths and execrations and wood of sticks—knocking at the sconces right and left, and every body shrinking and ducking when they saw him. In five minutes he had cleared the street of the combatants, and restored peace by his sole exertions. It was impossible to see the '*argumentum baculinum*' more energetically or more successfully used. 'He floored the fight in a crack,' as my servant had it. This vigorous peacemaker was Lord Enniskillen.

Loch Erne is the largest Lake, I believe, in Great Britain or Ireland, and eminently beautiful. It is full of green and wooded Islands, and abounds in fish—particularly Pike and Perch; and Trout in some parts. Salmon also run up in large numbers from Ballyshannon. The Trout are thinned by the rapacity of that fresh-water Shark, the Pike; and the stories told of this ravenous fish's boldness in Loch Erne, are almost incredible. One day, when landing a Trout of about a pound, a large Pike darted after it with such force, as to project himself two yards on the shelving sand; where he was made prisoner.

My friend, Colonel Nicol, gave a farewell party at Enniskillen Barracks when we received the route for Boyle, and the dancing was kept up vigorously till day-light. The 66th were always well-conducted and popular in quarters. We marched early the next morning, and half the population of the town escorted us for two miles, giving nine hearty cheers at parting.

In May, 1824, the Head Quarters of the 66th were stationed at Boyle, with three companies at Sligo.

Lord Palmerston has Estates in the County of Sligo, and in September 1824, he paid the town the honour of a visit to inspect their condition, when a large dinner-party was got up for him by Mr. Abraham Martin, a gentleman of wealth and enterprise residing in Sligo. The hour was seven o'clock – we came a quarter after and found the company assembled, but his Lordship had not yet arrived. Half-past seven, three-quarters – eight o'clock struck – still no Lord Palmerston. Then commenced a new quarterly series and went on to nine, but still no Lord. By this time we were all in abominable humour, and I, for one, was ravenous; but the appetite of many of the party had gone off, leaving behind disgust and lassitude and a sense of personal insult. Cake and wine were now handed round, and our sufferings were thus made endurable for another hour. But at the horrid sound of ten o'clock, the whole party rose in open rebellion, took the law in their own hands and rushed down stairs to what should have been dinner.

Half an hour after, when some signs of returning animation had become visible under the champaigne, in marched Lord Palmerston, and shuffling up to the head of the table, apologized to the Hostess for his want of punctuality – his hacks had knocked up – and then – putting on one of his blandest smiles, sat down, saying, 'But I'm glad you didn't wait!'

The regiment moved to Athlone in August 1825. From Athlone to Ballinasloe is only a ride, and two or three of us went to see the Fair. Fancy a huge dusty or muddy plain covered with twenty thousand cows and bullocks, and a hundred thousand sheep; with nine or ten thousand people poking their hands into their ribs – and you have Ballinasloe Fair before you.

We marched to Dublin in October 1825. When we arrived Sir Colquhoun Grant was in command of the Garrison; a strict disciplinarian and the terror of officers commanding corps. 'Your men ride like tailors, and awkward tailors too, Sir,' was a remark often applied by him to Cavalry Colonels—and 'Do you call that handful of men a regiment? Why it is only a detachment, and a dirty detachment, Sir,' would be a polite speech addressed to a *chef de bataillon* of Infantry. Yet, as they would say in his own country, 'his bark was aye waur than his bite'; and although he rather seemed to enjoy making a commanding officer of a regiment tremble in his shoes, or his boots, in front of his men, he was too upright and honest to do him an injury in a report to the Horse Guards, unless he richly deserved to be sent about his business.

We were much in society in Dublin the winter of 1825, which was a very gay season. The Marquis of Wellesley, then Lord Lieutenant, had fallen in love with a pretty American widow and married her sometime before. Being a Roman Catholic, the proceeding pleased the majority of the metropolitans, and the lady managed to disarm the Protestants of any different feeling by her very graceful deportment and fascinating manners. The Viceregal Court patronized the manufactures of the country, and several large parties were given with this object: amongst the rest a grand subscription ball was got up at the Rotunda, under the patronage of the Marchioness of Wellesley, where the ladies were all dressed in Irish tabinets. The 66th officers wore blue scarfs of that peculiar stuff, looped up with gold cords and tassels; which according to the first authority in the room, looked very elegant. We were rather inconveniently placed for enjoying the gaieties of Dublin, being quartered in the Richmond barracks, two miles off: notwithstanding, we managed to come in to two, three, and sometimes four parties a night.

About this time the Surgeon of the regiment, having imprudently indulged at a supper in some doubtful oysters, was attacked with indigestion which was followed by a bad fever that cost the poor fellow his life, notwithstanding the assistance of the Physician General and another Physician. The Writer succeeded to the Surgeoncy of the regiment.

Whilst we were quartered at the Richmond barracks the 58th occupied the other side of the square, and the greatest harmony prevailed between the two corps, who dined frequently together and had whist parties at each other's Mess Rooms. There was a billiard table at the bottom of the hill, on the road to Dublin, where we used often to meet. One day I had been playing with a remarkably fine young man of that corps, named Bell–quite an Apollo in face and figure, and much liked by all who knew him. We played till the dinner bugle sounded, and then agreed to meet at the same place for a conquering rubber next day. The morning after I cantered down the canal towards Portobello Strand, where I saw the 58th at ball-practice. As I rode up I perceived a group assembled, and individuals hurrying towards it from all parts. A vague presentiment of evil, which I have some-times felt before great calamities, came over my mind. On reaching the ground I was shocked beyond expression to find my poor friend Bell just breathing his last, with the blood streaming from his side! He had heedlessly passed in front of some awkward recruits that were firing, with their eyes intent upon the target, and was shot through the body.

In 1826, we were ordered to Birr–or as it is now called, Parsons Town, in honour of Lord Ross, the principal landlord, whose name was Sir Lawrence Parsons. I cannot say much in its favour, for one of our men had his skull broke by a stone held in a man's hand, and another was shot whilst on sentry. The ruffians, how-ever, failed in their murderous object, for both the men recovered.

Our residence at Parsons Town was enlivened by a certain fracas between a Catholic Priest named Crotty, and the Titular Bishop of the Diocese, against whom he had rebelled. Mr. Crotty had formed a party of the town's people in his favour, and, to conciliate the Protestants of the place, his adherents made their band play every night the most notorious Orange tunes; which, from them was almost as absurd as the silly act of pledging the 'Glorious and immortal Memory' in a bumper of Boyne water on the part of Mr. O'Connell. The refractory Priest told the Bishop that his spiritual instructions were as little calculated to benefit his Diocese as a farthing candle on the heights of Dover would be to illuminate Calais. There was no making light of this, so the Bishop excommunicated Mr. Crotty; but he was supported by the majority of the congregation: and when the new Priest, who happened to be the Bishop's nephew–arrived at Parsons Town, and prepared to officiate in the Catholic Chapel the following Sunday, he found Mr. Crotty already in possession, and could not get in. In this predicament he applied to Lord Ross, exhibited his credentials and asked for magisterial support. His Lordship called on Colonel Nicol for military assistance, and two hundred of the 66th were marched to the Chapel to put the right man in possession.

The regiment moved to Limerick in December—a good station, and a place of much intelligence and enterprise. (They had just finished a new Gaol and Lunatic Asylum; each a model in its line.) They had an admirable Club, formed after the regulations of the Kildare-street Club in Dublin, of which the Writer became a member. There were all manner of newspapers and periodicals—Billiards—Whist, but no Hazard—an erudite *Chef-de-Cuisine*, and a good and reasonable Cellar.

On the morning of Christmas Day an express was sent for the Writer from Killaloe, sixteen miles distant, to see one of our soldiers, who had his skull fractured in a fight in the streets the night before. The Surgeon in attendance had bled the patient, and was preparing to trephine—that is to bore a hole through the skull, near the injured part, so as to obtain a purchase by which to raise the fractured piece pressing on the brain—but waited for farther advice before undertaking so formidable a matter. The skull near the top of the head had been beat in, to the extent of half-a-crown, by the angle of a large stone, which a brutal ruffian had used, holding it in his hand; as is but too commonly done in Ireland. No bad symptoms had occurred, and the man was perfectly sensible, although there was a hollow in his skull that would hold half a large walnut. The *medico* wanted to set about boring his hole immediately, *secundem artem*, but was recommended to keep his trephine quiet for a little. In the morning he was advised to put it up altogether; the man having passed a good night, and the brain being evidently prepared to stow away its convolutions in a smaller compass, and accommodate itself to the diminished space. Finally, the patient recovered perfectly; though with an ugly hollow on his head that must sadly have bothered the subjacent organ of veneration.

One night after a party, as an officer of the regiment who had lately joined, and myself, were returning to the barracks, we heard an alarm of fire, and directed our steps towards the light, which was now beginning to spread far and wide. A large range of store-houses, seven or eight stories high, was bursting into a blaze. Immediately after, the Garrison was alarmed, and troops were put in motion to assist the firemen and protect property. We soon saw Sir C[harles] D[oyle] Commanding the District, on horseback, riding about among the crowd, very busy doing nothing, as was not unfrequently his wont. When he recognized us, he accosted my young companion–'Pray, Sir, what's your name?' 'H[eale]y, Sir.' 'Very well, Mr. H[eale]y, take that patrol of the 66th, and march them round yonder angle to protect those barrels of pork. Place a sentry on the west side of the store-house, one on the south and two on the north-east–Do you hear, Sir' 'Yes, Sir; but I don't know how to set about it.' 'Not know how, Sir–why, what the d— do you mean?' 'I mean exactly what I say, Sir C[harles], I joined yesterday, and have only been six days in the Service.' 'Oh, Oh, Mr. H[eale]y, that's very true–you can't know *much* about it yet–but get drilled, Sir; get drilled quick–in the meantime the Doctor will assist you.' So the sentries were posted with all due regularity.

The Salmon of the Shannon bear some proportion in size to the fine river they inhabit, and in the neighbourhood of Limerick they are in full possession of all their marine strength and vigour, but the stream is so broad that the best casts can only be fished from a boat. This takes away much of the zest of the sport; for when one hooks a fine fish it is pleasant to stand firmly on the solid rock, or to feel the turf of the bank springy under one's feet.

In March I commenced my fishing operations, proceeding in a skiff with an old guide, who was well acquainted with the haunts of the Salmon. We trolled through some beautiful holes for an hour without seeing a fish; at last I hooked one, but soon perceived by his want of liveliness and force, that it was a spent Salmon on his way down the river. I brought him to the shore, and landed him without injury; and although the old fisherman begged him as his lawful perquisite, I had compassion on his feebleness, and threw the poor valetudinarian back into the water, with an admonition to make the best of his way to the sea. Soon after I hooked another of the same description, and turned him also adrift. Next, a large Pike, at the imminent risk of my fly, which was a beauty of its kind–this fish was bestowed on the boatman, who appeared somewhat annoyed by the chivalry towards the distressed Salmon. Good actions by land or water are not always unrewarded, and the emancipation of the poor *Salmos* was recompensed by the good luck of hooking soon after a noble fish of twenty pounds, strong and active as a racer, which, after half an hour's interesting play, we secured; we then cut his gills and crimped him, and had him to dinner at the Mess the same day.

In April, we received orders to march to Buttevant, there to form our Depot, previous to embarkation for Canada. Here we were inspected by our old friend, Sir George Bingham, who dined with us at the Mess three days following. Poor Sir George—the grave has since closed over his warm and manly heart! He enjoyed himself with us at Buttevant, as one always does at a meeting with old and valued friends, and we gave him wine as generous as himself; for the last dozen of our noble Madeira, that had sailed with us on the Ganges twelve years before—ripened at St. Helena, and travelled with us ever since—here most appropriately exhaled its nectareous spirit.[42]

The regiment embarked at Cove in June 1827, on board the *Romney*, of fifty guns, and the *Arab* Transport, bound to Quebec. I sailed in the latter vessel.

12

Voyage to Canada · Quebec · The ambassador looks for the lavatory in the dining room · Salmon fishing · Montreal

WE stretched out into the Atlantic with a fine fair breeze, and went on all day as favourably as we could desire; but at night the wind chopped directly in our teeth, and we were obliged to stand away to the south. After this we had a succession of calms, and baffling little breezes, and all kinds of cross purposes, for nearly a month: by which time we were not more than two-thirds of our way.

At length we reached the Great Bank and got soundings, and one day when it was calm commenced cod-fishing. This was a bit of a novelty, but, after all, miserable angling. However we did much execution amongst these lubberly fish, which suffered themselves to be dragged out of the water without making the slightest resistance; killing three hundred of them; of which number twenty-five fell to my share. One of our officers amused himself in opening the stomachs, and a very odd and heterogeneous collection of items he discovered. One Gadus, who must have been an epicure in his way, had an oyster-knife in his stomach, but how he used it puzzled us all: another had a large Cuttle-fish—several had different kinds of shell-fish, and on examining one of the largest of them all a mouse was turned out, perfect, as if recently swallowed—probably an unfortunate fellow-passenger.

At length we saw the low, desolate Island of Anticosti at the mouth of the St. Lawrence, but were a week beating up the river. The little European rivers hide their diminished heads, compared with this magnificent stream. As we advanced, the shores grew bold, and wild, and primeval; with the pines and the rocks as they appeared a couple of centuries after the Flood. This savage uniformity at length became fatiguing to the eye, for nothing was visible but Firs and Granite—not a morsel of a clearance, nor smoke, nor human habitation. At length a straggling house began to peep out of the eternal forest on the Gaspé shore; and as we approached Kamouraska the mountains on that side receded from the shore, and the country became flat and alluvial, but only to an inconsiderable distance from the water. On the north shore the aspect was still abrupt, high and bold, and we could just see the extraordinary fissure, or deep ravine, through which the Saguenay pours its copious tribute. Then begin the long lines of white houses–and the narrow selvages of green along the banks, and every seven or eight miles a shining Church, and the picturesque islands–and the lofty cascade of Montmorency–till we drop anchor in the fine basin of Quebec.

We found the town an ugly cluster of houses, pitched on the extremity of a bald promontory–the streets narrow and crooked, and those built on made ground round the base disgracefully filthy–with zigzag wharves pushing irregularly into the noble stream, whose surface was dotted with shipping. But, after a day or two, we find the place improving in our estimation. We gain the Rampart and ascend to the Citadel, and are delighted with the glorious views on all sides that spread themselves out before us. We visit the numerous sweet spots in the immediate neighbourhood–ride along the pretty banks of the delicate little river, and luxuriate in the prospect of Quebec from Lorette–awake the sleeping echoes of that gem of Lakes–St. Charles–explore the bold rocks of the Chaudière–or gaze up with straining eyes at the lofty torrent at Montmorency. We consider also the historical memorials and associations with which the place is rich–as the scene of the first planting of Civilization and Christianity on this Continent–the toiling and patient Missionary–the listening and wondering Savage–then the transference of dominion to England –the Plains of Abraham–the triumph of the British arms–the refulgent name of Wolfe! Last, but not least, we appreciate it as the impregnable Bulwark of British power, and at length arrive at the conclusion, that in the mind of an Englishman there is no City in North America so classic or so celebrated as Quebec.

On our arrival the regiment was quartered in the Jesuits' Barracks, with the 79th Highlanders–a corps of great name and merit.

We found political agitation running very high when we reached Quebec. The Earl of Dalhousie, the Governor, finding the House of Assembly refractory, had just dissolved them; but he gained little by this step, as most of the old members were again returned, and the House once more chose Louis Joseph Papineau for their Speaker.

This person, since so notorious, had already made himself conspicuous in 1827, by violent attacks on the British Government and the Provincial Executive, both in Committees and at public meetings, altogether inconsistent with the moderation to be expected from the Speaker of the Assembly. The penetration of Lord Dalhousie saw even then the future Traitor in his true colours; for at his own table I well recollect hearing the Governor say–'Mark my words, gentlemen, that man is a political incendiary whose ambition will never be satisfied until he has hopelessly embroiled this Colony with Great Britain.'

The winter of 1827-8 came on early, and we prepared to meet it. At first the sensation of cold in a clear blue sky, illuminated by a bright unclouded sun, was cheerful and exhilarating; and our numerous pic-nic parties, under these circumstances were agreeable. There is no place near Quebec where the mellow and beautiful tints of the declining year are seen to more advantage than the fine woods surrounding St. Charles. This sweet little lake is shaped like an hour glass with a fine echo at the narrow part. It is a favourite resort of pic-nic parties, and abounds in trout, which form a very common dish on these occasions, whilst the echo affords an unfailing source of amusement. Much was the laughter of a bevy of pretty Quebec damsels at one of my idealess brother officers, who, when called upon by them to address the echo, could only draw upon his recollection of the manual and platoon exercise. How intense must have been the disgust of the nymph in her grotto, when forced by a spell she could not resist, to respond to such uncouth sounds as 'Shoulder Arms!' 'Order Arms!' 'With cartridge prime and load!' 'Return ramrods!'

Notwithstanding the Polar cold the Canadian winter is the healthiest season of the year. With the exception of frost-bites, and accidents from carting or chipping wood for the numerous stoves, we had scarcely any sick during the two first winters here. This ought, however, to be qualified by stating that eruptive diseases among the children are more common in winter than summer; and for several years after our arrival Small Pox was rife in the town and suburbs during some part of the cold season. Winter appears also to be unfavourable to canine health, and instances of hydrophobia are not uncommon.

On the 15th of November 1827, we were witnesses to a highly interesting ceremony in Quebec–namely, the laying of the first stone of a Monument to Wolfe and Montcalm, on a commanding eminence overlooking the river. The whole of the Garrison was assembled and fired a salute on this stirring occasion; and the interest of the scene was much heightened by the presence of one of Wolfe's soldiers, a Mr. James Thompson, who was in the action —now a fine-looking, silver-headed veteran, a hundred years old. With condescending attention to the brave old man's feelings, Lord Dalhousie paid him the compliment of presenting him the Masonic Mallet, and requesting him to give the three mystic strokes on the foundation stone.

My Irish countrymen of the lower orders improve much on exportation; and in this colony particularly, they became valuable members of society. They leave behind them much of their turbulence and combativeness, as well as of their mendacious and tipsifying attributes; work quietly, and honestly, and industriously, and generally speaking, get on very well. Several flourishing settlements of Irish are to be found in the country around Quebec; and in the city there is a very large congregation, who have a good and handsome Church, built a few years ago— partly by their own funds, assisted by the contributions of their Roman Catholic brethren in Montreal and Upper Canada; and essentially aided by the liberality of their Protestant friends. It was remarked that the French Canadians were of very little assistance in this matter; for Jean Baptiste is not very liberal of his money, nor has he much to spend—besides he is not very partial to the Irish, nor are they to him.

A virtuous Ecclesiastic, the Rev. Mr. McMahon, of whose tender and assiduous spiritual attentions to sick soldiers of his Communion I can bear testimony, officiates amongst his countrymen. This gentleman devotes himself to the temporal as well as spiritual interests of his flock, and, I believe, is eminently useful in inculcating quiet, sober and orderly habits, and restraining excess. Crowds of Emigrants surround his door at the opening of the navigation, in hopes of receiving advice and assistance from this good Priest; and his hand is open to them all, to the full extent of his limited means. In consequence of refusing to lend himself to the furtherance of Mr. Papineau's objects, and of his care in teaching fear of God, combined with honour of the constituted authorities, Mr. McMahon was long the object of virulent and calumnious attack on the part of that person's followers and the newspapers in his interest.

In the end of autumn 1828 Lord Dalhousie went home, and was succeeded by Sir James Kempt,[43] an admirable military officer, and a clever man. The demonstrations of attachment to his high-minded predecessor were strong and general here among the British part of the community. A grand entertainment was given him by the principal people of the town, a little before he embarked; and when he sailed, a Steam-boat full of Quebec ladies and gentlemen escorted the frigate which took his family home, a considerable distance down the river.

Sir James was a bachelor, and a Governor ought to be a married man for many reasons—one of which is, that the hospitalities of his roof would be more agreeable under the auspices of a lady than a gentleman. During the winter the pic-nic expeditions of Lady Dalhousie were a good deal missed. Her mode of assembling her party on these occasions was to send round a miniature whip, to be shewn to certain persons whom she wished to compose it, on the morning of the day selected. This was the well-known signal for the meeting of the carioles at the Château previous to starting; and the whip, like the torch of fire, soon produced a gathering.

The motion of gliding over the hard and smooth snow on a calm clear day, thermometer ten above zero, is very exhilarating and delightful; and few things in Canada are more joyous than the first burst of a Tandem Club of a dozen neat equipages, with good robing, good driving, a previous good lunch, harmonious bells, and an object.

We had friendly dinners and whist clubs, snug little dances often, with occasional balls. Then there were curling clubs and their dinners, and tandem clubs with their lunches, and snow shoe parties, and hutting or camping out parties, whose object was to acquire a more perfect enjoyment of the comforts of a good warm house by passing a night or two in the woods. As a climax to all, there was the fatiguing excitement of the moose hunt.

In the beginning of the summer of 1829, we had a visit from Mr. V[aughan] the British Ambassador at W[ashington]. His Excellency soon after his arrival, happening to eat fresh salmon rather too freely at dinner, with an accompaniment of new potatoes, *au naturel*, became indisposed in the course of the evening, and sent for the Writer. It so chanced that Sir C. and Lady Ogle from Halifax, were at the same time on a visit to Sir James Kempt, and residing at the Château as well as Mr. Vaughan. A large party was asked to meet the strangers at dinner the next day; but the disconsolate patient was kept on spoon diet and confined to his room by the Doctor. When dinner was over, the servants had retired, and Sir James was in the middle of a good story—the apparition of a pale man in a dressing gown and night-cap, with a bedchamber candle in his hand, and an expression of suffering in his face, stalked into the room. Lady Ogle was the first to observe him, and tittered incontinently at the odd figure: this was soon caught by the rest of the company, and ended in a loud and general laugh. The uproar brought the intruder to a stand still—then right about face, and a hasty retreat. It was the poor Plenipotentiary, who, not yet quite *au fait* as to the topography of the Château, had wandered into the dining room in the course of his evening explorations.

Ninety miles below Quebec, and nearly opposite Kamouraska on the South Shore, the Malbaie river enters the St. Lawrence. After an impetuous mountain course of two hundred miles, it escapes through a gorge, tumbles down a granite rock, and then winds very prettily along a cultivated valley, six or seven miles, until it meets the tide. There is a tolerable wooden bridge at its mouth, whose large abutments, loaded with great boulders, tell of the formidable floods that sometimes sweep down the valley.* A respectable Church with its long roof and glittering spire, and a tall elm or two, stands on an elevated point near the junction of the river with the St. Lawrence.

A very quiet and moral population of seven or eight hundred people inhabit this secluded valley. We are informed that after the Conquest a number of soldiers of Murray's Regiment settled here, intermarrying with the Canadians, and leaving traces of their larger stature and peculiar lineaments, which are still visible. Some of the customs of the good *habitans*, too—social family worship night and morning, for instance—may be of Scotch origin: for, however dissipated the life of a Scotch soldier may have been, he is apt towards the close to shew the salutary effect of former religious instruction. The good seed, whose early germination had been checked by the storms of his profession, seldom loses all

* This bridge was carried away by a flood last spring. (Author's footnote)

vitality, but often brings forth fruit when the turbulence of the military life is past. Be this as it may, the cross appears to have improved the breed considerably: the language of the military settlers, however, which may have been half Gaelic, half English—has yielded to that of the more numerous class, and the whole community now speak French.

Many of the Malbaie families are very large, and from fifteen to twenty children are not uncommon. They marry early—get a stripe of a concession from the Seigneur, and a house is run up for the young couple, *more Hibernico*, by their relations. They are then set adrift, but never separate far from their own connections. There is infinite social comfort in this custom; but the worst of it is that the bit of land is soon exhausted.

Their neighbours in the Bay of St. Paul, on the other side of a long mountain, have a very indifferent character; but the peasantry of this remote and pretty glen are the most virtuous people I have ever seen in any country. As to temperance with regard to spirituous liquors, our good philanthropists who are endeavouring to reform the world in this way would find their labours needless here. Among these primitive people, drunkenness is absolutely unknown; and whole families pass their lives without any individual ever having tasted intoxicating fluids. Some surprising instances of this kind have come to the Writer's knowledge.

I have been on four fishing expeditions to Malbaie, and hope that a short account of one of these may not be tiresome to the reader.

In the latter end of June, 1830, my friend, Major Wingfield,[44] of the 66th, and myself, set out from Montreal on a fishing trip to Malbaie. We embarked in buoyant spirits, well provided with choice apparatus, and taking with us *materiel* for preserving our fish—namely; salt, sugar, spices, and a large cask of vinegar. A good-natured American General, with his Aide-de-Camp, were our fellow-passengers in the steamboat to Quebec. They were heretics of the Utilitarian School, and thought it not a little extraordinary that we should make so long a journey to catch fish that might be so easily obtained in the market.

On reaching Quebec we found to our mortification the wind blowing up the river, strong against us, and no steamboat running whither we were bound. We were therefore obliged to wait there three days, and then take our passage in a miserable schooner from Kamouraska; the Captain engaging to land us at our destination on the opposite shore. The voyage was extremely tedious and disagreeable, lasting four interminable days and nights, though the distance was only ninety miles. Moreover, our lubberly skipper very nearly upset us half a dozen times by bad management during the gale from the eastward that lasted almost the whole voyage. To add to our misfortunes, we were half-starved as well as half-foundered; for our sea-stock was laid in under the anticipation of a few hours voyage, and consisted only of a loaf, a quarter of cold lamb and a bottle of wine. Thirty or forty dirty *habitans* from Kamouraska were on board and occupied the limited space below; we were therefore obliged to wrap ourselves in our cloaks and bivouac under the '*grande voile*' on deck. This was all very well as long as the weather continued dry, but on the third day the rain came down in torrents–often extinguishing our cigars; but we took fresh ones, still maintained our ground on deck, and puffed away bravely, in hope of better times. Towards the end of our wretched voyage sheer hunger made us purchase some bad salt pork, and sausages crammed with garlic, as our own barrels of provisions were hooped up, and if we broke bulk there might be a sorry account of them.

At length, with beards like Jews–cold, wet, half-starved and every way miserable, we reached the mouth of the Malbaie river, where we had bespoke lodgings, at the house of a Canadian, named Chaperon.

On our way from the shore we cast our hungry eyes on a salmon, just come in with the tide and floundering in a net: we incontinently licked our lips and purchased him. When we reached the house our servant handed the fish over to Madame Chaperon, with instructions to boil it for our breakfast–*not* alive, but as near as might be. Our toilet being finished we drew the table to the window, into which a rosebush in full bloom was peering from a flower-garden underneath. There, amidst the mixt aromata of flowers and fish, we commenced an attack on a pyramid of toast fit to form a new apex to that of Cheops–numerous dainty prints of fresh butter, some half gallon of thick cream, and half a bushel of new laid eggs–which was kept up vigorously for a couple of hours.

On Monday morning, July the 5th, we engaged a *calèche* with a good-looking Canadian boy, named Louis Panet, to attend us on our daily visits to the *Chute*, about six miles distant. The road up the valley is very good, following the winding course of the river, and overhung on the other side by green globular hills, very steep in many places. These are covered with a thin soil, which often after rain peels off in large patches, carrying down trees, fences, flocks, and even the houses, 'in hideous ruin and combustion' to the bottom. One of these frightful *eboulements* had fallen across our road lately, and the country people were still busy in clearing away the rubbish.

From my former experience, the first glance at the river assured me we should have good sport. Instantly our fishing rods were got ready, and taking Jean Gros with us we descended the steep bank, got into his crazy canoe, and were ferried across to the best part of the stream.

At the very first throw I rose a large salmon; but although he appeared greedy enough, he missed the fly. Giving my finny friend time to resume the position at the bottom he had quitted, and to compose himself, I then threw the fly lightly over him – communicating to it that slight motion which imitates life. He instantly darted at the glittering deception, and I found him fast on my line. After a moment's wonderment, he dashed madly across the river, spinning out the line merrily, and making the reel 'discourse eloquent music.' This fish did not stop in his career until nearly touching the opposite bank, when he turned – made another run for the middle, and then commenced a course of leaping, a yard or two out of the water. This is a dangerous time, and here unskilful anglers most frequently lose their fish; for each leap requires a corresponding movement of the arms and body to preserve the proper tension of the line. In fact, on these occasions a good angler will make a low *courtesy* to his fish. I played this active gentleman fully three quarters of an hour, when he gave up the contest, and I gaffed and secured my prize – a beautiful male fish, in fine season, weighing twenty-five pounds.

We continued at our sport till mid-day, when it became too hot and clear. By this time my companion had caught a number of large salmon trout, and I had picked up two more salmon and several trout of the same description; marked with the most brilliant colours. We then crossed to the shady side and reposed ourselves; and having discovered a copious spring bubbling through the gravel, close to the water's edge, we enlarged it into a well, into which we plumped our fish and a bottle of Hodson's Pale Ale; covering it with green boughs. We then employed ourselves in collecting strawberries for a dessert to our sandwich; and after lunch enjoyed our cigars, and chatted over our morning exploits.

When the shade of the high bank stretched across the river, we resumed our sport, and returned to a late dinner with our *calèche* literally full of fish. A goodly shew they made, as they covered two of Madame Chaperon's largest tables: the sum total being five salmon, weighing 105 pounds, and 48 trout, averaging three pounds a piece.

Next morning, after an early breakfast, we started for the Chute, taking a tent with us, which we pitched on a knoll overlooking our fishing ground. It proved, however, more ornamental than useful; the banks being so umbrageous that we did not require it by day, and we always returned to our lodgings in the evening.

Nothing mundane is without its alloy. Our enjoyments were great, with one serious drawback—the flies, those volant leeches that surrounded us—and notwithstanding our defence of camphorated oil smeared over our hands, faces and necks—sucked our blood without compunction. A fly is considered a stupid creature notwithstanding his powers of observation, but our Malbaie mosquitoes were insects of great sagacity, for they appeared to watch their opportunity to take us at a disadvantage, and when they saw us occupied in playing a fish, they made play too, and had fifty spears in our skins in half a minute. The little invisible sand flies, too, teased us extremely, and those insidious black wretches, who give no warning, like the honest mosquitoe—these crawled about our necks and up our sleeves, tracking their way with blood.

During our second day's fishing I had a little adventure which was not unattended with danger, though such was the excitement of the moment that I was scarcely conscious of it. Having observed a large salmon rising at a fly in the middle of the river, I got into the canoe and made old *Jean Gros* pole me out to the spot; kneeling as we were often obliged to do, for fear of upsetting the unmanageable little craft. I soon hooked the fish, and making my Charon stick his pole firmly into the bottom, we brought our tiny vessel athwart it, kept our position against the force of the current, which here ran very strong, and having a fine range of the open stream I played the fish for half an hour until he was quite subdued. *M. Jean* was then desired to weigh anchor and push for a shelving sandy bank where we had been accustomed to gaff our salmon. In pulling up the pole, which was shod with iron, the old man, by some inexplicable awkwardness, lost his hold of it—away the rapid stream bore us, whilst the long pole was left standing perpendicularly, vibrating still and shaking its head at us very ominously.

Jean Gros' shoulders elevated themselves to his ears instantly, and his wizened and corrugated face was elongated some three or four inches to the obliteration of manifold wrinkles that adorned it. It was irresistibly comic, and I could not help a loud laugh, though it was no joke. We had no paddle nor any thing else to assist us on board, and were running at six knots an hour towards the jaws of a dangerous rapid. My old *Voyageur*, after his first astonishment, uttered one or two indecent oaths, like a veritable French Colonist; then, apparently resigning himself to his fate, became paralysed with fear and began to mumble a prayer to some favourite Saint. In the meantime some good-natured *habitans*, who had been watching us playing the salmon, ran down the shore, parallel with us, when they saw us drifting down; flinging out to us every stick they met for the chance of our catching and using it as a paddle. All this time the salmon remained on the line, and my large rod occupied one hand entirely, and prevented much exertion in stretching for the floating timber; but as for abandoning rod or fish—neither was to be thought of for a moment. Once I overstretched myself and canoe and all were within an ace of being upset. At last success attended us—I secured a piece of board, and the first employment of it was the conferring a good sound thwack on *Jean Gros'* shoulders, accompanied with '*Ramez! s—, ramez!*' The effect was electrical—the old fellow seized the board and began to paddle vigorously, steering, as we approached an island, down the smaller branch, where the rapid could be passed with safety. By great good luck our co-voyageur in the water, took the same channel, and down the stream we all went merrily for half a mile. The rapid ended in a deep and quiet hole where the fish was soon gaffed; and after a little rest, and a *coup* of brandy to the old man, notwithstanding his delinquencies, he placed the canoe on his shoulders; I carried the fish and we returned by the bank.

We spent a delightful fortnight at Malbaie, killing many fine salmon, and a great number of magnificent trout; whilst we employed our servant, when we were fishing, in pickling, smoking or salting them. But the season became dry—the river fell, and the fish ceased to run in any considerable numbers. Towards the end of July we struck our tent, embarked in a large boat and proceeded twenty miles down the North Shore of the St. Lawrence, with the intention of exploring a small salmon stream, called 'La Riviere Noire,' which it was said, had never been fished.

The North Shore of the great Canadian Estuary, is an interesting field for the Geologist; and it has not yet been half explored. Indeed a comprehensive and scientific research through both these great Provinces is yet to be made; and would, I am persuaded, develop great natural riches, as well as many objects of curious enquiry.

It was a fine afternoon when we left Malbaie; the river was calm, and the white porpoises, those unwieldy looking creatures, were tumbling about in all directions. We had guns and tried a few shots without effect—the balls *ricochetting* off their smooth and oily skins, whenever they struck them. As it approached sunset our Canadian boatmen began a quartetto, by no means inharmonious, though the voices were rough enough—and kept it up with great spirit nearly all the rest of the voyage. At midnight we arrived at the mouth of the river, where we found a fine dry sandy beach, with a line of creamy surf rippling gently against it, in a wild and uninhabited country. We landed, found plenty of wood to kindle a large fire; ate our supper, which we shared with our *voyageurs*; for which they gave us another song under the exhilarating influence of a *coup* or two of brandy. We then wrapped ourselves in our cloaks, looked out for a soft stone for a pillow, placed our guns by our sides, put our feet to the fire and soon fell asleep.

The morning sun awoke us: we started up and took a refreshing swim in the salt water, whilst our attendants were getting breakfast ready. When the meal was over we prepared our rods and set out to reconnoitre the stream, the banks of which were covered with almost impenetrable jungle; but, after great exertions, we explored to the distance of four or five miles, yet only got one small salmon, which my friend caught, for our pains. The river, as far as we could reach, was a continuous succession of rapids and falls from one enormous granite rock to another.

On our return we disturbed a huge bear, who was busily employed in tearing up a large rotten pine to get at a colony of ants that inhabited it. We stopped and so did he; feeling, no doubt, as displeased as any christian, at being interrupted in his meal. He then walked away, and as we had left our guns at the boat, we felt no inclination to follow him.

Next day we returned to Chaperon's and the following morning visited the Chute, and found that a fresh batch of fine trout had made their way up the river, low as it was, which afforded us capital sport; rising greedily at our salmon-flies, and very lively and strong on the line—but we could see no salmon until late in the evening, when we noticed a very large one sucking at some small flies in the middle of the stream. We embarked in the canoe, and both covered him, endeavouring to tempt his palate by various flies resembling those on the water; using at the same time a single gut casting line, but all in vain. At last, just before starting for home, I tried one more cast over him, when he rose like a young whale, and I found him firm on the hook. The tackle was slender, no doubt, but the delicate fibre that held him prisoner was of the best description, and, though of nearly invisible tenuity, possessed great strength, which the flexibility of a long and admirable rod materially assisted. Great was the 'certaminis gaudium' during the exciting play of that noble fish, and many, many apprehensions had we of the result. But the staunch O'Shaughnessy kept its hold, and the tenacious gut failed not. Finally, after a glorious struggle of an hour and a quarter, this magnificent fish lay gasping on the sand. It weighed twenty-eight French pounds, or about thirty-one English.

On the 3rd of August, we returned to Quebec with two barrels of fish for distribution amongst our friends; and I guess if our utilitarian Yankee acquaintances had met us then, we should have been less the objects of their derision.

In the month of September 1829, The Honourable Matthew Bell, a gentleman residing at Three Rivers, took me up in the Boat to see his eldest son, who was in a bad state of health. Three Rivers is a straggling town, built on a sandy bank a little above the confluence of the St. Maurice with the great river, and deriving its name from the three mouths of this tributary. My kind host has a comfortable, well kept, and English-looking establishment here; and is the Lessee of the Government Forges, an Iron

Foundery five miles up the right bank of the St. Maurice, where he has a little colony of three hundred Canadians to whom he gives employment.

Two days after our arrival we visited the Forges. These are situated in a ferruginous tract of country, containing a considerable quantity of superficial patches of bog iron ore, lying in the vicinity of a forest which contains hard wood for charcoal. Mr. Bell obligingly conducted me over the premises, and pointed out all the mysteries of washing the ore, fusing, casting and hammering; processes on a smaller scale, but differing little otherwise from what the Writer had before seen in Scotland. Mr. Bell's workmen appeared contented and comfortable: they occupied good cottages with a small plot of garden attached to each. When we had seen all the lions of the place, we went to dinner in an old French mansion, finely perched on a high bank of the river, where we joined the ladies of the family.

There was talk during the meal of a bubbling spring at the bottom of the bank; and the Writer hazarded an opinion that the well might contain Carburetted Hydrogen, and would probably ignite if fire were applied. When the gentlemen were over their wine, the ladies, acting on the hint, made the workmen carry down a pan of live coals from one of the fires, and when we joined them afterwards, we found the spring blazing away briskly, surrounded by a large group of the Canadians with the greatest astonishment depicted in their black phizzes.

Our third winter in Canada commenced early and continued long without, however, favouring us with a *pont* across to Point Levi, which is a great desideratum at Quebec. In politics, the aspect of matters did not improve—on the contrary the financial difficulties began to thicken. The Home Government were willing to give up the King's Revenue, amounting to about one third of the fiscal income of the Province, to the disposal of the House of Assembly, on the reasonable condition of a small Civil List for the King's life, being voted; which should assure a certain degree of independence to the Governor, the Judges and three or four principal officers of the Government. But this arrangement, however rational and equitable, by no means suited Mr. Papineau, whose object was to concentrate all power in the Assembly, and to have every officer, from the Governor downwards, dependant for their bread on himself.

Towards the end of the session, it was plain to close observers, that Sir James Kempt was beginning to be not a little disgusted with Mr. Papineau, and to perceive that his own position, notwithstanding all the flummery and flattery at the beginning of his administration, was becoming daily more difficult. Foreseeing little good to be done in the work of reconciliation, where one of the parties was pre-determined to continue hostile, like a wise man he abandoned the scene of present strife and future mischief, and asked for permission to go home.

Desertion is a military crime of painfully frequent occurrence in the corps quartered in the Canadas. The vicinity of the States, and the high price of labour there, are sufficient inducements with the worthless characters that will be found in all regiments, to overcome all considerations of honour, all sense of duty and allegiance, and all fear of punishment. We suffered less than several other regiments; but still we lost many men, although every exertion was made to put a stop to this disgrace.

It would be the interest of the Government of the United States, as much as ours, to enter into some international arrangement for the discouragement and eventual suppression of desertion, by mutually giving up deserters. They suffer even in a greater proportion than ourselves; for according to several reports of different Secretaries at War, which the Writer has read, the number of desertions has averaged more than one-third of their whole Standing Army, for the years embraced by these official documents.

In May 1830, the regiment left Quebec for Montreal. During the stay of three years, the conduct of officers and men had been exemplary, and the Magistrates addressed a highly complimentary letter to the Commanding Officer at its departure to this effect. The evening was fine when we embarked; and as the steamboat passed under the Citadel, its lofty ramparts were crowned with the soldiers of the Garrison, and crowds of the inhabitants, who cheered us repeatedly as we shot up the river. These affectionate demonstrations were echoed and prolonged from the heights above the Coves, amongst numerous spectators, for a considerable distance above Quebec.

Montreal is a city of great merit and promise, built at the limit of the ship navigation; though even for this it is a little too high. It rejoices in the pretty little mountain from whence it derives its name – the pleasing Island of St. Helens – great intelligence and commercial enterprise, and a grand Roman Catholic Cathedral of modern erection, which towers superbly over the whole city, and

is, I believe, the most majestic Church on this Continent, east of Mexico. Montreal is built on the southern side of a large island, formed by the Ottawa and St. Lawrence at their junction. These two streams, although at last they blend harmoniously, keep a separate establishment for the first three our four miles after their union; and at Montreal, about a hundred yards from the bank, the line of demarcation between the clear water of the St. Lawrence and the dark current of the Ottawa, is very conspicuous.

The water of the river here disagrees with strangers, and produces unpleasant effects for the first week or two. Our regiment experienced this to a certain extent on our first arrival, but the inconvenience soon went off, and we found Montreal a healthy and agreeable quarter. Yet, according to statistical information collected by my friend Dr. Kelly, of the Royal Navy, from authentic sources, the duration of human life is shorter here than in Quebec, and both places are considerably behind the large towns in England, in point of salubrity. The violent extremes of temperature in the atmosphere, must here try the integrity of the weather organs, such as the lungs; and can scarcely fail of being unfavourable to longevity.

The Hôtel-Dieu both here and in Quebec, is admirably managed by the good Nuns. I love French Nuns.[45] They are a distinct and superior race to all the other European Sisterhood – most active and never to be fatigued in their beneficent labours, and of pure morals. Indeed such was the utter vileness of the other half of France at the Revolution, that the country might have now formed a lake similar to that of the Cities of the Plain, but for the redeeming virtue of many of the better sex. The Canadian Religieuses have not degenerated; and, notwithstanding the lying aspersions lately circulated, the establishments of these Sisters of Mercy here are the bright points on the aspect of French-Canadian society. 'The early history of Canada teems indeed with instances of the purest religious fortitude, zeal and heroism; of young and delicate females relinquishing the comforts of civilization to perform the most menial offices towards the sick – to dispense at once medical aid to the body and religious instruction to the soul of the benighted and wondering savage.'*

During our residence of a year at Montreal, I witnessed a scene of great religious scandal with much pain. A quarrel took place between two Presbyterian Clergymen officiating in the same Church, and there was a violent contest in consequence between their respective partizans as to the possession of it. One party had got in – early on a Sunday morning, too; barricaded the door, and there were blockaded by the other, who endeavoured to starve them into submission. But the besieged held out stoutly, and a supply of provisions having been obtained through a window in the course of the night, they shewed a determined front in the morning. All this time the crowd of Canadians in the street were laughing disdainfully at these disgraceful proceedings, and enjoying this extraordinary spectacle as a good joke. It was by no means

* Hawkins's Picture of Quebec. (Author's footnote.)

agreeable to my Protestant feelings to see persons of the greatest respectability committing themselves in this serio-comic manner; and when I beheld a most estimable medical friend, with whom I had dined the day before, figuring as ringleader in the fray, he appeared like the blind Sampson making sport for the Philistines.

It is but justice to the clerical gentlemen concerned, to add that they disapproved of these unseemly practices, and took no part in them.

13

Cholera at Kingston · Toronto · Diet of snipe for a sick man · Political situation deteriorates · Sir John Colborne appointed to command both provinces · American 'migration'

EARLY in May we left our pleasing Quarter for Kingston, in the Upper Province. This has been for many years an Artillery Station. We found two companies quartered in a neat little barrack, clean and very comfortable; as that superior and most respectable arm of the service soon makes itself every where – with a snug cottage on a pretty eminence for the Commandant, and the officers' mess-house on the ridge above, commanding a glorious view of the lake and the bay from the windows.

Our regiment occupied three points here – The Tête du Pont Barracks, Fort Henry and Point Frederick. For the first month or two we were very healthy, but as the summer advanced the malaria from the Rideau swamps began to act on the men; and we had a good deal of intermittent fever, generally of a mild description, that yielded readily to medicine.

After a few weeks, when we had looked about us a little, and reconnoitred our position, we began to bethink us that Lake Ontario was celebrated for its fish; and to take measures of hostility against the black bass, which we heard highly spoken of, as affording lively sport on the line and making a capital dish at table. So I bought a skiff, and prepared minnow tackle, struck the top-gallants of my salmon-rods; and, one fine day in June, crossed over to Garden Island, sitting in the stern of my pretty little craft, whilst my servant plied a tiny pair of oars.

I had a rod and line at each side, at right angles with the skiff, and another line astern. Having attached a minnow and a gaudy fly to each, I commenced trolling along, with the stern line rolled up as far as was necessary, on a stick in my pocket. We had not gone a hundred yards when one reel spun away merrily, and there was a bass of a couple of pounds on the minnow-look, leaping out of the water most vivaciously. Before I had secured this gentleman I felt a tug at my pocket, and discovered that another about the same size was fast on the stern-hook. I caught him also; and thus

we went on, amusingly enough, for three or four hours; and returned in the evening with three dozen of good bass, a few of
which were four pounds weight.

The bass is an excellent fish—firm, white and sweet at table,
and very lively on the hook; leaping out of the water like a salmon.
They are good either boiled or fried—at breakfast or dinner, and
make an admirable curry. During our stay on the shores of Lake
Ontario, I caught some thousands of them, and ate them constantly without satiety.

The question whether the pestilence, which under the name of
Asiatic Cholera, had spread through the British Islands in 1831
and 32, would be able to force its way across the broad barrier
of the Atlantic, was mooted in this remote Province with much
interest, some apprehension and a great difference of opinion.
The generality of my professional brethren, with myself, thought
the ocean was too vast to be passed; and that the new world
would continue happily exempt from the plague that was de-
vastating the old.

Unfortunately these sanguine hopes and speculations turned
out unfounded. The cholera crossed the Atlantic, and poured
over Canada and all North America, like a destroying flood. Indeed the mortality attending it was proportionately much greater
than in the mother country, or any part of Europe; and at
Montreal the disease was, for the population, four or five times
more deadly than in Paris.

On the 8th of June, the pestilence made its first appearance in
Quebec, having been apparently imported with a ship full of emigrants from Ireland. It proceeded up the river to Montreal, where
it burst out like a volcano on the 11th. Its course was capricious
and uncertain; some intermediate villages being ravaged, and
others passed over altogether. At Prescott, two deaths occurred
on the 15th, and on the 17th it reached Kingston.

The Director General of the Army Medical Department, Sir
James McGrigor, had providently issued orders to his officers
early in the year respecting the proper steps to be taken in preparing, as well as possible, for the approaching mischief; which
my friend, Dr. Skey,* at the head of the department here, was
indefatigable in enforcing; with the addition of such local directions as his perfect acquaintance with these Provinces, and long

* The Senior Army Medical Officer in Canada.

general experience elsewhere, might suggest. I have not the slightest doubt but that many lives were saved in the Canadas, by the preventive measure then taken throughout this command.

As soon as it was known that malignant cholera had really appeared in Quebec, it was plain enough that it would find its way to the shores of Lake Ontario. My old friend, Colonel Nicol, was our Commandant at Kingston; and I well knew what fearless energy might be expected from him in the midst of any epidemic, however deadly. We first had the barracks and hospitals most carefully cleaned and whitewashed: the duties and fatigues of the soldiers were lightened as much as possible, and they were daily inspected with great care by their medical officers. The canteen was placed under vigilant supervision, and preparations were made to isolate the barracks, and to remove the married soldiers resident in the town, with their families, to a camp on the other side of the bay.

On the morning of the 17th of June, a fatal case of undoubted cholera having occurred in the town, these precautions were carried into effect. A camp was formed on the hill near Fort Henry, and the barrack gates were shut.

Although the cholera raged in the town for the next fortnight, we had no case in the regiment till the 4th July, when two grenadiers were attacked with frightful spasms—I was sent for on the instant—bled them both largely, and they recovered. Ten other men of the regiment were taken ill, and treated in the same way: the agonizing cramps yielded to the early and copious bleeding, as to a charm, and they also all recovered.

Encouraged by the result of these, and several similar instances amongst the poor people of the town, I began vainly to imagine that this plan of treatment would be generally successful; and wrote confidently to this effect to Dr. Skey: but I was soon to be undeceived. Three men and a woman, of the 66th, were attacked the same night. I saw them immediately; and the symptoms being the same to all appearance, they were bled like the others, and all died within twelve hours of the first attack. The spot which their barrack at Point Frederick occupied was a promontory near the dock-yard, the air of which was vitiated by the neighbourhood of the rotting ships. The company quartered there was removed to camp on the hill the next morning, and had no more cholera.

The fact is, I believe that we had two different diseases, confounded together under the common name of cholera, to contend with: one of these maladies having very much the character of tetanus, or locked-jaw. This genus was marked by early, severe and universal spasms, affecting every muscle, and causing great torture. This appeared to be easily curable, and the early bleeding in this peculiar and asthenic type wrought miracles, when judiciously and fearlessly employed. In the other more dangerous form, when the malady stole on more quietly, the patients sank early into hopeless debility, and here medicine was of very little avail.

We all heard wonderful accounts of the effects of transfusion of saline fluid into the veins, and Dr. Sampson, the principal practitioner in Kingston, and a man of talent, was determined, as well as myself, to give it a fair trial.

We used it in twenty bad cases, but unsuccessfully in all—though the first effect in every instance was the apparent restoration of the powers of life; and in one remarkable case of a poor emigrant from Yorkshire, life was protracted seven days by constant pumping. Here the man almost instantaneously recovered voice, strength, colour, and appetite; and Sampson and myself, seeing this miraculous change, almost believed we had discovered the new elixir of life in the humble shape of salt and water.

The appearance of Kingston during the epidemic was most melancholy. No business was done, for the country people kept aloof from the infected town. The yellow flag was hoisted near the market place on the beach, and intercourse with the Steamboats put under Quarantine regulations. The conduct of the inhabitants was admirable, and reflected great credit on this good little town. The Medical men and the Clergy of all persuasions vied with each other in the fearless discharge of their respective dangerous duties; and the exertions of all classes were judicious, manly and energetic: for the genuine English spirit shewed itself, as usual, undaunted in the midst of peril, and rising above it.

We had thirty-six cases of bad cholera—besides a host of choleroid complaints, in the regiment. Of these we lost five men and two women. No child suffered.

During the prevalence of the disease it seemed to me that a number of errors in diet were generally entertained and acted on in our little community. Because unripe fruit, or excess in its use, does mischief, all fruit was now proscribed by common opinion; and vegetables of every description were placed under the same ban, so that the gardeners saw their finest productions rotting unsaleable. This was folly; for the stomach was more likely to suffer than to benefit from the want of its accustomed pabulum of mixed animal and vegetable substances. It was proper to live temperately—to avoid supper eating, or eating late in the day—as eight-tenths of the attacks came on in the night—to eschew excesses of all kinds—but, above all to be fearless and place confidence in Providence.

If, amidst so much distress, ludicrous ideas could be entertained, there was enough to excite them on this subject of abstinence from vegetables. Huge Irishmen who had sucked in the national root with their mother's milk, and lived on it all their lives, now shrank from a potato as poison. I heard a respectable and intelligent gentleman confess that he was tempted by the attractive appearance of a dish of green pease, and ate *one* pea, but he felt uncomfortable afterwards, and was sure it had disagreed with him. The disease ceased entirely, and the usual intercourse was restored between the Garrison and the Town in the middle of October.

We had tolerable shooting about Kingston. Partridges and woodcocks were common enough in the woods; snipe were abundant and even close to the town of Kingston there are marshes where one may pick up twenty couple of good fat snipes in the forenoon of October or November. But it is hard fag—the marsh being an extensive quagmire, covered with long, tough, matted grass, which gets entangled about one's ankles, and sometimes requires great exertion to burst through. Besides, if by a heavier step than usual, your foot penetrates the quaking stratum of thin soil, down you go, and the extended arms and the gun thrown across, are necessary to prevent disappearing altogether.

Nothing strikes a stranger more than the mute solitude of the woods in Canada; for no sound, except the chirp of a squirrel or the croak of a frog, is ever heard in the interminable forest: and these but rarely. Even woodpeckers are found on the skirts of the woods only, close to cultivated ground, where the sun vivifies the insects on which they feed. Yet the cause is obvious—the severity of the winter drives away the feathered tribes, and the migrating races either remain in the cleared country during the summer, or retire to breed in the most secluded depths of the mountain forest, far away from the haunts of man. An oppressive feeling of melancholy comes over one in passing through the gloomy recesses of a Canadian forest; seeing at every step the decay of vegetable nature – bestriding the rotten trees, and perceiving the living ones half-choked by pressure and confinement, and contending with each other for air and sunshine. No gay creepers entwine their trunks – no flowers gem the ground at their roots – no turf covers the earth about them. All is cheerless and unadorned, and monotonous gloom and silence.

In the young woods near the towns, the case is different. Animated life and abundance of wild flowers will here be met with, and the sportsman will find woodcocks and partridges in respectable numbers.

Our regiment soon became popular at Kingston. We flattered ourselves that we were all well conducted, and it is certain that the people were staunch in their British feelings, and well disposed and friendly to the military. Thus the main elements of kindly sentiments on both sides being in existence, it was easy to bring them into operation, and a degree of mutual attachment sprung up. We spent two years very pleasantly in our quiet quarters, partaking of much attention and hospitality. The first winter made us quite acquainted with our new friends; the second would have been still more agreeable, had it not been shaded a little by the recent ravages of the cholera.

In May, 1833, the 66th were ordered to York, now Toronto. We embarked in the fine steamboat the *Great Britain*, amidst loud and long continued cheering from our kind-hearted Kingston friends, and arrived the next day in the capital of Upper Canada.

The Indian names of places are not only soft and liquid, but exceedingly expressive; generally condensing in one musical word the distinctive and permanent local features. Toronto, in Mohawk, means 'trees growing in water,' and is happily significant of the appearance of parts of the lake shore near the town.

This is a long straggling place, recently redeemed from the forest, running two miles along the lake, where an inlet protected by a peninsula, forms a good harbour. The water, however, is scarcely deep enough, and depositions from the small and sluggish river Don, a little to the eastward of the town, and the debris of the crumbling clayey banks, threaten to fill it up at no very remote period, if not prevented by some scientific interposition.

In 1794 the Duke de Rochefoucalt Liancourt had visited York, which then only contained twelve small wooden houses, whose inmates, the Frenchman adds, were not of the best character. A more questionable authority, Mr. Gourlay, sneeringly says they have not improved much since. But this is a great mistake. The population of Toronto, in common with the vast majority of Upper Canada, is highly moral and respectable; and, so long as fidelity, forbearance under cruel injury, and exalted moral principle are esteemed in the world—this Province must possess a high and honourable name. When returning to the barracks from late parties in the town, our officers have often been struck with the profound quiet of the streets.

The Lieutenant Governor of Upper Canada in 1833, was Sir John Colborne,[46] a man, according to the historian Napier, 'of an extraordinary genius for war,' and not less admirably adapted for the discharge of the civil duties of a Governor. His attention to public business—the devotion of his whole time and all his energies, bodily and mental, to the improvement of this rising Province—his exertions in fostering emigration, and assisting and locating emigrants—were so conspicuous and unremitting, that they could not be denied by his most virulent political enemies. His affabiltiy, hospitality, and private virtues, and the wide spreading charity of his excellent wife, though devoid of all ostentation, were necessarily well known in a limited society like that of Toronto; and the estimation in which he is held in the Province, was signally demonstrated by the universal tribute of respect paid to him all along the road, when leaving his Government, on the arrival of Sir Francis Head.

Our Regiment had its Head Quarters in the barracks at Toronto, with detachments at four or five out-stations. The barracks are poor buildings, but agreeably situated on the bank of the lake, a mile and a half west of the town. All the principal people of the place called on us soon after our arrival; invitations followed quick; and our Commanding Officer, Major Baird—being a veteran of fine appearance and most gentlemanly manners—the other officers, also, quite what they ought to be, and the soldiers sober and well behaved—we found ourselves in a short time far advanced in the good opinion of the provincial metropolitans, and becoming favourites here, as we flattered ourselves had been the case at other quarters. To this desirable object the goodness of our band, which played *pro bono publico* two evenings in the week, did not a little contribute.

There was an old gentleman, Sir W— C—, formerly Chief Justice, a patient of mine at Toronto, who was sinking in a general decay of nature. My worthy patient became very weak towards the end of the year–his nights were restless–his appetite began to fail, and he could only relish tid bits. Medicine was tried fruitlessly, so his Doctor prescribed snipes. At the point of the sandy peninsula opposite the barracks, are a number of little pools and marshes, frequented by these delectable little birds; and here I used to cross over in my skiff and pick up the Chief Justice's panacea. On this delicate food the poor old gentleman was supported for a couple of months: but the frost set in–the snipes flew away, and Sir W— died.

There is a prodigious migration of pigeons in summer from the Southern States of America to the Canadian forests. Crossing over the upper end of Lake Ontario, innumerable columns of them hit the land close to the barracks, and continue to pass over in quick succession of flocks for three or four days. Many of these poor birds are quite young–the down on their bodies being still visible, and their tails not grown. The young birds, yet fearless of man, used to fly so close to the ground as to be knocked down by the soldiers with sticks; but the old ones, known by their long tails, kept their course high in the air. The slaughter about the barracks, and on the large common between them and the town, was enormous, and the whole country was covered with sharp-shooters during the time the birds were passing.

We had a garden belonging to the Mess at the barracks, in which there were a good number of fruit trees; and when we arrived these were in blossom, and appeared to be objects of great desire to the humming birds. I watched their manœuvres each morning with great pleasure about one large pear tree, although these beautiful little creatures flit about so rapidly as to require sharp sight to follow them, and manage to rifle the blossoms and flowers of their treasure always on the wing. What a pity the tiny beauties do not sing.

We were ordered back to Kingston in May 1834. The regiment embarked in the most perfect state of order and sobriety, and re-turned in the middle of the month to our good and quiet quarters.

Our numerous friends in Kingston received us on our return with a warm welcome. Our former stay of two years in their kind-hearted town had produced an almost affectionate intimacy. The place had improved in appearance, and several substantial houses, including a bank, had been built in the interval of our absence.

Again the two Provinces were destined to suffer severely from an invasion of cholera; and once more there were very discordant opinions amongst medical men as to the probable mischief it would occasion. Many persons supposed that the character of the disease was changing, and that its malignancy was on the decline generally throughout the world—consequently we should have it light this year. Besides, it was natural to suppose that its pathology was now better understood than formerly, and that the practice would be more successful. Now, though the community, generally, were less frightened than during the first epidemic, and paid more attention to preventive measures and the premonitions of the malady, and perhaps the practice was better—it turned out that the second attack of the pestilence was more fatal than the first. This town, with a population of about five thousand, lost two hundred in 1832, whilst not less than three hundred were carried off in 1834.

According to my own observation, the latter epidemic had more of the asthenic character than the former—that is to say, it was more marked by symptoms of debility and prostration immediately after the first attack, and less by violent spasms and extreme distress. It was thus more insidious and dangerous, and the patients sank sooner into a state of utter hopelessness. The same general feeling of discomfort and *malaise* was prevalent as before, and every one complained of loss of appetite and vigour, with nocturnal restlessness, or sleep without refreshment. I again noticed a ferruginous taste in the air; and this was observed in Paris and some other places in 1832. Fortunately the disease broke out late in the summer: the first case occurred at Kingston on the 26th of July.

Warned by the experience of 1832, no time was lost in isolating the Garrison as much as possible. When the first case of malignant cholera took place in the town, the barrack gates were shut as formerly—the married soldiers living in lodgings with their families were encamped near Fort Henry, on the same ground as before. The Royal Artillery having become sickly, were also sent to camp. These measures proved highly useful—the health of the numerous women and children was preserved, and that of the Artillery restored.

A strict hygeian police was established and sedulously maintained in the regiment, with the object of watching and crushing the first germ of the malady. Any deviation from the men's ordinary habits was at once noticed by steady non-commissioned officers appointed for this purpose, and reported to the surgeons. They were directed to observe the men at their meals carefully, and give notice if they should perceive loss of appetite in any individual. Drills and parades were discontinued, and all duties made as light as possible; but the men were marched a short distance in the cool of the evening by the Adjutant, after medical inspection. On hot days they were permitted to amuse themselves and cool the barracks by watering them and the square in which they stood with a fire engine, in which they enjoyed themselves much, making *jets d'eau* in the air *ad libitum*. Cleanliness of person, clothing, bedding and barrack rooms, was strictly enjoined and maintained. The men were allowed to take reasonable rest in the morning, and their sleep at that hour, which is generally the most refreshing after a hot night in a barrack room, was not abridged under a mistaken notion of the advantage of extreme early rising. No fastidiousness was practised as to their diet, which was not changed–the Writer conceiving, as before mentioned, that the stomach would be more liable to get out of order if deprived of the vegetables grateful to it, and to which it had been accustomed, than if they were permitted to be used. The canteen–that fruitful source of regimental mischief–was placed under strict watchfulness, and intemperance prevented as much as possible. It ought to be added that in this respect, and indeed every other, the conduct of the soldiers of the regiment during both epidemics was eminently good.

With these precautions, and early attention to premonitory abdominal disturbances, the disease touched us lightly, and we had only eight adult cases of cholera out of seven hundred and sixty-nine individuals. However, we had, besides, a host of bowel complaints, many of which, no doubt, would have merged in the pestilence but for early treatment. This was a ratio about twenty-fold less than amongst the civil population; and our total loss was fifty-fold less, or thereabouts; being only one man and two children.

There was a material difference at Kingston between the practice of 1832 and 1834. Laudanum, brandy and other stimulants, were administered now much more sparingly than before; when, probably, they had been used too freely. Bleeding, also, was not so common; for those violent tetanic spasms which it had so frequently relieved in the former year, were not now so general. Calomel had been given then very largely, but was now used less indiscriminately. In 1834, acetate of lead was employed in some nearly hopeless cases with benefit and Dr. Sampson, a clever and most worthy man, to whom I am under great obligations for professional assistance, found it highly useful in the last stages of the disease.

The Writer's favourite remedy was castor oil combined with a small quantity of laudanum, given in some grateful and demulcent fluid, as hot as possible—making the patient lie on his right side for the assistance of gravitation towards the pylorus. In some hundred cases, on this and the former occasion, he witnessed the most excellent effects from this remedy; and, moreover, experienced them himself in the early stage of two attacks of cholera he had at Kingston. Once, when attending a gentleman who died of the disease, the Writer was conscious of the very moment when he contracted it by the patient's bed-side—instantly went home and to bed, and took the oil and laudanum—when five minutes' delay might have cost him his life. For some time there was a terrible internal conflict—the heart and whole system laboured tumultuously, and the balance appeared to vibrate between the fatal rush of serum, or the thin fluid of the blood, to the coats of the intestines, and a salutary determination to the exterior. All this time the pulse could not be counted, and the feeling of anxiety and oppression was dreadful. At length the circulation became clamer; the shrivelling skin swelled out with grateful heat and warm moisture, and the crisis was past. Here, and in many similar instances, like oil on a stormy sea, this invaluable medicine soothed the internal commotion and effected a calm.

As on the former occasion, the conduct of the manly and intelligent community at Kingston was becoming the character of their town. Nobody shrank from kind offices to the sick—nobody ran away—a health committee sat daily, and the Doctors and Clergy of all persuasions did their duty nobly as before.

Although we have seen cholera following roads and rivers, and the great lines of human intercourse in various parts of the world, it has often left some favoured spots untouched, in a very capricious and unaccountable manner. In England, Exeter was never visited by the disease, though it prevailed in the neighbourhood. During the invasion here in 1834, the south shore of Lake Ontario was exempt, but not the north. Opposite to Kingston is a village on a height, called Barriefield, where numerous deaths took place from cholera; and another village or hamlet, half a mile distant and on a level with the lake, where the malady did not shew itself at all. We found it sticking pertinaciously to some houses, and occurring in them again and again; and those elevated parts of the town which had always been considered the most healthy suffered the most. By the middle of September the health of Kingston was restored, but half the inhabitants were in mourning.

It was necessary to relax and refresh a little after the anxieties and duties of those frightful times, when life was held by a tenure little better than a day's, or even an hour's purchase. I went, therefore, on a visit to some friends residing on the Bay of Quinté, having been promised good snipe shooting in that quarter.

The day after my arrival, another gentleman and I went to shoot in a marsh near the village of Wellington, seven miles from Picton. The day turned out singularly dark and gloomy, though without rain—the sky was like bronze, with here and there a patch better polished than the rest. We could scarcely see the snipes sometimes, but still had good sport—meeting with an extraordinary number, of great size and fatness, of which we bagged forty couple. After the first shots we discovered two hawks attending us, who continued our companions the whole day; hovering around as if on the watch for any birds we might miss: in fact they pursued and killed some of them before our eyes, though they always managed to keep out of range themselves. The falconry sometimes was most interesting—the snipes flew strong and swiftly and doubled beautifully; but their fine condition for the table was against them; they were thick winded and far too fat for a race.

In May we received the route for Quebec. The Magistrates of Kingston complimented Colonel Nicol and the 66th very highly on their departure after so long a residence amongst them—which was duly and courteously answered. We embarked amidst a burst of cheering; were towed to Prescott by a steamboat, shot down the rapids beautifully, and returned to Quebec after an absence of five years.

The situation of Lower Canada, when the regiment returned in 1835, was extraordinary and anomalous. Public affairs were fast verging on anarchy, whilst the great mass of the population was in a state of perfect quietness and order. The refusal of the supplies for the public service by the House of Assembly, for about two years and a half, had spread a great deal of distress amongst the officers of the Executive Government, who had now been long working without pay—had diminished their respectability and usefulness by throwing them deeply in debt; and was altogether painful to witness. For, whilst it gratified the malignant passions of the Speaker and his friends, it involved innocent persons in great anxiety and suffering, and was very derogatory to the character of the British Government.

The gaol was full of criminals, and the walls of the building were so thin that the felons bored holes and escaped continually. The soldiers who guarded it had no ball-cartridges—which the rogues knew well—and when an offer was made by the Commandant to place a sufficient quantity at the disposal of the Civil power there was a demur—a criminal might be shot in breaking out, and this would assuredly bring all the venom of the Assembly to bear on the head of the Sheriff. Thus the King's subjects could not put their noses outside the gates of Quebec at night without being robbed, and the reign of foot-pads revived every where. Two of our officers were rifled of their cash and stripped of their clothes close to the St. Louis Gate. Crime raised its audacious front rampant every where; and the respectable body of thieves and pickpockets drank Mr. Papineau's health with great propriety for producing general confusion, and creating for the fraternity such glorious saturnalia.

In the beginning of 1836, and in mid-winter, Sir John Colborne, was superseded in His Lieutenant Governorship of Upper Canada; and Sir Francis Bond Head,[47] a traveller and an author of some distinction, was appointed in his place. The former officer demurred at some instructions from the Colonial Secretary, most prejudicial to the true interests of the Province, and personally disrespectful to himself—and requested to be relieved. His desire was complied with in rather unseemly haste, considering the climate and unreasonable time of the year for removing his family; to say nothing of the awkwardness of disturbing the Head of the Provincial Government whilst the Parliament was in session. However to the great satisfaction of the well disposed in both Provinces, Sir John who had proceeded to New York to return to England, met there a despatch from home, complimenting him on the close of his labours as Lieutenant Governor, giving him the local rank of Lieutenant General, and offering him the military command of both Provinces. This was the *amende honorable*, and was frankly accepted; although I have reason to know that the health of this truly patriotic man was suffering at the time, under a complaint for which he was advised by his medical friends to repair to a milder climate. Well was it for every loyal British subject in these Provinces that his departure from America was thus critically prevented.

Quebec is the 'ultima Thule' of our good friends the travelling Americans in their annual migration to the north; where they begin to arrive a little after the swallows. It is pleasing to see them crowding the steamboats and hotels, and hastening through the streets to visit the Citadel and fine Ramparts; stare at the regularity and precision of the military parades, and admire the Bands. Notwithstanding that they have been a little naughty of late, one cannot help being gratified at viewing an occasional reunion of branches of the great family to which we both belong; and every lover of his species must earnestly desire that all sources of mutual bitterness may soon be dried up; and the only rivalry be henceforth which shall do most good to each other and the world.

Our fair Yankee visitors would be sometimes amusingly saucy. 'We are very much obliged to you,' a sweet girl from Boston one day said to Colonel Nicol–'for all the trouble and expense this fine Citadel has cost you, and for the care you take of it–we *are really*; you *know it's all for* us.' Great was the pity that my excellent friend, whose single demerit consists in being an old bachelor, did not try to secure this fair hostage for the future good behaviour of her countrymen.

In September 1836, we had a Brigade Field Day of three Regiments of the Garrison, the Royal, the 66th and 79th, on the celebrated battle ground, the Plains of Abraham. It attracted a very large number of spectators, and as the town was full of Americans, Brother Jonathan and his family mustered strong, and the female members were well dressed and looked very pretty–shewing no silly timidity but great good sense and courage during the firing. Altogether, considering the three good regiments–the scene of their evolutions–the character of the man who commanded, and the number of respectable people present–it was a fine sight. Unfortunately the elements appear to take no interest in such military spectacles–or, rather would seem to feel a pleasure in spoiling them; and before there was time for a dozen manœuvres the rain came down pitilessly and caused a general 'sauve qui peut'.

* * *

[Meanwhile, politically, the situation was deteriorating; In England the discussions in Parliament were interrupted by the death of William IV which gave M. Papineau and his friends a chance to organise resistance to Authority. Nor was the pro-Government element behind hand in its preparations for what appeared to be an imminent civil war. In July 1837 public meetings of about 6,000 people were held in both Quebec and Montreal where declarations of loyalty to the Crown were passed; but in October the local rebels gathered with small arms and cannon to enrol and arm themselves with the object of 'disfranchising their beloved country from all human authority, except the bold democracy residing within its bosom.' The dissident elements were only a small proportion of the French Canadians. In general they were discouraged by the Catholic Church, but they were joined by the usual crowd of malcontents who will gather round any standard which appeals to their emotions or their pockets. Editor.]

* * *

The plot now began to thicken apace. On the 23rd of October a large meeting of five confederated counties was held at St. Charles, a village on the Richelieu, about thirty miles from Montreal, which was soon destined to obtain an unenviable celebrity. Here, in 1830, in Sir James Kempt's time there had been a meeting, expressing dissatisfaction with his administration, when all the rest of the Province was busy complimenting him; and another similar assemblage in 1831. Here, also, had flourished a seditious newspaper–the 'Echo du Pays,'–perverting and corrupting all within its circle. This, then, was the very centre and focus of disaffection, now ripening fast into treason: and in the signal chastisement *here* first inflicted, we may without presumption recognize a measure of that retributive justice, which is seen occasionally to interpose in regulating the affairs of the world.

Mr. Wolfred Nelson, a distiller of St. Denis, was chosen by Mr. Papineau to preside at this meeting, on account of his influence in the neighbourhood, ardent character and English name. Here the representatives of five counties, under salutes of cannon and musketry, in language the most treasonable, bound themselves to form one great confederation, as a centre of union for the whole Province – to oppose the Government as far as they safely might – to elect their own magistrates and militia officers – enrol and arm themselves and invite all the rest of Lower Canada to join their patriotic league. Amongst other ferocious resolutions there was one urging the soldiers to desert, and pledging the Canadians to assist them, which was pre-eminently infamous, but even more silly and impotent than wicked.

Mr. Papineau knew not the character of the British soldier whom he wished to make a recreant perjurer like himself. When exposed to great sufferings and privations, the instant there is a prospect of action he ever rises superior to the surrounding difficulties; his conduct purifies itself in danger, and is always best when his full energies are called into play. The same imminent personal risk that enfeebles and paralyses weaker natures, only brings him up to the full tension and vigour of his faculties, mental, moral and corporeal. Desertion in time of peace is, unfortunately, too common in the Canadas; but after this open and disgraceful incitement, it ceased as if by magic. Throughout the first winter there was scarcely one solitary instance, and this public outrage on the character of the British Army stands on record only as a piece of brutal and useless folly. It has been deeply atoned. One short month after the insult was offered – *and on the very spot* – it was expiated in blood!

14

Insurrection · The fighting at St. Charles and St. Denis · 'Le bon Dieu n'est pas patriote' · Reinforcements · Insurrection quashed · The author is promoted · The 66th leaves Canada

THE Commander of the Forces, Sir John Colborne, foresaw the coming storm and prepared to meet it. At once assuming a heavy responsibility, he directed the fortifications of Quebec to be repaired and thoroughly armed – ordered horses to be purchased for the Artillery, magazines of provisions and ammunition to be established – barracks to be built, and new corps of loyal men to be raised. He sent for troops from the Upper Province and New Brunswick, and concentrated the small force he had in hand at Montreal, as the chief *point d'appui* of his operations.

In the beginning of November, as the shipping dropped down the St. Lawrence, the disaffected began every where to assume a more insolent tone, particularly in that populous tract along the River Richelieu, and on the banks of the Lake of the Two Mountains; a bold expansion of the Ottawa. Bands of armed men, masked and disguised, now began to roam about the country at night, terrifying their more quiet neighbours into enrolment amongst the illegal confederacy, and extorting by violence the resignation of commissions – to be inserted in the next *Minerve* or *Vindicator** as voluntary acts.

There is every reason for believing that Mr. Papineau had no wish to carry matters farther, for the present, than these minacious demonstrations – to be adroitly used afterwards in any treaty between the Government and himself: and no general insurrection, in all likelihood, would have taken place until a better organization of the *habitans* had been effected. Happily, a premature contest began almost by accident, and the arch-traitor then found, as might be expected, the evil spirits he had evoked, soon beyond his control.

A band of five or six hundred of the '*Fils de la Liberté*' had been accustomed to meet on three or four successive Sundays for military training, in a field adjacent to the city of Montreal; and

* *Revolutionary Newspapers.* (Editor.)

had once or twice marched through the streets at night to display their strength, until the magistrates at length interfered and forbade the assemblage. A corps of opposite politics, called the 'Doric Club,' had also been for some time enrolled, though without the same offensive parade of their numbers, who longed very much for an opportunity of interchanging a few hard fisticuffs with the young heroes of liberty. At length the collision took place–the juvenile patriots made a sorry fight and were beaten out of town. Several excesses were committed by both parties–the *Vindicator* Office was broken into and the press and types destroyed; and Mr. Papineau's house was only saved by the military, who were called out in strong force to put down the riot. The destruction of the *Vindicator* press was, no doubt, richly merited, but should not have thus taken place. Violence is always wrong–creates a factitious sympathy for its objects, and thus defeats its own ends. The arm of the law ought to have suppressed this nefarious print long before.

At this time the Author was on a professional visit to the family of Sir John Colborne, at Sorel; and for several days that he remained, hourly reports of a general insurrection about to break out were brought. Nelson at this period was fortifying his house at St. Denis to the great annoyance of the ladies of the family, who saw their beautiful flower pots and pianos put aside, to make room for guns and pikes and barricades. We had constant intelligence of his proceedings, as well as what was going on in other Quarters; and Sir John only awaited his Staff coming up from Quebec to move to Montreal. When the despatch was brought containing the news of this riot, he came into the drawing-room with the letter in his hand, exclaiming 'Well, thank God, there's no blood shed–though the fight's begun. I must be off by tonight's boat.'

On the 10th November, Sir John ordered a small body of volunteer cavalry to patrol as far as St. John's. They discovered some armed *habitans* at St. Athanase, on the other side of the Richelieu, who forbade their advance, but dispersed the next day on the approach of a Company of Infantry from Montreal.

On the 16th November a constable, escorted by a small party of volunteer cavalry, proceeded to St. John's, with warrants for the arrest of Messrs. Demaray and D'Avignon, accused of treason. Having accomplished this object they were attacked on their return by a large body of armed men, posted judiciously behind the fences on each side of the road: the prisoners were liberated, and the cavalry driven back—a few of them being wounded.

Men's minds had been gradually preparing for violence and bloodshed, yet this outrage excited intense interest in Montreal. No time was lost in endeavouring to avenge it, and next morning Lieut. Colonel Wetherall[48] commanding the Royal Regiment, with four companies, two guns and some cavalry, was ordered to move from Longueuil to Chambly, scouring the country as he went along. Some of the volunteers who had been wounded in the affair of the day before, accompanied this expedition. The Colonel dispersed one or two armed bands, taking a few prisoners, but his chief difficulty was the bad road.

A degree of artificial confidence had now been raised in the minds of the vain peasantry in the neighbourhood; and the slight success of liberating two state prisoners and repulsing a handful of cavalry, puffed them up with the most extravagant ideas of ultimate success in the approaching struggle with the Government. In the meantime warrants had at length been issued for the apprehension of Papineau, O'Callaghan and several others, who immediately repaired to the great rendezvous ordered at the village of St. Charles.

The news of the rescue of Messrs. Demaray and D'Avignon was rapidly spread along the populous banks of the Richelieu, and excited great rejoicings amongst the *habitans*. Large masses of them soon began to assemble at two points on the right bank— St. Charles and St. Denis. At St. Charles twelve hundred rebels commanded by an American named Brown, commenced stockading the village, cutting down Mr. Debartzch's beautiful trees for this purpose; killing and salting his cattle, luxuriating amongst his fat poultry, and regaling themselves with his wines.

At St. Denis, seven miles down the river, Wolfred Nelson, learning that a warrant was out for his apprehension, collected a large mass of the neighbouring *habitans*, variously armed, and made preparations to resist the law. The number of men under his command cannot be easily ascertained, as reinforcements were constantly arriving; but it is believed at least to have amounted to eleven or twelve hundred—the majority bearing firearms. These Mr. Nelson posted in the strongest houses in the village, distributed an ample allowance of his whiskey amongst them, and bade defiance to the Government.

Mr. Papineau, O'Callaghan, and two or three other leaders repaired secretly to this neighbourhood as soon as they found measures taking for their apprehension; and continued at St. Denis or St. Charles until the approach of Colonel Wetherall's column, when Papineau crossed the river and remained on the other side during the action. In this he took no part personally—having been always—'A dog in forehead, but in heart a deer.'

Under these grave circumstances, with the whole dense population of the six Counties, perhaps of the whole Province, ripe for insurrection, no time was to be lost in attacking these strong holds. A combined military movement was therefore ordered by the Commander of the Forces; and on the 22nd November, two columns of troops, as strong as could then be detached from Montreal, were directed to move from Chambly and Sorel, on St. Charles and St. Denis.

At Sorel the navigable river Richelieu joins the St. Lawrence. The detachment ordered hence on St. Denis, eighteen miles distant on the same bank, consisted of nearly three hundred men of the 24th, 32nd and 66th regiments, with a few volunteer cavalry and a howitzer, under the command of Colonel Gore,[49] the Deputy Quarter Master General: having a small steamboat at his disposal for the conveyance of ammunition and provisions.

Colonel Gore commenced his march at ten o'clock of a very stormy night; making a detour to his left when leaving Sorel to conceal his object. The weather was as bad as possible—the cold benumbed, and the thick snow-drift blinded the men, whilst the tenacious mud of the execrable road pulled off their boots and mocassins. The column, however, persevered, and on approaching St. Ours, avoided that village, and turned up a Concession road to the left. After a most toilsome and miserable night-march of twelve hours the troops arrived half frozen at St. Denis. Here they were received by a hot fire from the outskirts of the village, which warmed and animated them; and in the excitement of combat the fatiguing exertions of the dreary night were soon forgotten.

The enemy's chief strength lay in some high stone houses at the east end of the village, from the numerous windows of which they poured an incessant fire. The defenders were well covered, and the officer of artillery could make little impression with his light gun;

although one lucky shot, entering by a window, killed a dozen of the rebels. In the meantime several men had fallen amongst the troops; and an officer of the 32nd, named Markham,[50] distinguished by his romantic gallantry, was pierced by four balls, yet without mortal injury. The whole detachment, covering themselves as they might, persisted bravely in their endeavour to overpower the fire of their adversaries; and the 66th Light Company being good marksmen, in an effective position, and commanded by a cool and brave man, Crompton, brought down a number of the enemy. Amongst others less distinguished, Mr. Ovide Perrault, a Member of the Assembly, fell under their fire.

After gallantly, though fruitlessly, persevering for four hours, until his ammunition began to fail; whilst additional numbers were pouring in from the neighbourhood to reinforce the insurgents—Colonel Gore found himself unable to carry the village with his small force, and retired to Sorel; having the mortification of leaving his gun behind sticking in the frozen mud, and with a loss of twenty men, killed and wounded.

It may be somewhat presumptuous in the Writer to criticise military operations, yet an old Peninsular Officer cannot avoid expressing his regret that Colonel Gore should not have economised his men's strength more on the advance. Brought up in the Wellington school, and distinguished for personal intrepidity in the Peninsula, he was eager to push on in obedience to his orders to join Colonel Wetherall: yet physical impossibilities are not to be surmounted, and orders however peremptory, *must* be sometimes discretionary. Had he kept the line of the river, in communication with his boat, and rested his column at St. Ours instead of avoiding it—thus bringing the troops comparatively fresh into action, there would have been, in all probability, a different result. As it was, the consequences were most calamitous —the whole detachment was put *hors de combat*, the gun was lost, and the steam-boat being fired on at St. Ours, was only saved by the good conduct of an officer of the Commissariat, who overawed the cowardice or treachery of the Canadian Master, and conducted the boat back safe to Sorel.

Yet good arose from the evil. The check at St. Denis gave confidence to the rebels at St. Charles, and tended to make the chastisement they received there, the more exemplary and complete.

And here I must pause a moment to deplore the fate of Lieutenant Weir of the 32nd regiment. This fine young man had been despatched by land from Montreal to Sorel; but from the badness of the roads could not reach that place until some hours after Colonel Gore's column had set out. He then started in a calèche in pursuit of the troops; but fatally followed the high road, passing them in the dark, who were then struggling through the Concession road far to his left; and on reaching St. Denis was made a prisoner by Nelson. This man, however misguided, is of a generous nature and treated the officer with courtesy; but on the approach of Colonel Gore, he directed him to be conveyed to St. Charles under the charge of a person named Jalbert. Mr. Weir was most barbarously murdered in the village, and his mutilated remains were afterwards found sunk under a load of stones in the river. They were removed to Montreal and honoured by a distinguished public funeral. The general character of Wolfred Nelson, and his kindness to some wounded soldiers who were made prisoners, repel the supposition that he was privy to this atrocity. But they who wantonly release men from the restraints of legal and social obligations are morally responsible for the excesses they commit. Jalbert was lately tried in Montreal for the murder of Mr. Weir, but the Jury composed of nine French Canadians and three of British or American origin, would not agree and were dismissed. The evidence on the trial appeared strongly criminatory of the prisoner.

Colonel Wetherall's detachment when leaving Chambly, consisted of four Companies of the Royal Regiment, one of the 66th, two six pounders, and a detachment of Montreal Cavalry, amounting to about 350 men. They too started on the same dark and tempestuous night, and so great were the difficulties of moving troops at such a season that the ammunition wagon broke down on the short road to the upper ferry, and the column took five hours to cross the river. It reached St. Mathias at 4 a.m. having been four hours in marching three miles.—Here, the troops being already exhausted by fatigue, the Colonel halted for two or three hours—resumed his march at 7 a.m. on the 23rd November, and reached St. Hilaire at 11. Conceiving that Col. Gore must have experienced the same difficulties as himself, and was probably halting at St. Ours, a messenger was now despatched to inform him of the position of the Chambly column, and that Colonel

Wetherall intended attacking St. Charles, eight miles distant, the next morning.

At 2 a.m. on the 24th, the messenger returned, not having been able to pass St. Denis, bringing the disastrous news of the repulse of the Sorel people, which Colonel Wetherall could scarcely credit –yet prudently acted on its truth: sending a courier with the intelligence to Montreal, and directing Major Warde of the Royal to join the column immediately with the Grenadier Company from Chambly. This order was obeyed with great expedition, boats having been found to bring the men down the river.

At 7 p.m. Colonel Wetherall made a feigned march of a couple of miles towards St. Charles, with the object of alarming the enemy, discovering their signals and harassing them by keeping them on the alert. As soon as he discovered that a chain of torches and blue lights had telegraphed his movements to the insurgents, he brought back his column to St. Hilaire, and gave the troops a good night's rest, whilst the rebels were watching all night. Thus the ruse succeeded admirably.

At 10 a.m. on the 25th November, no intelligence having been received from Montreal, Colonel Wetherall marched on St. Charles. He found all the houses along the road deserted and barricaded, and all the bridges broken down. The last bridge crossed a deep ravine with wooded banks–affording a good military position, which had been stockaded and occupied immediately before the arrival of the troops–the rebels' dinners being found on the fires. Half a mile farther on was another skilful stockade which was also deserted.

When within half a mile of St. Charles the column was fired at from the other side of the Richelieu and from some barns. The fire was returned by the advanced guard and a barn was burned. Colonel Wetherall then halted to reconnoitre, and was immediately received by a loud cheer of defiance from the stockaded village, Mr. Debartzch's house and the opposite bank of the river, followed by a heavy fire.

The Light Infantry were now extended to the left of the road, and the main body of the column moved to the right; whilst one gun was playing with cannister and grape shot on the stockade to the left, and another with round and grape on the loop-holed house; from whence a well directed fire was kept up, but with little effect, as the men were well sheltered.

Thus things continued for half an hour, when the whole column was advanced to a rail fence and ditch about a hundred yards from the stockade; a body of sixty or seventy rebels now had the temerity to advance from their cover and attempt to turn the Colonel's right flank, but were repulsed with loss; and the fire being now very hot from the stockade, and every mounted officer having had his horse killed or wounded, a general charge and advance was ordered, and after some fifteen minutes' smart work, the stockade was stormed, the loop-holed houses set on fire, and nearly two hundred of the rebels bayonetted or shot.

From a Journal found in the house of Mr. Blanchette, the Priest of St. Charles, it appeared that the insurgents, alarmed by Colonel Wetherall's feigned march from St. Hilaire, had been under arms the whole night in expectation of an attack. It was also established that this recreant Clergyman had assembled the rebels in the Church of St. Charles on the morning of the action, and given them his benediction.

Sunday, the 26th, was employed in burying the dead; a few of whom were given up to their relations who came to seek them. In the course of the day several despatches were received from St. Hilaire, stating that a strong force of the rebels was assembling in that neighbourhood, prepared to cut off Colonel Wetherall's retreat from Chambly. It now became a question, therefore, whether the Colonel should follow the fugitives to St. Denis, or attack the more formidable body in his rear. After due deliberation he decided on the latter, and marched early on the 27th.

Having carefully conducted his wounded to St. Hilaire, and left a guard to protect them, Colonel Wetherall, on the morning of the 28th, advanced on a body of one thousand insurgents strongly posted near St. Mathias, with two guns, which he attacked and dispersed, with the loss of their guns and four or five killed. He then re-crossed the Richelieu and returned to Chambly the same evening.

Colonel Wetherall is a very fortunate man, but also one of the class who deserve good fortune. At this critical time the fate of the Province may be truly said to have depended on his capacity and exertions, and he proved himself equal to the responsibility. Throughout this perplexing march—cut off from all communication with Head Quarters—deprived of the co-operation of his colleague, and isolated amidst masses of a furious insurgent peasantry, his conduct commands unmixed admiration. In the determination to attack St. Charles alone, even when the rebels were flushed with their recent success, and in the actual assault, we recognize sagacity and intrepidity—the firm nerve and undisturbed judgment of a consummate soldier.

Nor should an humbler name be passed unnoticed. Lieut. Johnston who led the company of the 66th, (left being in front,) was the first officer, and nearly the first individual, who cleared the fence, cheering on his men beautifully, and eliciting from the high-minded Commander the compliment—'Well done 66th!'

The news of Colonel Gore's disaster diffused the greatest alarm in Montreal, for it was coupled with the expectation of a general rising throughout the Province. In fact, the most fatal consequences might have followed but for the instantaneous corrective afforded by the success of Colonel Wetherall. As soon as the news arrived much uneasiness was felt at Head Quarters respecting the latter officer, and courier after courier was despatched to recall him: happily they were all intercepted, and the silly captors, who rejoiced as the successive messengers fell into their hands, little knew what irreparable injury they were thus doing their own cause.

On the 5th of December, Martial Law was proclaimed in the District of Montreal, and rewards were offered for the apprehension of Papineau and several of the instigators of the rebellion.

Early in the month, Colonel Gore, eager to revenge and retrieve his misfortune, entered St. Denis and St. Charles at the head of a stronger force; recovered his gun and some wounded, and found the dead body of poor Weir. He then burned the houses of the chief rebels, penetrated to St. Hyacinthe, collected arms, received the submission of many of the *habitans*, pacified all that country and left garrisons in some of the most disaffected villages.

After the rout at St. Charles some of the rebel chiefs fled across the lines into the United States, and were received with open arms by the inhabitants of the border towns of Vermont. Subscriptions were raised for them—arms supplied—including two brass guns stamped with the American Eagle, and the fair borderers taxed themselves to provide the patriots, as they called themselves, with colours. In fact, the ladies of Swanton worked a handsome pair, which they presented to Mr. Bouchette, son of the Surveyor General of Lower Canada, who had ungratefully espoused the rebel cause. These, with Bouchette himself, who was wounded, the guns, several muskets and some treasure, were captured by the gallant yeomanry of Missiquoi Bay, Lake Champlain, on the first irruption of the rebels and their American friends into the Province.

When the repulse at St. Denis was known at Montreal, emissaries of mischief were despatched from thence to different parts of the Province, but without raising the population any where except in that disaffected section of the country about the Lake of the Two Mountains. Throughout the rest of Lower Canada, the Clergy, the principal Seigneurs and most influential French Canadians discountenanced these criminal proceedings; and only the immediate circle about Papineau, contaminated by his sedition, awed by his boldness, fascinated by his eloquence and perverted by the long impunity attending his career—rose in rebellion: the rest of the Canadians maintained a passive integrity.

In the meantime the men of British origin and the American settlers in the Province behaved nobly. The latter came forward prominently to warn their brethren in the States against joining the insurgents; to disabuse them of the erroneous notions they had entertained respecting British rule in Canada, and to pledge themselves to support the just and mild Government under which they lived. The English, Irish and Scotch, acted with characteristic energy and rose against this foul rebellion as one man. Corps of volunteers were enrolled everywhere; and in Montreal and Quebec five thousand brave men were armed, trained and put on garrison duty in the short space of a winter month. There was much moral beauty and interest in this simultaneous burst of genuine patriotism; and it was delightful to see these ardent civilians drilling diligently even amidst the intense cold of this hyperborean climate, and afterwards rivalling in steadiness and military proficiency their companions in arms of the line.

The Head Quarters with two companies of the 66th remained during the winter in Quebec, whilst the other four had been sent up the river in October, and had done good service in the affairs of St. Denis and St. Charles. Our old friend and Commanding Officer, Colonel Nicol, was promoted in the brevet of 1837, and in quitting the corps bore with him its warmest good wishes and affectionate regret.

The county of the Lake of the Two Mountains had been one of

the chief scenes of Mr. Papineau's declamations during the summer, and the population was so generally perverted, that at the meeting of the five counties their arrangements for military enrolment, the election of magistrates, and other illegal acts, were highly praised, and made the model for the rest. Thither, therefore, after the St. Denis repulse a certain Swiss adventurer, named Girod, repaired; making St. Eustache, the principal village, his Head Quarters: where by exaggerations and lies, and promises of the plunder of Montreal, he soon induced a large number of men to raise the standard of rebellion.

For some weeks M. Girod met with no interruption, for the operations to the south of the St. Lawrence absorbed all the disposable troops. Many excesses and robberies, consequently, were committed on the few loyal people in and about St. Eustache, who mostly fled to Montreal, terrified by M. Girod's threats and exactions. As soon, therefore, as the organization of the volunteers was well advanced, and that important place could be safely left to their guardianship, Sir John Colborne resolved to do this daring bandit the honour of marching against him in person.

Accordingly, on the 13th December three British Regiments, the Royal, 32nd and 83rd, a squadron of Volunteer Cavalry, a Corps of Infantry and Rifles, with six guns and a Rocket Brigade— forming a force of sixteen or seventeen hundred men, marched out of Montreal amidst the rapturous cheering of the British population. Besides the main body from Montreal, two companies of the 24th Regiment (a corps indefatigable in its exertions this winter,) quartered at the Carillon Rapids of the Ottawa, with some militia and volunteers, were directed to move on Grand Brûlé, a post of the rebels, and co-operate with the principal force.

One bridge over the branch of the Ottawa, between Ile Jésus and the Island of Montreal, had been secured by a detachment; but another over the northern arm was destroyed by Girod. This, however, during operations in a Canadian winter is not of much consequence. Two short marches brought the troops to the broken bridge, when it was found necessary to move three or four miles farther down the river to find a gentler current, with ice strong enough to cross. By good fortune it had frozen very keenly the preceding three days, so that little difficulty was experienced. Indeed the weather had been most adverse to the rebel cause throughout, so that the superstitious *habitans* had some reason for their peevish and impious exclamation–'*Le bon Dieu n'est pas patriote!*' The winter appeared to relax his grasp on the St. Lawrence, on purpose that troops and munitions of war might be conveyed from Quebec to Montreal much later than usual; and now a severe frost occurred exactly when necessary for the furtherance of military operations.

Before crossing the river some shots were fired on the troops from the Church of St. Eustache, which had been barricaded and strongly garrisoned. Some other buildings were also occupied, but the stone Church was the rebel-citadel. Six or seven hundred armed men mustered in the place that morning; however, on the approach of the troops, three or four hundred of the faint-hearted fled; and it was thus a melancholy spectacle to witness so hopeless a struggle.

As soon as the Artillery crossed the river arrangements were made for the assault of the place, and two of the guns were planted against the Church. The greater part of the Infantry was placed in cover, and different houses and positions around the town were occupied to command the fire of the insurgents and intercept the runaways. The guns were light and could do nothing against the massive walls or their defenders, except disturbing and blinding them with dust, when a bullet entered by a door or window and pulverized the thick plaster coating the inside. This must have been one reason why the garrison fired so badly; for, though the guns were within half-musket range, no Artilleryman was touched during the last half hour. At length the Sacristy and the Church itself were set on fire and stormed by Major Ward and the Royal Regiment, with scarcely any loss. The rebels then attempted to escape, but about a hundred, with Dr. Chenier their leader, were killed and many taken prisoners. More than half of this beautiful village was now reduced to ashes.

M. Girod abandoned the poor wretches he had betrayed soon after the beginning of the action, wandered about the country for some days, but finding it impossible to escape, shot himself. Girouard, a principal chief and instigator of the rebellion, with one or two others, were soon after apprehended and lodged in gaol.

Next morning, the 15th of December, the Commander of the Forces marched to St. Benoit, a disaffected village, where he found a body of three hundred penitent rebels drawn up in line–many on their knees; with grounded arms, each having a white rag in his hand. The arms were secured and the *habitans* pardoned and dismissed.

Almost immediately after the arrival of the Montreal troops, the column of the 24th from Carillon made its appearance; a simultaneous precision that would have been of considerable importance had Girod defended the post of Grand Brulé as was expected.

The insurrection here being thus effectually crushed, Colonel Maitland with the 32nd Regiment and two guns was sent on to St. Scholastique and St. Thérèse, two rebel villages, to receive the submission of the peasantry and collect arms. The insurgents here also surrendered unconditionally and were pardoned—the salutary severity of St. Eustache, like the chastisement at St. Charles, having pacified all the neighbourhood. Sir John Colborne then returned to Montreal; the whole business having only occupied four days.

Soon after his return a large portion of the prisoners taken in action, against whom no previous charge could otherwise be alleged, were liberated from gaol. Indeed the utmost clemency on the part of the Government and its civil and military officers, was a pleasing and marked characteristic during the whole of the first rebellion; and justice was only permitted to claim a portion of her rights at the close of the second, because the previous mercy had been so grossly abused.

Quebec, under its vigilant Commandant, Colonel Rowan,[51] enjoyed comparative quiet during these stirring times. Early in November five or six French Canadians were apprehended on charges of sedition, put in gaol four or five days, and then released on bail. On their liberation a crowd of their countrymen—principally from the large suburb of St. Roch—collected to cheer them, when a riot on a small scale took place between the Irish and Canadians—a few heads and windows were broken, and after a desultory skirmish the suburbans were chased out of the gates. The Magistrates then interfered and prohibited all assemblages in the street.

One dark and gloomy morning about an hour before day-break, three alarm guns were fired from the Artillery Bastion, which were answered immediately from the Citadel, according to previous arrangements. The Garrison turned out instantly—the Volunteers mustered and repaired to their alarm posts—the bombardiers stood to their guns—the guards at the different gates listened for the approaching enemy—mounted officers repaired to the Commandant for orders—and every body longed for day-light. Day at length broke, but no enemy appeared; and it turned out that all this pother arose from the servants of the Hôtel-Dieu having set fire to some straw to scald a pig.

Great manifestations of loyalty now broke out amongst the French Canadians, and numerous meetings were held throughout the Province, from which warm, and even fulsome addresses were sent to the Governor, which he interpreted as favourably as they could desire. It was amusing to contrast some of these with their Papineau resolutions three or four months before. However, it is wise not to be too inquisitive as to motives when the overt act is correct, and men are sometimes kept honest by the belief of their integrity. The fact is certain that the Districts of Quebec and Three Rivers have remained quiet, whilst only the serfs of Papineau, in a part of the District of Montreal rose in rebellion.

On the 9th of May, Quebec was enlivened by the arrival of the *Edinburgh* 74, the *Inconstant* frigate, and the *Apollo* and *Athol* troop-ships, having on board Major General Sir James Macdonell[52] and a Brigade of Guards, composed of the Grenadier and Coldstream Regiments. Soon after, these splendid Battalions disembarked and marched to the Citadel and Jesuits' Barracks, where they took up their quarters as the permanent garrison of the city. In thus sending some of the *élite* of her troops to occupy the chief bulwark of her power on this Continent, Great Britain gave no uncertain pledge of her determination to exert her strength for the preservation of this valuable portion of her vast Empire.

As soon as this fine Brigade reached Quebec, the regiments quartered there were sent up the river. Our Head Quarters moved to Three Rivers, where they remained during the summer. Troops now poured into the St. Lawrence—two Regiments of Cavalry—several Corps of Infantry, with strong reinforcements for those already in these Provinces, arrived in the early part of the summer; and our rural and quiet quarters at Three Rivers were animated by the frequent passage of the steamboats, covered with red coats, and musical with bugles and bands. Including the regiments from Nova Scotia and New Brunswick that had arrived early in the year, the additional force amounted to about ten thousand men.

The 66th passed a quiet summer at Three Rivers and Sorel. At the former place the King's Dragoon Guards—a superb corps recently arrived from England—were also quartered.

Towards the end of autumn reports of coming disturbances began to thicken, and intelligence to crowd in from all quarters of a dangerous and wide spread plot against the peace of these Provinces. Extensive preparations had been for some months going on in the border States for a fresh invasion of the Canadas, and this formidable conspiracy was no longer confined to the demoralized rabble on the frontiers. Respectable persons in all classes of society at once considered themselves released from the obligations of morality, the restraints of conscience and the specific engagement of the national faith, in a treaty of friendship with England. Large sums of money were raised—depôts of arms and provisions prepared—numerous secret societies, with fictitious names and objects, formed—and sixty thousand names enrolled in Vermont, New York, Michigan, Ohio, Kentucky and one or two other States, with the object of wresting the Canadas from the dominion of Great Britain.

But many traitors, as might be expected, were found amongst this wicked confederacy, and the base covetousness which first set it on foot defeated its own objects. Sir John Colborne and Sir George Arthur soon had secret and accurate information of what was going on, and made their preparations accordingly. The Writer has seen several communications of this description received from various persons living far apart, but all concurring; and on the whole no less than thirteen or fourteen documents—some of much length—were received from persons residing in the States above-mentioned, who were sworn members of the lodges; not from any proper motive, but, as they all confessed, for the sake of a reward, though at the risk of their lives. In these very minute statements were given the numbers, means, arrangements and objects of the conspirators; and it was remarkable how nearly they all agreed in the great outlines of the plot. Several civil and military officers of the United States and of the State Governments, acting from honourable motives, furnished corroborating intelligence of the wide-spread confederacy, whilst they lamented their own inability to put it down.

Simultaneously with this vast conspiracy numerous emissaries traversed the Lower Province, exciting to rebellion, exaggerating the great preparations making in the States, and threatening all who would not swear to rise when warned, with proscription and death. About thirty thousand *habitans* in the Montreal District are believed to have been included in the list of insurrection—bound solemnly to rise in arms when they should receive the order; and many others were intimidated into a promise to remain quiet and make no opposition.

The second insurrection, like the first, broke out prematurely. Late in October Sir John Colborne had gone to Quebec and it was believed this duty would detain him there a week. The conspirators fixed on Saturday, the 3rd of November, for a general rising throughout the western part of the Montreal District; and it was intended to collect an overwhelming force, attack the garrisons of Laprairie, St. John's, Chambly and Sorel, and obtain military possession of all the right bank of the St. Lawrence, from the boundary line to the mouth of the Richelieu, before the Commander of the Forces would have returned from Quebec, or any military strength could be sent across from Montreal.

But the war-worn chief with whom they had to do was too vigilant and too active for their calculations, and before they supposed half his work was done at Quebec, he suddenly appeared at Montreal on Sunday morning, the 4th of November—instantly proclaimed Martial Law, caused several suspected persons to be arrested, and began preparations for crossing the river at the head of a strong force.

On Saturday night the bulk of the population in the County of Laprairie, along the Chateauguay river, and the greater part of L'Acadie and Beauharnois, rose in arms. They attacked the houses of several isolated loyalists, murdered a man named Walker, at La Tortu, near Laprairie; invested the seignorial mansion of Mr. Ellice at Beauharnois, captured his son, his agent, Mr. Brown, and some ladies; and soon after got possession of a steamboat which touched at the village. On the morning of the 4th November, some bands of insurgents from Verchères, Contrecœur and that neighbourhood, moved towards the Richelieu, expecting to find depôts of arms in the villages along its banks, as had been promised, and hoping to raise the people. An enterprising fellow named Malhiot was at the head of this movement, and intended, it was said, to attack Sorel if he could muster the force he anticipated.

We had the 66th, about six hundred strong, at this important post, together with a hundred volunteers. A good deal of alarm was felt by the population at the vicinity of the rebels, who remained five or six days in possession of St. Ours, and even pushed an advanced guard within five miles of Sorel: several of the French Canadians, in consequence, ran away from the village. But there was little ground for apprehension; for with proper military management of such a garrison, no number of miserable half-armed insurgents could have taken the place, nor was it very probable that they would presume to attack it.

On the 8th November we received orders, at Sorel, for the advance of the 66th up the valley of the Richelieu, to clear it entirely of Malhiot's bands, and open the communication with St. John's. It had rained incessantly for nearly three days, and the streets of the village and the roads were more navigable for a skiff than passable for pedestrians. In seven or eight hours after the receipt of the route, Lieutenant Colonel Johnston,[53] at the head of a strong column, composed of the 66th, half a battery of Artillery under Captain Tylden, which had arrived from Quebec the day before, and a detachment of Volunteer Cavalry, marched or rather *waded* out of Sorel in the direction of St. Ours, in admirable order—as far as the knees. As the column was leaving the village a steamboat came to the wharf, with some companies of the Grenadier Guards on board, on their way to Montreal, who began to cheer merrily. This was answered by our people, and repeated and re-echoed by the Guards, the other passengers, and a crowd of spectators, until the troops were out of hearing; whilst in the mind of the Writer this stirring scene linked itself with reminiscences of battle fields of days of yore.

Malhiot occupied a strong position on the Boucherville Mountain, but the hearts of his people quailed on the approach of the troops, and they abandoned their post. The 66th found three guns, some muskets and pikes, and a considerable quantity of ammunition.

This absurd insurrection being effectually quashed, prisoners were brought in, in great numbers, and the Montreal gaol was soon filled. The great lenity of the Government on the former occasion having been so grossly misunderstood, and so criminally abused, it now became an act of the clearest necessity as well as justice to make some examples. As it was plain that proceedings in the ordinary courts would be nugatory, a military court was ordered to assemble at Montreal for the trial of the most guilty of the prisoners.

The Court Martial consisted of fourteen Field Officers and Captains in the Army, with Major General Clitherow,[54] their President. It met on the 19th November, sat nearly four months, was abused by an injudicious and violent press for the cautious regularity of its proceedings, and tried one hundred and twelve prisoners, ninety-nine of whom were convicted of high treason and rebellion on the clearest evidence. Twelve of the most criminal convicts were executed–two of whom had been implicated in the murder already adverted to–several were pardoned and fifty-four had their sentence of death commuted into transportation.

The Author, having been promoted on the medical Staff of the army, had the grief of parting with his old and gallant corps, the 66th, in November this year, when it embarked for England. The severance of an old officer from a regiment in which he has passed the greater part of an active life, is only faintly and imperfectly represented by the separation of a member from the rest of the family; yet is there no other human relationship so analogous. Through the four quarters of the globe, in war and peace, in ardent youth and mature manhood, during all the changes of eight and twenty years, its hospitable messroom had been to him a happy home. His feelings may be imagined when, from the lofty citadel he watched the ship, bearing away his fine old corps, passing Point Levi, and disappearing in the distance. Brave and steady Berkshire! May your course be ever as at Oporto, and Talavera, and Vittoria, and your other hundred fields; and worthy of the day when your conduct elicited from the great Captain of the age the memorable comment, 'They fought like lions!' Beloved Corps farewell! Be ye ever found '*quo fas et gloria ducunt.*'

THE END

APPENDIX 1

Notes

1. There is very little that I have been able to discover about Walter Henry's forbears. The local records were all burnt in the fire in the Four Courts in Dublin. The name Walter Henry of the Abbey, county-Donegal, whose mother's Christian name was Katherine, appears in a will of 1741 as benefiting by the lease of two mills. As both these Christian names were used in the author's generation there may be a connection, but the evidence is slight and the half dozen families still living in the vicinity, whose surname is Henry, have no knowledge of him. An advertisement in the *Donegal Democrat* produced no replies.

2. According to Pigott's Directory of 1824 his uncle was a Dr. Rolston, a surgeon of Donegal.

3. Henry was not only a keen fisherman; he studied the biology of his prey and his paper, 'Observations on the Habits of the Salmon Family', was published in 1837 by the Literary and Historical Society of Canada. It is one of the early Canadian papers on fish biology. In addition he wrote two letters to the *Albion* (New York), under the pseudonym Piscator, which were published.

4. The modern theory, that the musical march round the city was a cover plan to drown the sound of the sappers undermining the walls, would have interested Henry even more. He was sceptical of miracles.

5. Sir Everard Home was born in 1756. From 1804 to 1813 he was Professor of Anatomy and Surgery at St. George's Hospital. He gave a course of lectures in 1810. Henry's attack on his moral character is based on the charge that Home used the original research of his brother-in-law, John Hunter, as a basis for his own theses, and then burnt the originals. He was a good practical surgeon but his influence at St. George's was 'great and not always beneficial'.

6. Sir Benjamin Brodie was assistant surgeon at St. George's Hospital from 1808 to 1822 when he became surgeon there. Later he was President of the Royal College of Surgeons and also of the Royal Society. He was a favourite of George IV and became serjeant Surgeon to William IV.

7. Major General Warren M. Peacocke late of the Coldstream Guards had seen service in the Netherlands and Egypt. He was too experienced a soldier to take umbrage at Henry's impertinence.

8. Martindale, James Ward, served as Assistant Surgeon in the 67th Foot and later as Surgeon of the 17th Foot. He died in New South Wales in January 1832.

9. Dr. B—. The only doctor whose career appears to identify itself with this incident is Abraham Bolton, a Deputy Inspector of Hospitals since 1804, who died in Ireland in 1818.

10. Goldie, General Sir George, was commissioned in 1803. He was a captain in 1806 and promoted Major on 20th June 1811. He received the brevet of Lieutenant Colonel on 12th August 1819, but owing to Colonel Nicol's long tenure of command he could not get substantive promotion in his own Regiment. He commanded the 35th Foot (1st. Bn. Royal Sussex) as a Lieutenant Colonel from 1834 to 1837 when he was promoted to Colonel in the 11th Foot (Devons). He was subsequently made a Major General (1846), Lieutenant General (1854) and General (1862). He received a Gold Medal for the Peninsula, the C.B. and a Knighthood. He was seriously wounded on 30th June 1813 by a musket ball which lodged in his lung and remained there until his death fifty years later.

11. Dodgin, Lieutenant Colonel Daniel, got his captaincy in the 66th Foot in July 1803 and was promoted Major three years later. He received the brevet of Lieutenant Colonel in June 1813. For his services in the Peninsula he was awarded a gold medal and two bars and the C.B. He died in 1837.

12. The author appears to be charging the 88th Connaught Rangers with these excesses, but he cannot have had a comprehensive view of the whole sorry affair. The 88th Regiment was conspicuous throughout the campaign for its gallantry and *élan*: qualities which lead to trouble when discipline is relaxed. Napier selects no individual corps for particular censure.

13. General 'Slade as a cavalry leader was deplorable, always rash when he should have been cautious, and timid when he should have been bold. He was a byword for inefficiency throughout the army' (Fortescue). This unhappy episode was, however, redeemed a few days later by a detachment of the same Regiments under Lieutenant Sternowitz who captured twenty French Dragoons.

14. The military scandal-monger can make what he likes of this clue. Six of the assaulting regiments had yellow facings, the 9th, 30th, 38th, 44th, 77th and 88th.

15. Charles Nicol was commissioned into the 16th Foot in June 1795; he transferred four years later to the 66th Foot in the rank of Captain, was promoted Major in 1806, Lieutenant Colonel in 1811, Colonel in 1825, Major General in 1837, Lieutenant General in 1846. He died in 1850. He was awarded a gold medal for his services at the battle of Nive and was made a C.B. He never married but devoted his whole life to his Regiment, which he commanded for so many years.

16. Lord Fitzroy Somerset was Wellington's brilliant Military Secretary who later became Field Marshal Lord Raglan. Popular histories have treated unkindly one of the greatest men and best soldiers this country has ever produced.

17. The origin of the word batman is uncertain. The Universal Military Dictionary of 1779 defines batmen as 'servants hired in war time to take care of the horses belonging to the train of artillery, bakery, baggage etc. They generally wear the King's livery during their service.' A hundred years later the Military Dictionary and Gazetteer of 1881 noted that 'The term is now applied in the English Service to a soldier who acts as servant to an officer'. The old French word *bast* meant a pack-saddle and this seems to be its most probable derivation, but bats and battels were, and still are, words in common use at Winchester and Oxford. There may be a connection between the two.

18. Jonathan Wild (1682?–1725) was a notorious receiver of stolen goods. He built up a successful practice amongst the thieves of London whom he organized into gangs with special spheres of work. He also opened a house for the recovery of lost property so that he could return, at a price, to their owners the goods which his minions had stolen. He operated from large premises in the Old Bailey and later opened two branch offices. He was merciless to anyone who double-crossed him and brought to justice murderers and thieves who were not in his employ. He petitioned the Corporation of London for a grant of its freedom in recognition of his services. However, justice eventually caught up with him and he was hanged at Tyburn on 24th May 1725.

19. The Commissariat was in fact a department of the Treasury and responsible to Whitehall. However, on operations the Commander in Chief had considerable powers which the Duke of Wellington exercised with tact and firmness. By the end of the Campaign the service was good

but the Treasury allowed it to fall to pieces in the peace that followed and must bear, under Parliament, the blame for the logistic failures of the early days of the Crimean War.

20. John Wasdell was appointed Assistant Surgeon in the 57th Foot, 3rd December 1803, and became Surgeon to the 66th Foot in January 1810. He was promoted on the Staff in May 1812 and retired on half pay four years later. He died *circa* 1819.

21. Sir James McGrigor M.D., was born in 1771 and purchased a commission as Surgeon in the 88th Foot in 1793. He served as a medical officer in Flanders, the West Indies, India, Ceylon, Egypt and the United Kingdom before being appointed Chief of the Medical Staff of the Duke of Wellington's Army in the Peninsula, where he remained from January 1812 until peace was signed. Wellington said of him, 'He is one of the most industrious, able and successful public servants I have ever met with.' In June 1815 he was appointed Director General of the the Army Medical Department, a post he held with great distinction until 1851. It was only after his retirement with a knighthood and a baronetcy that the Treasury was able to undo the excellent work he had done and create, by short-sighted parsimony, the conditions which were to cost the country so dearly in the Crimean War. In particular the 'sprung waggons' provided for the wounded had been abolished. The heavy country carts which were all that could be collected in front of Sevastopol caused them unimaginable suffering.

22. Surgeon Henry seems to be accusing the 57th Regiment of this ingenuity, particularly as he does not appear to censure the culprits more than Victorian decency demands. He would naturally take a lenient view of any misdemeanours by the Die-Hards of Albuera.

23. The British Army in the Peninsula was always well fed and well found, as it always is towards the end of a war. It is a tragedy that the administrative services are allowed to fall to bits between wars through short sighted economies. But it always happens.

24. It was about this time that an interesting custom was initiated in the 66th Foot. The story goes that the officers were invited to a ball by a distinguished French lady. The Commanding Officer, out of considera-tion for a defeated enemy, ordered that plain clothes would be worn. However, the exigencies of the campaign had reduced the officers' wardrobes, and some of them could not produce anything but uniform. They were promptly ordered to obtain civilian dress; and to ensure that they kept it with them it was ordained that the whole mess should dine

in plain clothes once a year. This custom was honoured as long as the Regiment retained its identity and was known as 'White tie night,' at least until after the Second World War. In the bet and fine book (see note 26) there are a number of instances of officers being fined for not observing this custom.

25. Henry records a number of instances in which he undertook private practice. In Ireland particularly, at that time, an experienced and competent physician would have been most welcome. He never mentions where he got the drugs which he prescribed but presumably they came from military resources, an early and unofficial example of the health service.

26. The 66th had a book in which all bets and fines made at the Mess table were recorded. It started in 1814 and was in continuous use throughout the Regiment's existence. Surgeon Henry's name occurs on several occasions – usually as a winner. His earliest recorded bet was on the 26th November 1816, when he won half a dozen bottles of Maderia from Lieutenant Bullen. In May 1818 he bet Lieutenant Roberts one dozen of wine that he beat him by four feet in a running hop, step and leap. He won that one too. Eleven years later he took another half dozen off Lieutenant Healey at billiards.

27. The barracks at Poonamalee have long since disappeared but the 66th Foot bivouacked there for some months during the Second World War. It was no more prepossessing than in Surgeon Henry's day.

28. In some villages in India the peacock is regarded as sacred, in others as vermin. The sportsman in search of an addition to his rations was always advised to consult the local headman before shooting the neighbouring woods. Surgeon Henry seems to have beem lucky. Some of his successors have been chased back to their barracks bereft of both dignity and dinner.

29. The author's memory has played him false here. His dhobi washed his clothes. The water carrier was a Bheesti; but when he was writing Kipling was still unborn and Gunga Din unwritten. His Khitmugar was his butler and his Mnausalgee his cook.

30. A hundred miles in ten days is certainly not an arduous march. The distance was, however, dictated by the capacity of the commissariat bullocks on which a unit depended for the movement of its baggage, and which could only manage twelve miles in a day. Henry's description of his route could be equally applied to similar marches down to the Second World War, except that game was less plentiful.

31. The Bangywalla was a purveyor of *cannabis indica*, or pot as it is called today. Nautch girls were professional dancers who did not always combine their art with an older trade, for which professionals were usually available.

32. This regiment was probably the 11th Bengal Native Infantry, the Runseet Ka Paltan. When the mutiny broke out in Meerut, where it was stationed, it succumbed to the threats of retaliation by the ringleaders of the 3rd Cavalry and 20 BNI, but connived in the escape of its British Officers, and very few of its members took an active part. After the mutiny Bengalis were banned from the Indian Army, and regarded as worthless soldiers; but it must be remembered to their credit that they had fought well in earlier wars under good British Officers.

33. Dr. Sangrado is a character in Le Sage's *Gil Blas*. The name of this 'tall withered, wan executioner of the sisters three' was a symbol for the kind of pitiless bloodletting which was rife in the seventeenth century.

34. The controversy about Sir Hudson Lowe's treatment of Napoleon – and vice versa – has given employment to many pens. In the Canadian edition of his work Surgeon Henry, though generally supporting the Governor, makes some charges of lack of good temper and self control. In the English edition he withdraws them unreservedly as a result of letters received from officers in a better position to judge the case than he was. Both the charges and the amend are ommitted from this edition. Students of the quarrel will find a great deal about it in the English edition, a copy of which is in the Library of the Royal United Services Institution in Whitehall.

35. This was a reference to the lace on the officers' uniforms. It was changed to gold a few years later, not in deference to Napoleon but as part of a general exercise in military millinery which increased expense, hampered movement and was inimical to efficiency.

36. The English edition enlarges upon this incident. Apparently Sir Hudson Lowe had formed the opinion that O'Meara's conversation in the Mess was subversive to his authority and requested the commanding Officer to withdraw the privilege of being an honorary member. Colonel Nicol was on leave in England and the officer acting for him, without mentioning it to his officers, sent O'Meara a note saying that his society was no longer desired by the Regiment. Notwithstanding, he dined in the Mess that night and solicited, and got a certificate signed by the officers as to his good behaviour in the Mess. He subsequently produced it in his book *Napoleon in Exile* (London, 1822).

37. It appears that Surgeon Henry's object in inserting this order in this part of his narrative is to give weight to the subsequent paragraphs in which he comments on the general conditions on the island as they affected health. It was the contention of Napoleon's admirers that he was sent to one of the most unhealthy military stations in the Empire in the hope that he would soon die and so rid the British Government of a Security risk. The author is at pains to contradict this absurd charge, which, however, still obtains at least limited credence. See *Napoleon's St. Helena* by Gilbert Martineau (Murray, 1968).

38. This unfortunate individual must have had difficulty in justifying his existence. Sir Hudson Lowe looked after every detail of Napoleon's security and there was little for the troops to do except find innumerable guards and picquets. It was only natural that he should turn to farming to fill in his time, for his family, Pine-Coffin, comes of landed stock, but his attempt to enter the field of commerce was ill judged – to put it mildly. He was not, however, the bucolic boor whom Henry depicts. He had translated and published Stutterheim's account of the battle of Austerlitz ten years before.

39. Sir Hudson Lowe held Surgeon Henry in high esteem both as a man and a doctor. In 1823 he wrote to him asking for a full report on the state of Napoleon's body as revealed at the post mortem. He received a most detailed and technical reply, dated 12th September 1823, from Cavan where Henry was then serving. The original, signed and in his own handwriting, is preserved with the Lowe Papers, British Museum, Additional Manuscripts Vol. No. 20214 folios 200–1. An exact copy will be found in *Napoleon Immortal* by James Kemble (Murray, 1959).

40. The author had not yet been promoted from Assistant Surgeon and was consequently shown in the Army List as Ass. Surgeon, an aspersion which would not be tolerated in these enlightened days when the Director General of Abbreviations and Nomenclature, or some such highly paid bureaucrat, would have assembled a Working Party to devise a less ambiguous title. His promotion to Surgeon came shortly afterwards.

41. The morbid fear of military intervention in politics originated with Cromwell's rule of the Major Generals. It is deeply embedded in the British constitution to this day and still causes grave inconvenience and lack of efficiency. Its historical origins and growth to that date were clearly set forth in Clode's classic *Military Forces of the Crown*.

42. Madeira was always supposed to improve by being taken on a

voyage, and no respectable Regiment would embark without a generous supply amongst its baggage. A dozen bottles spread over three nights, would not have gone far in a mess of twenty or so officers but perhaps the subalterns were fobbed off with less travelled vintages. The modern method of maturing madeira is by subjecting it to heat in special buildings for some months. This gives it its characteristic taste which was so popular in the early part of the nineteenth century and is considerably cheaper than sending it on a voyage round the world.

43. General Sir James Kempt had had a varied and distinguished career in the Army. He had seen service in the Netherlands and in Egypt, Italy and Sicily before being appointed to the Staff of the Army in the Peninsula in 1811. He was severely wounded leading the assault at Badajoz but recovered in time to fight at Vittoria, Nivelle, Nive, Orthez and Toulouse. At Waterloo he succeeded to the command of Picton's division on the latter's death. After his service in Canada he was Master General of the Ordnance from 1834–38. He died in London in 1854 at the age of 90.

44. Major C. L. Wingfield had seen service with the 13th Light Infantry in Burma. He transferred to the 66th by purchase.

45. In the English edition the words 'esteem and respect' have been substituted for love. I suspect the publisher. Love is much more descriptive of Henry's warm and generous Christianity.

46. Sir John Colborne, first Baron Seaton, 1778–1863, started his military career as an ensign in the 20th Foot at the age of 16. He was promoted on merit and without purchase through each rank to Lieutenant Colonel in the 66th Foot. In 1811 he transferred to the 52nd. His attack on the flank of the French Guard at Waterloo had an important, some say decisive, effect on the outcome of the battle. His last appointment was Commander of the Forces in Ireland from which he retired at the age of 72 with the rank of Field Marshal.

47. Sir Bond Head was a colourful character. He was descended from a Portuguese Jew called Mendez who had come to England as a physician to Catherine of Braganza. His grandfather changed his name to Head when he married an heiress of that name. Bond was educated at Rochester and the RMA Woolwich before being gazetted into the Royal Engineers in 1811. He served in the Mediterranean and during the Waterloo campaign was in charge of a pontoon unit. In 1825 he went on half pay and travelled extensively in South America as a mining engineer. After leaving Canada he received a baronetcy and retired to

his home, Duppas Hall, Croydon, where he wrote extensively on a variety of topics. A keen horseman he rode hard to hounds up to the age of 75.

48. Lieutenant Colonel George Augustus Wetherall started in the 7th Royal Fusiliers and saw active service in the east Indies, including the attack and capture of Java. He later became Deputy Adjutant General in Canada. For his service in that country he was awarded the C.B. and appointed ADC to the Queen. He was later Adjutant General to the Forces.

49. Colonel the Hon. Charles Gore, C.B., K.H., served in the Peninsula for which he received nine clasps to his medal. He was also at Quatre-Bras and Waterloo where he had no less than four horses shot under him, whilst principal ADC to Sir James Kempt. His duties were roughly comparable to those of Brigade Major today. He was undoubtedly a very gallant officer but appears to have had little technical sense.

50. Major Frederick Markham was later promoted to Lieutenant Colonel and went to India where he commanded a Brigade in the Punjab campaign of 1848–49 including the siege of Mooltan and the battle of Goojerat.

51. Colonel William Rowan had served in the Peninsula and at Waterloo. His duties, though impeccably performed, were probably not very arduous as the bulk of the population was loyal. He was promoted Major General in Command in Canada in 1846.

52. Major General Sir James Macdonell was an old Coldstreamer. He served with the expedition to Naples and Calabria, including the battle of Maida, for which he received a gold medal, and subsequently in the Peninsula and at Waterloo. He was promoted Lieutenant General in 1841.

53. Lieutenant Colonel Thomas Henry Johnston who succeeded Colonel Nicol was not gazetted as Ensign until 1822, when his predecessor had already commanded for 11 years. He purchased his promotion rapidly and got command after 16 years' service. He was promoted Major General in 1857. He must have found the take-over a difficult one.

54. Major General John Clitherow was a Scots guardsman, at that time known as the Scots Fusilier Guards. He served in the disastrous Walcheren expedition of 1809 and subsequently in the Peninsula. He was severely wounded at the battle of Fuentes d'Onoro and again at Burgos. He was promoted Lieutenant General in 1841.

Brief Chronology of Surgeon Henry's Life

1st Jan.	1791	Born in Donegal.
11th April	1811	Appointed Hospital Mate for General Service.
16th May	1811	Landed at Lisbon for active service.
19th Dec.	1811	Appointed Assistant Surgeon 66th Foot.
7th April	1812	Visited Badajoz on the morrow of its storming.
21st June	1813	Present at Battle of Vittoria,
25th July	1813	The surprise of Maya,
14th Nov.	1813	The passage of the Nive,
13th Dec.	1813	The affair before Bayonne,
14th Feb.	1814	The affair at Garris and
27th Feb.	1814	The Battle of Orthes.
18th April	1814	Soult submitted to Wellington.
July	1814	Left Bordeaux with 66th Foot for England.
3rd April	1815	Sailed for India.
22nd July	1815	Arrived Madras.
2nd Nov.	1815	Joined 1/66th at Dinapore en route for Nepaul.
17th Feb.	1816	Accompanied 66th into Nepaul.
4th Mar.	1816	Gurkhas accepted Peace terms.
8th Mar.	1816	Withdrawal to India commences.
28th Mar.	1816	Arrived Dinapore.
7th Aug.	1816	Arrived Cawnpore.
2nd April	1817	Embarked at Calcutta.
5th July	1817	Arrived St. Helena.
1st Sept.	1817	Interview of officers of the 66th with Napoleon.
5th May	1821	Death of Napoleon.
21st May	1821	Embarked with 66th for England.
31st July	1821	Arrived Spithead, went on leave, rejoined 66th in
May	1822	at Hull until ordered to Ireland in
Mar.	1823	In various stations in Ireland during which
8th June	1826	he was promoted Surgeon of the 66th and
June	1827	embarked with them for Canada. Stationed in Quebec until
May	1830	when the battalion moved to Montreal and thence in
May	1831	to Kingston where on

17th June 1832 Cholera broke out.

May 1833 moved to Toronto but in

May 1834 returned to Kingston where on

26th July 1834 Cholera again visited the Regiment. In

May 1835 he accompanied the 66th back to Quebec.

23rd Nov. 1837 Action at St. Denis, (author not present).

25th Nov. 1837 Action at St. Charles (author not present).

4th Jan. 1839 Surgeon Henry promoted Staff Surgeon.

Nov. 1839 66th embarked for England.

16th Dec. 1845 Staff Surgeon Henry appointed Deputy Inspector General Army Medical Service for Canada.

12th Mar. 1852 Granted local rank of Inspector General.

4th June 1855 Retired from the Army.

27th June 1860 Died in Canada.

APPENDIX 3

Notes on Regiments

Originally Regiments were known by the name of their Colonel; thus Hepburn's, Kirk's, Trelawney's, etc. When Officers of the same name commanded different Regiments they were distinguished by the colour of the facings, hence the Buffs and the Green Howards. By Surgeon Henry's time nearly all were known by numbers, though a few clung to their old titles. One of the last to retain its Commanding Officer's name was the 28th Gloucesters commanded by an old fire-eater called Bragg. It is told of him that they were once brigaded with the 2nd Queens and 8th Kings Regiment. On a ceremonial parade when it came to his turn, on the left of the line, to call his Regiment to attention to receive the inspecting officer he bawled out 'Nor Kings, nor Queens, nor Royal Marines, but old Braggs the 28th atten—shun.'

At times some Regiments had two battalions each, the remainder normally only one. During an emergency second battalions were raised. Sometimes these were disbanded when things returned to normal, sometimes they were amalgamated with their first battalions and sometimes they were renumbered as units in their own right.

In 1811, when Henry joined the Army, in addition to colonial and foreign corps, garrison and veteran battalions, the Army List shows 104 Regiments of Infantry of the Line, many of which had second Battalions. There were also, but these are not shown in the Army List, the European Regiments of the East India Company which were taken on to the British Establishment after the Indian Mutiny. They were then given the numbers of some of the Regiments which had been disbanded after the Peninsular War. After Waterloo the first twenty five Regiments were allowed to keep their second battalions, the remainder were single battalion Regiments until the Cardwell reforms of the late nineteenth century when battalions were linked to form two battalion Regiments. The idea behind this was that one should serve at home and one abroad, the former being used to keep the latter up to strength.

The Infantry Regiments mentioned by numbers in *Surgeon Henry's Trifles*, with the titles they bore in the First and Second World War are given below. Cavalry titles were not affected by the Cardwell Reforms in this respect.

1st The Royal Scots (The Royal Regiment).
3rd The Buffs (Royal East Kent Regiment).
5th The Royal Norththumberland Fusiliers.
11th The Devonshire Regiment.
15th The East Yorkshire Regiment.
20th The Lancashire Fusiliers.
24th The South Wales Borderers.
28th 1st Bn. The Gloucestershire Regiment.
31st 1st Bn. The East Surreys.
32nd 1st Bn. The Duke of Cornwall's Light Infantry.
34th 1st Bn. The Border Regiment.
39th 1st Bn. The Dorsetshire Regiment.
43rd 1st Bn. The Oxfordshire & Buckinghamshire Light Infantry.
44th 1st Bn. The Essex Regiment.
50th 1st Bn. The Royal West Kent Regiment.
57th 1st Bn. The Middlesex Regiment.
58th 2nd Bn. The Northamptonshire Regiment.
60th The Kings Royal Rifle Corps.
66th 2nd Bn. The Royal Berkshire Regiment.
71st 1st Bn. The Highland Light Infantry.
77th 2nd Bn. The Middlesex Regiment.
79th 1st Bn. The Queen's Own Cameron Highlanders.
83rd 1st Bn. The Royal Ulster Rifles.
85th 2nd Bn. The King's Shropshire Light Infantry.
87th 1st Bn. The Royal Irish Fusiliers.
92nd 2nd Bn. The Gordon Highlanders.

INDEX

Abraham, Plains of, 211, 241
Abrantes, 38
Accoah, 118
Ackland, Maj Dudley, 57th
    Regt, 84
Adour, R., 92, 94
Aire, 94, 95
Alava, General, Spanish Army, 58,
    59
Albuera, 25, 37
Albuquerque, 39–41, 51
Alcantara, 58, 59
Aldea Galaga, 33, 35, 36
Alen-tejo, 39, 41
Alhandra, 38
Allagon, R., 60, 61
Allahabad, 130, 137, 138
Almandralejo, 47
Almaraz, 47
Altar de Chao, 41
Angoulême, Duc d', 98, 99
Anticosti, Island of, 210
Antommarchi, Dr, 167, 177, 178,
    181, 182, 185, 189, 190, 194
Antonio, 26, 33, 34, 36, 38–40, 44,
    55–60, 64, 81, 90, 99, 110
Apollo, Transport, 257
Arab, Transport, 209
Archambault, 156
Arnott, Dr Archibald, 20th Regt,
    179
Arran, Earl of, 9
Arthur, Sir George, 258
Artois, Compte d', 101
Ascension Island, 167, 185
Athlone, 204
Athol, Troopship, 257

Badajos, 38–42, 46, 48–52, 93
Baird, Capt James, 66th Regt.,
    151, 157, 234

Balcombe, Mr, 160
Ballinasloe, 204
Ballyshannon, 203
Balmaine, Count, 172, 173
Baños, 63
Barriefield, 239
Barrioplano, 81, 82
Bastan, Vale of, 73, 78
Baxter, Dr, 166
Bayonne, 83, 87, 88, 90, 98, 102
Beauharnois, 259
Bejace, 98
Belem (Port), 22, 25, 36
Bell, Hon. Mathew, 222, 223
Bell, Lieut Henry, 58th Regt, 206
Benares, 127, 139
Benguela, 167
Beresford, Marshal, 25, 145, 152
Bertrand, Countess, 148, 168, 183,
    185–187, 189, 190, 192–194
Bertrand, Marshall, 147–149, 153,
    154, 166, 178, 181–183, 185, 187,
    190, 194
Bettiah, 124
Bhastee Rhamm, 110, 120, 121,
    125, 127
Bhicknee Pass, 115, 116
Bhurtpore, 125, 138
Bidassoa, R., 62
Bingham, Sir George, Lieut-Col
    53rd Regt, 148, 149, 152–154,
    176, 209
Bingham, Lady, 173
Birr, 206
Black Prince, The, 68, 72, 87
Blakeney, Capt Henry, 66th Regt,
    187
Blanchette Rev, 251
Bolton, Dr, 24, 30
Bonavista, Dr, 178
Bordeaux, 98, 99
Borghese, Princess, 179

Boston, 241
Bouchette, Mr, 252, 253
Boucheville Mts, 260
Boyle, 204
Bristol, 99
Brodie, Sir Benjamin, 19
Brown, Mr, 246
Buchanan, Cpl. James, 13th Light Dragoons, 95
Bull, Captain Robert, RHA, 71
Bulstrode, Captain Augustus, 66th Regt, 89
Bulwee, 112
Buonaparte, Napoleon, 7, 61, 70, 76, 96, 97, 101, 104, 105, 136, 144 ff., 192
Burgos, 56, 58, 65
Buttevant, 209
Byng, General John, 47, 58, 60, 84, 86, 87, 97, 91, 94, 98, 119, 198

Cadiz, 20, 58
Cadogan, Lieut-Col. the Hon. Henry, 71st Regt, 70
Caesar, Rev Julius, 124
Calcutta, 101, 104, 106, 108, 127, 136, 137, 139, 152
Cambo, 85–87, 89
Camel, S.S., 185, 192, 194
Cameron, Colonel, 78 n
Campo Mayor, 39, 41–44
Canning, Mr, 168
Carcassone, 97, 98
Carillon Rapids, 254, 256
Caroline, Queen of Naples, 179
Cato, 17, 18
Cavan, 201
Cawnpore, 127, 131–133, 135
Ceclavin, 60
Ceylon, 104
Chambly, 246, 247, 249–251, 259
Champlain, Lake, 253
Chaperon, M & Mde, 217, 219, 222
Charles V, Emperor, 40
Chateauguay, R., 259
Chatham, 100, 102, 195

Chatham, H.M.S., 99
Chaudière, R., 211
Chenier, Dr, 255
Cintra, 23, 36
Ciudad Rodrigo, 38
Clitheroe, Major-General John, 261
Clitherow, Captain William, 3rd Foot Guards, 91, 102
Coimbra, 25, 27–29, 36–38, 99
Colborne, General Sir John, 234, 240, 241, 244, 245, 254, 256, 258, 259
Conqueror, H.M.S., 158, 166
Contrecœur, 259
Coria, 58–63
Cove, 99, 209
Crabbe, Ship's Captain, 101, 105, 108
Crompton, Captain William, 66th Regt, 248
Crothy Rev, 206
Currie, Lieut-Colonel Edward, 90th Regt, 89
Cypriani, 161, 162

Dalhousie, Earl of, 211–214
Dalhousie, Lady, 214
Dalmatia, Duke of (see Soult, Marshal)
D'Avignon, 245, 246
Davy, Lieut William, 66th Regt. 63, 158
Debartzch, Mr, 246, 250
Demaray, M., 245, 246
D'Erlon, Count, (see Drouét)
Dinapore, 107–110, 113, 121, 124, 125, 137, 139
Dodgin, Colonel Daniel, 66th Regt, 40, 48, 93, 94, 147, 150, 156, 160
Don R., 233
Don Benito, 54
Donegal, 8
Dorah, S.S., 139, 140
Douro, R., 65
Doyle, General Sir Charles, 208

INDEX

Drouét (General Count D'Erlon) 77, 79
Dublin, 19, 200, 204, 205
Dudgeon, Major Ralph, 71st Regt, 56
Duncan, Captain Peter, 66th Regt, 152
Dunn, Ensign William, 66th Regt, 84
Dunne, Captain J. D., 66th Regt, 151
Dupré, Madame, 85
Durham, 199

Ebro, R., 65, 67, 68, 76
Edinburgh, 19
Edinburgh, H.M.S., 257
Edwards, Mr Commissary, 60, 199
El Bordon, 28
Elizonda, 73, 74, 76, 78 n, 79
Ellice, Mr, 259
Ellis, Captain John, 66th Regt, 151
Elvas, 33, 36, 39, 44, 45, 56–58
Enniskillen, 202, 203
Enniskillen, Lord, 203
Erne, Loch, 203
Eske, R., 8, 9, 14, 15, 100
Espelette, 85, 89, 90
Estramadura, 25, 38, 44, 50, 52
Exeter, 239

Farquhar, Sir Robert, 140
Ferdinand VII, King, 54
Fesch, Cardinal, 178
Figueras, 25, 29
Fo, 171
Frith, Rev, 71
Fuentes d'Onore, 25
Fuentes del Maestro, 53
Fung Mun Rhin Ko Chinn, 171

Galba, 40
Galisteo 62
Ganges, R., 108, 127–131, 139

Garden Island, 228
Garrone, R., 97, 98
Garris, 91, 102, 198, 199
Gave, R., 92
Gaviao, 39
Gazan, Count de, 98
George III, 97
George IV, 192, 193
Ghazepore, 127
Ghent, Treaty of, 101
Gimont, 96
Girod, M, 254, 255
Girouard, M., 258
Goa, 124
Goldie, General Sir George, 66th Regt, 37, 82, 201
Gore, Colonel the Hon. Charles, 43rd Regt, 247–249, 252
Gorrequer, Maj Gideon, 19th Regt, 180
Gosport, 99
Gourgaud, General, 148
Graham, General Sir Thomas, 64
Grand Brulé 254, 256
Grant, General Sir Colquhoun, 204
Granville, Dr, 199
Great Britain, Steamboat, 233
Grenoble, 101
Guadiana, R., 40, 43, 50, 54

Harispe, General, 91
Harvey, Lieut Thomas, 66th Regt, 108
Head, Sir Francis Bond, 234, 240
Healey, Ensign Robert, 66th Regt, 208
Heir, Surgeon Mathew, 152, 153
Hill, General Sir Rowland, 41, 47, 48, 54, 58, 60, 63, 64, 68, 73, 74, 76, 77, 79–81, 83, 85, 87–89, 91, 92, 98
Hogg, John, Ship's Captain, 21
Home, Sir Everard, 19
Hoogly, R., 108
Hornachos, 47
Hunn, Captain, R. N., 168

Ibbetson, Commissary, 160, 185
Inconstant, Frigate, 257
Iphigenia, Frigate, 159
Isle of Bourbon, 141
Isle of France (*see* Mauritius)
Isle of Wight, 109, 193

Jalbert, 249
James's Town, 142 ff.–184
Johanna, Island of, 104
Johnston Lieut-Col Thomas, 66th Regt, 260
Johnston, Lieut John, 66th Regt, 252
Johnstone, Miss, 173
Jordan, Captain John, 66th Regt, 151
Joseph Buonaparte, King, 71
Josephine, Empress, 96
Juan Fernandez, 143
Jumna, R., 130
Junot, Marshall, 23, 33
Juttshugee Bummaunjhee, 159

Kamouraska, 210, 215, 217
Kelly, Dr, R.N., 226
Kelly, Pte Patrick, 66th Regt, 144
Kempt, General Sir James, 214, 215, 224, 242
Kentucky, 258
Khatmandoo, 122, 123
Kien Long, Emperor, 172
Kingston, 228–233, 235, 236, 238, 239

L'Acadie, 259
Lake, General Lord, 125
L'Allemande, General, 47
Lambrecht, Lieut John, 66th Regt, 102, 118 119, 139
Lampton, Mr, 198
Languedoc Canal, 97
Lantz, 79
Laprairie, 259

Las Cases, Count, 169, 187
Lascelles, Lieut-Col Edmund, 66th Regt, 150
La Tortu, 259
La Urbada, 64
Leith, Lieut-Col Alexander, 31st Regt, 84, 90
l'Estrange, Lieut John, 108, 151, 155
Liberdade, 38, 62
Limerick, 207, 208
Lincoln, 195
Lisbon, 20, 22, 25, 29, 30, 32, 33, 36, 38, 39, 155
L'Isle en Jourdain, 96
Liverpool 19, 199, 200
Llerena 53, 54
London, 19
Longueuil, 246
Louis XVIII, 96, 97
Lord Melville, Indiaman, 100, 106
Lorette, 211
Los Alduides, 77
Lowe Lady, 129, 147, 173, 184
Lowe, General Sir Hudson, 145, 147, 159, 163, 165–167, 169, 173, 174, 179, 180, 184, 185
Lyons, 101, 104

M'Carthy, Lieut Charles, 66th Regt, 150, 155
Macdonald, Marshall, 101
Macdonell, General Sir James, 257
McDougall, Lieut Robert, 66th Regt, 158
McGrigor, Sir James, 69, 95, 229
Macleod, Lieut-Col Donald, 11th Bengal N.I., 125, 126, 137
McMahon, Rev, 213
Madagascar, 141
Madeira, 102
Madras, 101, 104, 105
Madrid, 54
Maitland, Col the Hon. John, 32nd Regt, 256
Malbaie, R., 215, 216, 221
Malhiot, 259, 260

Marie-Louise, Empress, 96, 177
Markham, Maj Frederick, 32nd
    Regt, 248
Martin, Mr Abraham, 204
Martindale, J. W., 20
Martinez, Don Juan Joze, 50
Mascagni, Dr, 177
Mascarenhas, Don Manoel, 23, 32,
    33, 36
Massena, Marshall, 19, 38, 155
Masterman, Capt W. T., 34th
    Regt, 72
Mauritius, 140, 141
Maunsell, Capt, 22
Marchand 185
Maya, 74–77, 78 n, 83
Melville, H.M.S., 159, 160
Mendizabal, 46
Merida, 38–40
Michigan, 258
Mirabeau, 7
Mirande, 95, 96
Missiquoi Bay, 253
Moffatt, Lieut Thomas, 66th
    Regt, 153, 155
Mondego. R., 25, 28, 29
Montbrun, 93
Montcalm, General, 213
Montchenu, Marquis de, 172, 174,
    175
Montholon, General Count, 148,
    163, 167, 169, 178, 181–183, 185,
    187, 190, 194
Montmorency, 211
Montreal, 213, 216, 224–226, 229,
    242, 244–247, 249, 250, 252–257,
    259–261
Moralejo, 58, 60
Morillo, General, Spanish Army,
    68, 69, 85
Muckawnpore, 120–122, 132

Napoleon (*see* Buonaparte)
Nelson, Mr Wolfred, 243, 245, 246,
    249
Nepaul, Rajah of, 110, 122
New Brunswick, 244, 257

Newport, 100
New York, 241, 258
Nicol, Lt.-Gen. Charles, 66th
    Regt, 53, 84, 86, 115–120, 122,
    132, 139, 148–150, 154, 155, 163,
    165, 177, 185, 190, 204, 207, 230,
    239, 241, 253
Nive, R., 86, 87, 89, 102
Nivelle, R., 83
Noire, R., 221
Nova Scotia, 257

O'Callaghan, Colonel the Hon.
    R. W., 39th Regt, 69, 70
O'Callaghan, Mr, 246, 247
Ochterlony, Major-General Sir
    David, 112, 120
Ogle, Sir Charles and Lady, 215
Ohio, 258
O'Meara, Dr, 147, 148, 156, 161–
    164, 166, 169, 182, 194
O'Neill, Earl, 9
Ontario, Lake, 228–230, 235
Oporto, 37, 261
Orthes, 92, 95
Ottawa, 225, 226, 244, 254

Paget, Sir Charles, 193
Paley, Rev, 195, 196
Palmerston, Lord, 204
Pampeluna, 72, 76, 79–83
Pancorvo, 65
Panet, Louis, 217
Papineau, Joseph Louis, 211, 213,
    223, 224, 240, 242–247, 252–254,
    257
Paris, 7, 101, 229, 236
Parson's Town (*see* Birr)
Peacocke, Maj General W. M., 20
Perrault, Mr Ovide, 248
Phillippon, General, 39
Picton, General Sir Thomas, 42
Picton, Village of, 239
Pine-Coffin, Brigadier, J., 268
Pitt, 7
Placentia, 62, 63

Point Levi, 223, 261
Poonamalee, 105, 106, 134
Port Lewis, 140
Portsmouth, 20, 192, 193
Prescott, 229, 240
Princess Charlotte, Frigate, 101
Puebla, 68
Puebla del Prior, 47
Puente d'Arenas, 65
Punhete, 38

Quebec, 209, 211, 212, 216, 222–228, 230, 239–242, 244, 245, 253, 255–257, 259, 260
Quinte, Bay of, 239

Rapté, R., 118, 119
Reade, Lieut-Col Sir Thomas, 27th Regt, 165
Rhaamoh Saamhe, 134
Rhamnahgur, 115
Richardson, Dr, 113
Richlieu, R., 242, 244–247, 250, 251, 259, 260
Rideau Swamps, 228
Rio Janeiro, 150, 167
Robespierre, 7
Rochefoucalt Liancourt, Duke de, 234
Rodney, H.M.S., 99
Rolston, Calherine, 2, 17, 18
Rolston, Dr, 10
Rome, King of, 96
Romney, H.M.S., 209
Roncesvalles, 76, 83
Ross, Lord, 206
Rowan, Col William, 58th Regt, 256

Saccavem, 38
Saguenay, R., 211
St Athanase, 245
St Benoit, 255
St Charles, Village, 242, 246–253, 256

St Charles, Lake, 211, 212
St Cristoval, 46
St Denis, Isle of Bourbon, 141
St Denis, Village, 243-254
St Eustache, 254–256
St Helena, 129, 136, 139, 142 ff., 193
St Helens, Is., 225
St Hilaire, 249–251
St Hyacinthe, 252
St Jean de Luz, 88
St Jean Pied de Port, 87
St John's, 245, 259, 260
St Lawrence, R., 210, 215, 221, 225, 226, 244, 247, 254, 255, 257, 259
St Maurice, R., 222, 223
Santa Martha, 52
St Mathias, 249, 251
St Ours, 247–249, 260
St Palais, 91, 92, 198
St Paul, Bay of 216
St Roch, 256
St Scholastique, 256
St Sebastian, 76, 79, 83
St Thérèse, 256
Salamanca, 63, 64, 151
Salvatierra, 72
Sampson, Dr, 231, 238
Sanchez, Don Julian, 59
"Sangrado, Dr," 132, 200
Saunderson, Col, 201
Saunderson, Capt Bassett, 44th Regt, 201
Shannon, R, 208
Shekelton Dr, 82
Shipp, John, 120
Shortt, Dr, 181
Sierra Morena, 47, 54
Sieyes, Abbé 7
Simon, 12–14, 145
Skey, Dr Joseph, Medical Department, 229, 230
Slade, General John, 47
Sligo, 204
Spithead 191, 192
Solvielta, Don Ignacio, 51

Solvielta Donna Thereza, 39, 40
    46
Somerset, Lord Fitzroy, 59
Sorel, 245, 247–250, 258–260
Soult, Marshal, Duke of Dalmatia,
    41, 46, 56, 76, 88, 89, 96–98
Spithead, 99, 191
Stewart, General Sir William 76,
    77, 78 n
Stokoe, Surgeon, 166
Sturmer, Baron, 172
Subijana d'Aliva, 69–72
Sunderland, 195, 196, 198
Sussex, Duke of, 198
Swanton, 252

Tagus, R., 22, 33, 38, 47, 54, 58–60
Talavera, 151, 261
Thomar, 38
Thompson, James, 213
Thoulouse, 96–99, 151
Three Rivers, 222, 257, 258
Toledo, 38
Tolosa, 71
Tormes, R., 63, 64
Toro, 65
Toronto, 233, 234
Torres Vedras, 19, 38, 58
Trajan, 40, 58
Truxillo, 54–56
Two Mountains, Lake, 244, 253
Tylden, Capt John, R.A., 260

Usagre, 47

Vaughan, Mr, 214, 215
Verchères, 259
Verling, Dr, 166, 167
Vermont, 252, 258
Vieux Mougerre, 87, 88, 90
Vignali, Dr, Abbé, 178, 183, 185,
    190, 194

Vigo, H.M.S., 159
Ville Franche, 97, 98
Vittoria, 65, 67, 68, 70, 71, 81–83,
    119, 150, 261

Walker, General G.T., 48
Walker, Mr, 259
Warde, Major Henry, 1st Royal
    Regt, 250
Wardell, Ensign William, 66th
    Regt, 154
Wasdell, Staff Surgeon John, 67,
    74, 81
Waterloo, 70
Webb, Capt, R.N., 190
Weir, Lieut George, 32nd Regt,
    249, 252
Wellesley, Marquis of, 58, 205
Wellesley, Sir Arthur (see
    Wellington, Duke of)
Wellington, 1st Duke of, 19, 23,
    30, 36, 37, 39, 46, 58, 59, 63, 77,
    80, 83, 89, 91, 93, 97, 98, 152,
    155
Wellington, Village of, 229
Wetherall, Lieut-Col George, 1st
    Royal Regt, 246–252
Whiskey, 159, 160
Wild, Jonathan, 60, 64, 110
William IV, King, 242
Wingfield, Major C. L., 66th Regt,
    216
Wolfe, General, 70, 211, 213
Worcester, Marquis of, 54

York, Duke of, 150
Yu, 171

Zadorra R., 68
Zafra, 47
Zarza Mayor, 59, 60
Zezere, 38